Graduate Texts in Mathematics **86**

Graduate Texts in Mathematics

continued after index

J.H. van Lint

Introduction to
Coding Theory

Second Edition

Springer-Verlag
Berlin Heidelberg New York London Paris
Tokyo Hong Kong Barcelona Budapest

J.H. van Lint
Eindhoven University of Technology
Department of Mathematics
Den Dolech 2, P.O. Box 513
5600 MB Eindhoven
The Netherlands

Mathematics Subject Classifications (1991): 94-01, 11T71

Library of Congress Cataloging-in-Publication Data
Lint, Jacobus Hendricus van, 1932–
    Introduction to coding theory, 2^d ed. / J.H. van Lint.
    p.   cm. — (Graduate texts in mathematics; 86)
    Includes bibliographical references and index.
    ISBN 0-387-54894-7. — ISBN 3-540-54894-7 (Berlin)
    1. Coding theory. I. Title. II. Series.
QA268.L57   1992
003′.54—dc20   92-3247

Printed on acid-free paper.

Production managed by Dimitry L. Loseff; manufacturing supervised by Robert Paella.
Typeset by Asco Trade Typesetting Ltd., Hong Kong.
Printed and bound by R.R. Donnelley & Sons, Harrisonburg, VA.
Printed in the United States of America.

9 8 7 6 5 4 3 2 1

ISBN 3-540-54894-7 Springer-Verlag Berlin Heidelberg New York
ISBN 0-387-54894-7 Springer-Verlag New York Berlin Heidelberg

Preface to the Second Edition

The first edition of this book was conceived in 1981 as an alternative to outdated, oversized, or overly specialized textbooks in this area of discrete mathematics—a field that is still growing in importance as the need for mathematicians and computer scientists in industry continues to grow.

The body of the book consists of two parts: a rigorous, mathematically oriented first course in coding theory followed by introductions to special topics. The second edition has been largely expanded and revised. The main editions in the second edition are:

(1) a long section on the binary Golay code;
(2) a section on Kerdock codes;
(3) a treatment of the Van Lint-Wilson bound for the minimum distance of cyclic codes;
(4) a section on binary cyclic codes of even length;
(5) an introduction to algebraic geometry codes.

Eindhoven   J.H. VAN LINT
November 1991

Preface to the First Edition

Coding theory is still a young subject. One can safely say that it was born in 1948. It is not surprising that it has not yet become a fixed topic in the curriculum of most universities. On the other hand, it is obvious that discrete mathematics is rapidly growing in importance. The growing need for mathematicians and computer scientists in industry will lead to an increase in courses offered in the area of discrete mathematics. One of the most suitable and fascinating is, indeed, coding theory. So, it is not surprising that one more book on this subject now appears. However, a little more justification and a little more history of the book are necessary. At a meeting on coding theory in 1979 it was remarked that there was no book available that could be used for an introductory course on coding theory (mainly for mathematicians but also for students in engineering or computer science). The best known textbooks were either too old, too big, too technical, too much for specialists, etc. The final remark was that my Springer Lecture Notes (#201) were slightly obsolete and out of print. Without realizing what I was getting into I announced that the statement was not true and proved this by showing several participants the book *Inleiding in de Coderingstheorie*, a little book based on the syllabus of a course given at the Mathematical Centre in Amsterdam in 1975 (M.C. Syllabus 31). The course, which was a great success, was given by M.R. Best, A.E. Brouwer, P. van Emde Boas, T.M.V. Janssen, H.W. Lenstra Jr., A. Schrijver, H.C.A. van Tilborg and myself. Since then the book has been used for a number of years at the Technological Universities of Delft and Eindhoven.

The comments above explain why it seemed reasonable (to me) to translate the Dutch book into English. In the name of Springer-Verlag I thank the Mathematical Centre in Amsterdam for permission to do so. Of course it turned out to be more than a translation. Much was rewritten or expanded, problems were changed and solutions were added, and a new chapter and several new proofs were included. Nevertheless the M.C. Syllabus (and the Springer Lecture Notes 201) are the basis of this book.

The book consists of three parts. Chapter 1 contains the prerequisite mathematical knowledge. It is written in the style of a memory-refresher. The reader who discovers topics that he does not know will get some idea about them but it is recommended that he also looks at standard textbooks on those topics. Chapters 2 to 6 provide an introductory course in coding theory. Finally, Chapters 7 to 11 are introductions to special topics and can be used as supplementary reading or as a preparation for studying the literature.

Despite the youth of the subject, which is demonstrated by the fact that the papers mentioned in the references have 1974 as the average publication year, I have not considered it necessary to give credit to every author of the theorems, lemmas, etc. Some have simply become standard knowledge.

It seems appropriate to mention a number of textbooks that I use regularly and that I would like to recommend to the student who would like to learn more than this introduction can offer. First of all F.J. MacWilliams and N.J.A. Sloane, *The Theory of Error-Correcting Codes* (reference [46]), which contains a much more extensive treatment of most of what is in this book and has 1500 references! For the more technically oriented student with an interest in decoding, complexity questions, etc. E.R. Berlekamp's *Algebraic Coding Theory* (reference [2]) is a must. For a very well-written mixture of information theory and coding theory I recommend: R.J. McEliece, *The Theory of Information and Coding* (reference [51]). In the present book very little attention is paid to the relation between coding theory and combinatorial mathematics. For this the reader should consult P.J. Cameron and J.H. van Lint, *Designs, Graphs, Codes and their Links* (reference [11]).

I sincerely hope that the time spent writing this book (instead of doing research) will be considered well invested.

Eindhoven   J.H. VAN LINT
July 1981

Second edition comments: Apparently the hope expressed in the final line of the preface of the first edition came true: a second edition has become necessary. Several misprints have been corrected and also some errors. In a few places some extra material has been added.

Contents

CHAPTER 1

Mathematical Background

In order to be able to read this book a fairly thorough mathematical back-ground is necessary. In different chapters many different areas of mathematics play a rôle. The most important one is certainly algebra but the reader must also know some facts from elementary number theory, probability theory and a number of concepts from combinatorial theory such as designs and geo-metries. In the following sections we shall give a brief survey of the prerequi-site knowledge. Usually proofs will be omitted. For these we refer to standard textbooks. In some of the chapters we need a large number of facts concerning a not too well-known class of orthogonal polynomials, called Krawtchouk polynomials. These properties are treated in Section 1.2. The notations that we use are fairly standard. We mention a few that may not be generally known. If C is a finite set we denote the number of elements of C by $|C|$. If the expression B is the definition of concept A then we write $A := B$. We use "iff" for "if and only if". An identity matrix is denoted by I and the matrix with all entries equal to one is J. Similarly we abbreviate the vector with all coordinates 0 (resp. 1) by $\mathbf{0}$ (resp. $\mathbf{1}$). Instead of using $[x]$ we write $\lfloor x \rfloor :=$ $\max\{n \in \mathbb{Z} \mid n \leq x\}$ and we use the symbol $\lceil x \rceil$ for rounding upwards.

§1.1. Algebra

We need only very little from elementary number theory. We assume known that in $\mathbb{N}$ every number can be written in exactly one way as a product of prime numbers (if we ignore the order of the factors). If a divides b, then we write $a \mid b$. If p is a prime number and $p^r \mid a$ but $p^{r+1} \nmid a$, then we write $p^r \| a$. If

$k \in \mathbb{N}, k > 1$, then a representation of n in the base k is a representation

$$n = \sum_{i=0}^{l} n_i k^i,$$

$0 \le n_i < k$ for $0 \le i \le l$. The largest integer n such that $n|a$ and $n|b$ is called the greatest common divisor of a and b and denoted by g.c.d.(a, b) or simply (a, b). If $m|(a - b)$ we write $a \equiv b \pmod{m}$.

(1.1.1) Theorem. *If*

$$\varphi(n) := |\{m \in \mathbb{N} | 1 \le m \le n, (m, n) = 1\}|,$$

then

(i) $\varphi(n) = n \prod_{p|n} (1 - 1/p)$,
(ii) $\sum_{d|n} \varphi(d) = n$.

The function φ is called the *Euler indicator*.

(1.1.2) Theorem. *If* $(a, m) = 1$ *then* $a^{\varphi(m)} \equiv 1 \pmod{m}$.

Theorem 1.1.2 is called the Euler–Fermat theorem.

(1.1.3) Definition. The *Moebius function* μ is defined by

$$\mu(n) := \begin{cases} 1, & \text{if } n = 1, \\ (-1)^k, & \text{if } n \text{ is the product of } k \text{ distinct prime factors,} \\ 0, & \text{otherwise.} \end{cases}$$

(1.1.4) Theorem. *If f and g are functions defined on $\mathbb{N}$ such that*

$$g(n) = \sum_{d|n} f(d),$$

then

$$f(n) = \sum_{d|n} \mu(d) g\left(\frac{n}{d}\right).$$

Theorem 1.1.4 is known as the *Moebius inversion formula*.

Algebraic Structures

We assume that the reader is familiar with the basic ideas and theorems of linear algebra although we do refresh his memory below. We shall first give a sequence of definitions of algebraic structures with which the reader must be familiar in order to appreciate algebraic coding theory.

(1.1.5) Definition. A *group* $(G, \cdot)$ is a set G on which a product operation has been defined satisfying

(i) $\forall_{a \in G} \forall_{b \in G} [ab \in G]$,
(ii) $\forall_{a \in G} \forall_{b \in G} \forall_{c \in G} [(ab)c = a(bc)]$,
(iii) $\exists_{e \in G} \forall_{a \in G} [ae = ea = a]$,
    (the element e is unique),
(iv) $\forall_{a \in G} \exists_{b \in G} [ab = ba = e]$,
    (b is called the inverse of a and also denoted by a^{-1}).

If furthermore

(v) $\forall_{a \in G} \forall_{b \in G} [ab = ba]$,

then the group is called *abelian* or *commutative*.

If $(G, \cdot)$ is a group and $H \subset G$ such that $(H, \cdot)$ is also a group, then $(H, \cdot)$ is called a subgroup of $(G, \cdot)$. Usually we write G instead of $(G, \cdot)$. The number of elements of a finite group is called the *order* of the group. If $(G, \cdot)$ is a group and $a \in G$, then the smallest positive integer n such that $a^n = e$ (if such an n exists) is called the *order* of a. In this case the elements $e, a, a^2, \ldots, a^{n-1}$ form a so-called *cyclic* subgroup with a as *generator*. If $(G, \cdot)$ is abelian and $(H, \cdot)$ is a subgroup then the sets $aH := \{ah | h \in H\}$ are called *cosets* of H. Since two cosets are obviously disjoint or identical, the cosets form a partition of G. An element chosen from a coset is called a *representative* of the coset. It is not difficult to show that the cosets again form a group if we define multiplication of cosets by $(aH)(bH) := abH$. This group is called the *factor group* and indicated by G/H. As a consequence note that if $a \in G$, then the order of a divides the order of G (also if G is not abelian).

(1.1.6) Definition. A set R with two operations, usually called addition and multiplication, denoted by $(R, +, \cdot)$, is called a *ring* if

(i) $(R, +)$ is an abelian group,
(ii) $\forall_{a \in R} \forall_{b \in R} \forall_{c \in R} [(ab)c = a(bc)]$,
(iii) $\forall_{a \in R} \forall_{b \in R} \forall_{c \in R} [a(b + c) = ab + ac \wedge (a + b)c = ac + bc]$.

The identity element of $(R, +)$ is usually denoted by 0.
    If the additional property

(iv) $\forall_{a \in R} \forall_{b \in R} [ab = ba]$

holds, then the ring is called *commutative*.

The integers $\mathbb{Z}$ are the best known example of a ring.

(1.1.7) Definition. If $(R, +, \cdot)$ is a ring and $\emptyset \neq S \subseteq R$, then S is called an *ideal* if

(i) $\forall_{a \in S} \forall_{b \in S}[a - b \in S]$,

(ii) $\forall_{a \in S} \forall_{b \in R}[ab \in S \wedge ba \in S]$.

It is clear that if S is an ideal in R, then $(S, +, \;)$ is a subring, but requirement (ii) says more than that.

(1.1.8) Definition. A *field* is a ring $(R, +, \;)$ for which $(R \setminus \{0\}, \;)$ is an abelian group.

(1.1.9) Theorem. *Every finite ring R with at least two elements such that*

$$\forall_{a \in R} \forall_{b \in R}[ab = 0 \Rightarrow (a = 0 \vee b = 0)]$$

is a field.

(1.1.10) Definition. Let $(V, +)$ be an abelian group, $\mathbb{F}$ a field and let a multiplication $\mathbb{F} \times V \to V$ be defined satisfying

(i) $\forall_{\mathbf{a} \in V}[1\mathbf{a} = \mathbf{a}]$,

   $\forall_{\alpha \in \mathbb{F}} \forall_{\beta \in \mathbb{F}} \forall_{\mathbf{a} \in V}[\alpha(\beta \mathbf{a}) = (\alpha\beta)\mathbf{a}]$,

(ii) $\forall_{\alpha \in \mathbb{F}} \forall_{\mathbf{a} \in V} \forall_{\mathbf{b} \in V}[\alpha(\mathbf{a} + \mathbf{b}) = \alpha\mathbf{a} + \alpha\mathbf{b}]$,

   $\forall_{\alpha \in \mathbb{F}} \forall_{\beta \in \mathbb{F}} \forall_{\mathbf{a} \in V}[(\alpha + \beta)\mathbf{a} = \alpha\mathbf{a} + \beta\mathbf{a}]$.

Then the triple $(V, +, \mathbb{F})$ is called a *vector space* over the field $\mathbb{F}$. The identity element of $(V, +)$ is denoted by $\mathbf{0}$.

We assume the reader to be familiar with the vector space $\mathbb{R}^n$ consisting of all n-tuples $(a_1, a_2, \ldots, a_n)$ with the obvious rules for addition and multiplication. We remind him of the fact that a *k-dimensional subspace* C of this vector space is a vector space with a *basis* consisting of vectors $\mathbf{a}_1 := (a_{11}, a_{12}, \ldots, a_{1n})$, $\mathbf{a}_2 := (a_{21}, a_{22}, \ldots, a_{2n})$, $\ldots$, $\mathbf{a}_k := (a_{k1}, a_{k2}, \ldots, a_{kn})$, where the word basis means that every $\mathbf{a} \in C$ can be written in a unique way as $\alpha_1 \mathbf{a}_1 + \alpha_2 \mathbf{a}_2 + \cdots + \alpha_k \mathbf{a}_k$. The reader should also be familiar with the process of going from one basis of C to another by taking combinations of basis vectors, etc. We shall usually write vectors as *row vectors* as we did above. The *inner product* $\langle \mathbf{a}, \mathbf{b} \rangle$ of two vectors $\mathbf{a}$ and $\mathbf{b}$ is defined by

$$\langle \mathbf{a}, \mathbf{b} \rangle := a_1 b_1 + a_2 b_2 + \cdots + a_n b_n.$$

The elements of a basis are called *linearly independent*. In other words this means that a linear combination of these vectors is $\mathbf{0}$ iff all the coefficients are 0. If $\mathbf{a}_1, \ldots, \mathbf{a}_k$ are k linearly independent vectors, i.e. a basis of a k-dimensional subspace C, then the system of equations $\langle \mathbf{a}_i, \mathbf{y} \rangle = 0$ ($i = 1, 2, \ldots, k$) has as its solution all the vectors in a subspace of dimension $n - k$ which we denote by $C^\perp$. So,

$$C^\perp := \{\mathbf{y} \in \mathbb{R}^n | \forall_{\mathbf{x} \in C}[\langle \mathbf{x}, \mathbf{y} \rangle = 0]\}.$$

These ideas play a fundamental role later on, where $\mathbb{R}$ is replaced by a finite field $\mathbb{F}$. The theory reviewed above goes through in that case.

(1.1.11) Definition. Let $(V, +)$ be a vector space over $\mathbb{F}$ and let a multiplication $V \times V \to V$ be defined that satisfies

(i) $(V, +, \ )$ is a ring,
(ii) $\forall_{\alpha \in \mathbb{F}} \forall_{\mathbf{a} \in V} \forall_{\mathbf{b} \in V} [(\alpha \mathbf{a}) \mathbf{b} = \mathbf{a}(\alpha \mathbf{b})]$.

Then we say that the system is an *algebra* over $\mathbb{F}$.

Suppose we have a finite group $(G, \cdot)$ and we consider the elements of G as basis vectors for a vector space $(V, +)$ over a field $\mathbb{F}$. Then the elements of V are represented by linear combinations $\alpha_1 g_1 + \alpha_2 g_2 + \cdots + \alpha_n g_n$, where

$$\alpha_i \in \mathbb{F}, \qquad g_i \in G, \qquad (1 \leq i \leq n = |G|).$$

We can define a multiplication $*$ for these vectors in the obvious way, namely

$$\left(\sum_i \alpha_i g_i\right) * \left(\sum_j \beta_j g_j\right) := \sum_i \sum_j (\alpha_i \beta_j)(g_i \cdot g_j),$$

which can be written as $\sum_k \gamma_k g_k$, where γ_k is the sum of the elements $\alpha_i \beta_j$ over all pairs (i, j) such that $g_i \cdot g_j = g_k$. This yields an algebra which is called the *group algebra* of G over $\mathbb{F}$ and denoted by $\mathbb{F}G$.

EXAMPLES. Let us consider a number of examples of the concepts defined above.

If $A := \{a_1, a_2, \ldots, a_n\}$ is a finite set, we can consider all one-to-one mappings of S onto S. These are called *permutations*. If σ_1 and σ_2 are permutations we define $\sigma_1 \sigma_2$ by $(\sigma_1 \sigma_2)(a) := \sigma_1(\sigma_2(a))$ for all $a \in A$. It is easy to see that the set S_n of all permutations of A with this multiplication is a group, known as the *symmetric group of degree n*. In this book we shall often be interested in special permutation groups. These are subgroups of S_n. We give one example. Let C be a k-dimensional subspace of $\mathbb{R}^n$. Consider all permutations σ of the integers $1, 2, \ldots, n$ such that for every vector $\mathbf{c} = (c_1, c_2, \ldots, c_n) \in C$ the vector $(c_{\sigma(1)}, c_{\sigma(2)}, \ldots, c_{\sigma(n)})$ is also in C. These clearly form a subgroup of S_n. Of course C will often be such that this subgroup of S consists of the identity only but there are more interesting examples! Another example of a permutation group which will turn up later is the *affine permutation group* defined as follows. Let $\mathbb{F}$ be a (finite) field. The mapping $f_{u,v}$, when $u \in \mathbb{F}$, $v \in \mathbb{F}$, $u \neq 0$, is defined on $\mathbb{F}$ by $f_{u,v}(x) := ux + v$ for all $x \in \mathbb{F}$. These mappings are permutations of $\mathbb{F}$ and clearly they form a group under composition of functions.

A *permutation matrix P* is a $(0, 1)$-matrix that has exactly one 1 in each row and column. We say that P corresponds to the permutation σ of $\{1, 2, \ldots, n\}$ if $p_{ij} = 1$ iff $i = \sigma(j)$ $(i = 1, 2, \ldots, n)$. With this convention the product of permutations corresponds to the product of their matrices. In this way one obtains the so-called matrix representation of a group of permutations.

A group G of permutations acting on a set Ω is called *k-transitive* on Ω if for every ordered k-tuple $(a_1, \ldots, a_k)$ of distinct elements of Ω and for every

k-tuple $(b_1, \ldots, b_k)$ of distinct elements of Ω, there is an element $\sigma \in G$ such that $b_i = \sigma(a_i)$ for $1 \leq i \leq k$. If $k = 1$ we call the group transitive.

Let S be an ideal in the ring $(R, +, \cdot)$. Since $(S, +)$ is a subgroup of the abelian group $(R, +)$, we can form the factor group. The cosets are now called *residue classes mod S*. For these classes we introduce a multiplication in the obvious way: $(a + S)(b + S) := ab + S$. The reader who is not familiar with this concept should check that this definition makes sense (i.e. it does not depend on the choice of representatives a resp. b). In this way we have constructed a ring, called the *residue class ring R mod S* and denoted by R/S. The following example will surely be familiar. Let $R := \mathbb{Z}$ and let p be a prime. Let S be $p\mathbb{Z}$, the set of all multiples of p, which is sometimes also denoted by (p). Then R/S is the ring of integers mod p. The elements of R/S can be represented by $0, 1, \ldots, p - 1$ and then addition and multiplication are the usual operations in $\mathbb{Z}$ followed by a reduction mod p. For example, if we take $p = 7$, then $4 + 5 = 2$ because in $\mathbb{Z}$ we have $4 + 5 \equiv 2 \pmod 7$. In the same way $4 \cdot 5 = 6$ in $\mathbb{Z}/7\mathbb{Z} = \mathbb{Z}/(7)$. If S is an ideal in $\mathbb{Z}$ and $S \neq \{0\}$, then there is a smallest positive integer k in S. Let $s \in S$. We can write s as $ak + b$, where $0 \leq b < k$. By the definition of ideal we have $ak \in S$ and hence $b = s - ak \in S$ and then the definition of k implies that $b = 0$. Therefore $S = (k)$. An ideal consisting of all multiples of a fixed element is called a *principal ideal* and if a ring R has no other ideals than principal ideals, it is called a *principal ideal ring*. Therefore $\mathbb{Z}$ is such a ring.

(1.1.12) Theorem. *If p is a prime then $\mathbb{Z}/p\mathbb{Z}$ is a field.*

This is an immediate consequence of Theorem 1.1.9 but also obvious directly. A finite field with n elements is denoted by $\mathbb{F}_n$ or $GF(n)$ (Galois field).

Rings and Finite Fields

More about finite fields will follow below. First some more about rings and ideals. Let $\mathbb{F}$ be a finite field. Consider the set $\mathbb{F}[x]$ consisting of all polynomials $a_0 + a_1 x + \cdots + a_n x^n$, where n can be any integer in $\mathbb{N}$ and $a_i \in \mathbb{F}$ for $0 \leq i \leq n$. With the usual definition of addition and multiplication of polynomials this yields a ring $(\mathbb{F}[x], +, \cdot)$, which is usually just denoted by $\mathbb{F}[x]$. The set of all polynomials that are multiples of a fixed polynomial $g(x)$, i.e. all polynomials of the form $a(x)g(x)$ where $a(x) \in \mathbb{F}[x]$, is an ideal in $\mathbb{F}[x]$.

As before, we denote this ideal by $(g(x))$. The following theorem states that there are no other types.

(1.1.13) Theorem. $\mathbb{F}[x]$ *is a principal ideal ring.*

The residue class ring $\mathbb{F}[x]/(g(x))$ can be represented by the polynomials whose degree is less than the degree of $g(x)$. In the same way as our example

$\mathbb{Z}/7\mathbb{Z}$ given above, we now multiply and add these representatives in the usual way and then reduce mod $g(x)$. For example, we take $\mathbb{F} = \mathbb{F}_2 = \{0, 1\}$ and $g(x) = x^3 + x + 1$. Then $(x + 1)(x^2 + 1) = x^3 + x^2 + x + 1 = x^2$. This example is a useful one to study carefully if one is not familiar with finite fields. First observe that $g(x)$ is *irreducible*, i.e., there do not exist polynomials $a(x)$ and $b(x) \in \mathbb{F}[x]$, both of degree less than 3, such that $g(x) = a(x)b(x)$. Next, realize that this means that in $\mathbb{F}_2[x]/(g(x))$ the product of two elements $a(x)$ and $b(x)$ is 0 iff $a(x) = 0$ or $b(x) = 0$. By Theorem 1.1.9 this means that $\mathbb{F}_2[x]/(g(x))$ is a field. Since the representatives of this residue class ring all have degrees less than 3, there are exactly eight of them. So we have found a field with eight elements, i.e. $\mathbb{F}_{2^3}$. This is an example of the way in which finite fields are constructed.

(1.1.14) Theorem. *Let p be a prime and let $g(x)$ be an irreducible polynomial of degree r in the ring $\mathbb{F}_p[x]$. Then the residue class ring $\mathbb{F}_p[x]/(g(x))$ is a field with p^r elements.*

PROOF. The proof is the same as the one given for the example $p = 2, r = 3$, $g(x) = x^3 + x + 1$. □

(1.1.15) Theorem. *Let $\mathbb{F}$ be a field with n elements. Then n is a power of a prime.*

PROOF. By definition there is an identity element for multiplication in $\mathbb{F}$. We denote this by 1. Of course $1 + 1 \in \mathbb{F}$ and we denote this element by 2. We continue in this way, i.e. $2 + 1 = 3$, etc. After a finite number of steps we encounter a field element that already has a name. Suppose, e.g. that the sum of k terms 1 is equal to the sum of l terms 1 $(k > l)$. Then the sum of $(k - l)$ terms 1 is 0, i.e. the first time we encounter an element that already has a name, this element is 0. Say 0 is the sum of k terms 1. If k is composite, $k = ab$, then the product of the elements which we have called a resp. b is 0, a contradiction. So k is a prime and we have shown that $\mathbb{F}_p$ is a subfield of $\mathbb{F}$. We define linear independence of a set of elements of $\mathbb{F}$ with respect to (coefficients from) $\mathbb{F}_p$ in the obvious way. Among all linearly independent subsets of $\mathbb{F}$ let $\{x_1, x_2, \ldots, x_r\}$ be one with the maximal number of elements. If x is any element of $\mathbb{F}$ then the elements $x, x_1, x_2, \ldots, x_r$ are not linearly independent, i.e. there are coefficients $0 \neq \alpha, \alpha_1, \ldots, \alpha_r$ such that $\alpha x + \alpha_1 x_1 + \cdots + \alpha_r x_r = 0$ and hence x is a linear combination of x_1 to x_r. Since there are obviously p^r distinct linear combinations of x_1 to x_r, the proof is complete. □

From the previous theorems we now know that a field with n elements exists iff n is a prime power, providing we can show that for every $r \geq 1$ there is an irreducible polynomial of degree r in $\mathbb{F}_p[x]$. We shall prove this by calculating the number of such polynomials. Fix p and let I_r denote the number of irreducible polynomials of degree r that are *monic*, i.e. the coefficient of x^r is 1. We claim that

(1.1.16)
$$(1 - pz)^{-1} = \prod_{r=1}^{\infty} (1 - z^r)^{-I_r}.$$

In order to see this, first observe that the coefficient of z^n on the left-hand side is p^n, which is the number of monic polynomials of degree n with coefficients in $\mathbb{F}_p$. We know that each such polynomial can be factored uniquely into irreducible factors and we must therefore convince ourselves that these products are counted on the right-hand side of (1.1.16). To show this we just consider two irreducible polynomials $a_1(x)$ of degree r and $a_2(x)$ of degree s. There is a 1–1 correspondence between products $(a_1(x))^k (a_2(x))^l$ and terms $z_1^{kr} z_2^{ls}$ in the product of $(1 + z_1^r + z_1^{2r} + \cdots)$ and $(1 + z_2^s + z_2^{2s} + \cdots)$. If we identify z_1 and z_2 with z, then the exponent of z is the degree of $(a_1(x))^k (a_2(x))^l$. Instead of two polynomials $a_1(x)$ and $a_2(x)$, we now consider all irreducible polynomials and (1.1.16) follows.

In (1.1.16) we take logarithms on both sides, then differentiate, and finally multiply by z to obtain

(1.1.17)
$$\frac{pz}{1 - pz} = \sum_{r=1}^{\infty} I_r \frac{rz^r}{1 - z^r}.$$

Comparing coefficients of z^n on both sides of (1.1.17) we find

(1.1.18)
$$p^n = \sum_{r|n} r I_r.$$

Now apply Theorem 1.1.4 to (1.1.18). We find

(1.1.19)
$$I_r = \frac{1}{r} \sum_{d|r} \mu(d) p^{r/d} > \frac{1}{r} \{ p^r - p^{r/2} - p^{r/3} - \cdots \}$$

$$> \frac{1}{r} \left(p^r - \sum_{i=0}^{r/2} p^i \right) > \frac{1}{r} p^r (1 - p^{-r/2+1}) > 0.$$

Now that we know for which values of n a field with n elements exists, we wish to know more about these fields. The structure of $\mathbb{F}_{p^r}$ will play a very important role in many chapters of this book. As a preparation consider a finite field $\mathbb{F}$ and a polynomial $f(x) \in \mathbb{F}[x]$ such that $f(a) = 0$, where $a \in \mathbb{F}$. Then by dividing we find that there is a $g(x) \in \mathbb{F}[x]$ such that $f(x) = (x - a)g(x)$. Continuing in this way we establish the trivial fact that a polynomial $f(x)$ of degree r in $\mathbb{F}[x]$ has at most r zeros in $\mathbb{F}$.

If α is an element of order e in the multiplicative group $(\mathbb{F}_{p^r} \setminus \{0\}, \ )$, then α is a zero of the polynomial $x^e - 1$. In fact, we have
$$x^e - 1 = (x - 1)(x - \alpha)(x - \alpha^2) \cdots (x - \alpha^{e-1}).$$

It follows that the only elements of order e in the group are the powers α^i where $1 \leq i < e$ and $(i, e) = 1$. There are $\varphi(e)$ such elements. Hence, for every e which divides $p^r - 1$ there are either 0 or $\varphi(e)$ elements of order e in the field. By (1.1.1) the possibility 0 never occurs. As a consequence there are elements of order $p^r - 1$, in fact exactly $\varphi(p^r - 1)$ such elements. We have following theorem.

(1.1.20) Theorem. *In* $\mathbb{F}_q$ *the multiplicative group* $(\mathbb{F}_q \backslash \{0\},\ )$ *is a cyclic group.*

This group is often denoted by $\mathbb{F}_q^*$.

(1.1.21) Definition. A generator of the multiplicative group of $\mathbb{F}_q$ is called a *primitive element* of the field.

Note that Theorem 1.1.20 states that the elements of $\mathbb{F}_q$ are exactly the q distinct zeros of the polynomial $x^q - x$. An element β such that $\beta^k = 1$ but $\beta^l \neq 1$ for $0 < l < k$ is called a *primitive kth root of unity*. Clearly a primitive element α of $\mathbb{F}_q$ is a primitive $(q - 1)$th root of unity. If e divides $q - 1$ then α^e is a primitive $((q - 1)/e)$th root of unity. Furthermore a consequence of Theorem 1.1.20 is that $\mathbb{F}_{p^r}$ is a subfield of $\mathbb{F}_{p^s}$ iff r divides s. Actually this statement could be slightly confusing to the reader. We have been suggesting by our notation that for a given q the field $\mathbb{F}_q$ is unique. This is indeed true. In fact this follows from (1.1.18). We have shown that for $q = p^n$ every element of $\mathbb{F}_q$ is a zero of some irreducible factor of $x^q - x$ and from the remark above and Theorem 1.1.14 we see that this factor must have a degree r such that $r|n$. By (1.1.18) this means we have used all irreducible polynomials of degree r where $r|n$. In other words, the product of these polynomials is $x^q - x$. This establishes the fact that two fields $\mathbb{F}$ and $\mathbb{F}'$ of order q are isomorphic, i.e. there is a mapping $\varphi: \mathbb{F} \to \mathbb{F}'$ which is one-to-one and such that φ preserves addition and multiplication.

The following theorem is used very often in this book.

(1.1.22) Theorem. *Let* $q = p^r$ *and* $0 \neq f(x) \in \mathbb{F}_q[x]$.

(i) *If* $\alpha \in \mathbb{F}_{q^k}$ *and* $f(\alpha) = 0$, *then* $f(\alpha^q) = 0$.
(ii) *Conversely: Let* $g(x)$ *be a polynomial with coefficients in an extension field of* $\mathbb{F}_q$. *If* $g(\alpha^q) = 0$ *for every* α *for which* $g(\alpha) = 0$, *then* $g(x) \in \mathbb{F}_q[x]$.

PROOF.

(i) By the binomial theorem we have $(a + b)^p = a^p + b^p$ because p divides $\binom{p}{k}$ for $1 \leq k \leq p - 1$. It follows that $(a + b)^q = a^q + b^q$. If $f(x) = \sum a_i x^i$ then $(f(x))^q = \sum a_i^q (x^q)^i$.
   Because $a_i \in \mathbb{F}_q$ we have $a_i^q = a_i$. Substituting $x = \alpha$ we find $f(\alpha^q) = (f(\alpha))^q = 0$.
(ii) We already know that in a suitable extension field of $\mathbb{F}_q$ the polynomial $g(x)$ is a product of factors $x - \alpha_i$ (all of degree 1, that is) and if $x - \alpha_i$ is

one of these factors, then $x - \alpha_i^q$ is also one of them. If $g(x) = \sum_{k=0}^{n} a_k x^k$ then a_k is a symmetric function of the zeros α_i and hence $a_k = a_k^q$, i.e. $a_k \in \mathbb{F}_q$.

If $\alpha \in \mathbb{F}_q$, where $q = p^r$, then the *minimal polynomial* of α over $\mathbb{F}_p$ is the irreducible polynomial $f(x) \in \mathbb{F}_p[x]$ such that $f(\alpha) = 0$. If α has order e then from Theorem 1.1.22 we know that this minimal polynomial is $\prod_{i=0}^{m-1}(x - \alpha^{p^i})$, where m is the smallest integer such that $p^m \equiv 1 \pmod{e}$. Sometimes we shall consider a field $\mathbb{F}_q$ with a fixed primitive element α.

In that case we use $m_i(x)$ to denote the minimal polynomial of α^i. An irreducible polynomial which is the minimal polynomial of a primitive element in the corresponding field is called a *primitive polynomial*. Such polynomials are the most convenient ones to use in the construction of Theorem 1.1.14. We give an example in detail.

(1.1.23) EXAMPLE. The polynomial $x^4 + x + 1$ is primitive over $\mathbb{F}_2$. The field $\mathbb{F}_{2^4}$ is represented by polynomials of degree <4. The polynomial x is a primitive element. Since we prefer to use the symbol x for other purposes, we call this primitive element α. Note that $\alpha^4 + \alpha + 1 = 0$. Every element in $\mathbb{F}_{2^4}$ is a linear combination of the elements $1, \alpha, \alpha^2$, and α^3. We get the following table for $\mathbb{F}_{2^4}$. The reader should observe that this is the equivalent of a table of logarithms for the case of the field $\mathbb{R}$.

Table of $\mathbb{F}_{2^4}$

$$
\begin{array}{lllll}
0 & = & & & = (0\ 0\ 0\ 0) \\
1 & = & 1 & & = (1\ 0\ 0\ 0) \\
\alpha & = & \alpha & & = (0\ 1\ 0\ 0) \\
\alpha^2 & = & & \alpha^2 & = (0\ 0\ 1\ 0) \\
\alpha^3 & = & & & \alpha^3 = (0\ 0\ 0\ 1) \\
\alpha^4 & = & 1 + \alpha & & = (1\ 1\ 0\ 0) \\
\alpha^5 & = & & \alpha + \alpha^2 & = (0\ 1\ 1\ 0) \\
\alpha^6 & = & & \alpha^2 + \alpha^3 & = (0\ 0\ 1\ 1) \\
\alpha^7 & = & 1 + \alpha & + \alpha^3 & = (1\ 1\ 0\ 1) \\
\alpha^8 & = & 1 & + \alpha^2 & = (1\ 0\ 1\ 0) \\
\alpha^9 & = & & \alpha & + \alpha^3 = (0\ 1\ 0\ 1) \\
\alpha^{10} & = & 1 + \alpha + \alpha^2 & & = (1\ 1\ 1\ 0) \\
\alpha^{11} & = & & \alpha + \alpha^2 + \alpha^3 & = (0\ 1\ 1\ 1) \\
\alpha^{12} & = & 1 + \alpha + \alpha^2 + \alpha^3 & & = (1\ 1\ 1\ 1) \\
\alpha^{13} & = & 1 & + \alpha^2 + \alpha^3 & = (1\ 0\ 1\ 1) \\
\alpha^{14} & = & 1 & + \alpha^3 & = (1\ 0\ 0\ 1) \\
\end{array}
$$

The representation on the right demonstrates again that $\mathbb{F}_{2^4}$ can be interpreted as the vector space $(\mathbb{F}_2)^4$, where $\{1, \alpha, \alpha^2, \alpha^3\}$ is the basis. The left-hand column is easiest for multiplication (add exponents, mod 15) and the right-hand column for addition (add vectors). It is now easy to check that

$$m_1(x) = (x - \alpha)(x - \alpha^2)(x - \alpha^4)(x - \alpha^8) \qquad = x^4 + x + 1,$$

$$m_3(x) = (x - \alpha^3)(x - \alpha^6)(x - \alpha^{12})(x - \alpha^9) \qquad = x^4 + x^3 + x^2 + x + 1,$$

$$m_5(x) = (x - \alpha^5)(x - \alpha^{10}) \qquad = x^2 + x + 1,$$

$$m_7(x) = (x - \alpha^7)(x - \alpha^{14})(x - \alpha^{13})(x - \alpha^{11}) \qquad = x^4 + x^3 + 1,$$

and the decomposition of $x^{16} - x$ into irreducible factors is

$$x^{16} - x = x(x - 1)(x^2 + x + 1)(x^4 + x + 1)$$
$$\times (x^4 + x^3 + 1)(x^4 + x^3 + x^2 + x + 1).$$

Note that $x^4 - x = x(x - 1)(x^2 + x + 1)$ corresponding to the elements 0, 1, α^5, α^{10} which form the subfield $\mathbb{F}_4 = \mathbb{F}_2[x]/(x^2 + x + 1)$. The polynomial $m_3(x)$ is irreducible but not primitive.

The reader who is not familiar with finite fields should study (1.1.14) to (1.1.23) thoroughly and construct several examples such as $\mathbb{F}_9$, $\mathbb{F}_{27}$, $\mathbb{F}_{64}$ with the corresponding minimal polynomials, subfields, etc. For tables of finite fields see references [9] and [10].

Polynomials

We need a few more facts about polynomials. If $f(x) \in \mathbb{F}_q[x]$ we can define the *derivative* $f'(x)$ in a purely formal way by

$$\left(\sum_{k=0}^{n} a_k x^k \right)' := \sum_{k=1}^{n} k a_k x^{k-1}.$$

The usual rules for differentiation of sums and products go through and one finds for instance that the derivative of $(x - \alpha)^2 f(x)$ is $2(x - \alpha)f(x) + (x - \alpha)^2 f'(x)$. Therefore the following theorem is obvious.

(1.1.24) Theorem. *If $f(x) \in \mathbb{F}_q[x]$ and α is a multiple zero of $f(x)$ in some extension field of $\mathbb{F}_q$, then α is also a zero of the derivative $f'(x)$.*

Note however, that if $q = 2^r$, then the second derivative of any polynomial in $\mathbb{F}_q[x]$ is identically 0. This tells us nothing about the multiplicity of zeros of the polynomial. In order to get complete analogy with the theory of polynomials over $\mathbb{R}$, we introduce the so-called *Hasse derivative* of a polynomial $f(x) \in \mathbb{F}_q[x]$ by

$$f^{[k]}(x) := \frac{1}{k!} f^{(k)}(x);$$

$$\left(\text{so the } k\text{-th Hasse derivative of } x^n \text{ is } \binom{n}{k} x^{n-k}. \right)$$

The reader should have no difficulty proving that α is a zero of $f(x)$ with multiplicity k iff it is a zero of $f^{[i]}(x)$ for $0 \le i < k$ and not a zero of $f^{[k]}(x)$.

Another result to be used later is the fact that if $f(x) = \prod_{i=1}^{n}(x - \alpha_i)$ then $f'(x) = \sum_{i=1}^{n} f(x)/(x - \alpha_i)$.

The following theorem is well known.

(1.1.25) Theorem. *If the polynomials $a(x)$ and $b(x)$ in $\mathbb{F}[x]$ have greatest common divisor 1, then there are polynomials $p(x)$ and $q(x)$ in $\mathbb{F}[x]$ such that*

$$a(x)p(x) + b(x)q(x) = 1.$$

PROOF. This is an immediate consequence of Theorem 1.1.13.   □

Although we know from (1.1.19) that irreducible polynomials of any degree r exist, it sometimes takes a lot of work to find one. The proof of (1.1.19) shows one way to do it. One starts with all possible polynomials of degree 1 and forms all reducible polynomials of degree 2. Any polynomial of degree 2 not in the list is irreducible. Then one proceeds in the obvious way to produce irreducible polynomials of degree 3, etc. In Section 9.2 we shall need irreducible polynomials over $\mathbb{F}_2$ of arbitrarily high degree. The procedure sketched above is not satisfactory for that purpose. Instead, we proceed as follows.

(1.1.26) Lemma.

$$3^{\beta+1} \| (2^{3^\beta} + 1).$$

PROOF.

(i) For $\beta = 0$ and $\beta = 1$ the assertion is true.
(ii) Suppose $3^t \| (2^{3^\beta} + 1)$. Then from

$$(2^{3^{\beta+1}} + 1) = (2^{3^\beta} + 1)\{(2^{3^\beta} + 1)(2^{3^\beta} - 2) + 3\},$$

it follows that if $t \geq 2$, then $3^{t+1} \| (2^{3^{\beta+1}} + 1)$.   □

(1.1.27) Lemma. *If m is the order of 2 (mod 3^l), then*

$$m = \varphi(3^l) = 2 \cdot 3^{l-1}.$$

PROOF. If $2^\alpha \equiv 1$ (mod 3) then α is even. Therefore $m = 2s$. Hence $2^s + 1 \equiv 0$ (mod 3^l). The result follows from Theorem 1.1.2 and Lemma 1.1.26.   □

(1.1.28) Theorem. *Let $m = 2 \cdot 3^{l-1}$. Then*

$$x^m + x^{m/2} + 1$$

is irreducible over $\mathbb{F}_2$.

PROOF. Consider $\mathbb{F}_{2^m}$. In this field let ξ be a primitive (3^l)th root of unity. The minimal polynomial of ξ then is, by Lemma 1.1.27

$$f(x) = (x - \xi)(x - \xi^2)(x - \xi^4)\cdots(x - \xi^{2^{m-1}}),$$

a polynomial of degree m. Note that

$$x^{3^l} + 1 = (1 + x)(1 + x + x^2)(1 + x^3 + x^6)\cdots(1 + x^{3^{l-1}} + x^{2\cdot 3^{l-1}}),$$

a factorization which contains only one polynomial of degree m, so the last factor must be $f(x)$, i.e. it is irreducible.   □

Quadratic Residues

A consequence of the existence of a primitive element in any field $\mathbb{F}_q$ is that it is easy to determine the squares in the field. If q is even then every element is a square. If q is odd then $\mathbb{F}_q$ consists of 0, $\frac{1}{2}(q - 1)$ nonzero squares and $\frac{1}{2}(q - 1)$ nonsquares. The integers k with $1 \le k \le p - 1$ which are squares in $\mathbb{F}_p$ are usually called *quadratic residues* (mod p). By considering $k \in \mathbb{F}_p$ as a power of a primitive element of this field, we see that k is a quadratic residue (mod p) iff $k^{(p-1)/2} \equiv 1$ (mod p). For the element $p - 1 = -1$ we find: -1 is a square in $\mathbb{F}_p$ iff $p \equiv 1$ (mod 4). In Section 6.9 we need to know whether 2 is a square in $\mathbb{F}_p$. To decide this question we consider the elements 1, 2, ..., $(p - 1)/2$ and let a be their product. Multiply each of the elements by 2 to obtain 2, 4, ..., $p - 1$. This sequence contains $\lfloor (p - 1)/4 \rfloor$ factors which are factors of a and for any other factor k of a we see that $-k$ is one of the even integers $> (p - 1)/2$. It follows that in $\mathbb{F}_p$ we have $2^{(p-1)/2} \, a = (-1)^{(p-1)/2 - \lfloor (p-1)/4 \rfloor} \, a$ and since $a \neq 0$ we see that 2 is a square iff

$$\frac{p - 1}{2} - \left\lfloor \frac{p - 1}{4} \right\rfloor$$

is even, i.e. $p \equiv \pm 1$ (mod 8).

The Trace

Let $q = p^r$. We define a mapping $\mathrm{Tr}: \mathbb{F}_q \to \mathbb{F}_p$, which is called the *trace*, as follows.

(1.1.29) Definition. If $\xi \in \mathbb{F}_q$ then

$$\mathrm{Tr}(\xi) := \xi + \xi^p + \xi^{p^2} + \cdots + \xi^{p^{r-1}}.$$

(1.1.30) Theorem. *The trace function has the following properties:*

  (i) *For every $\xi \in \mathbb{F}_q$ the trace $\mathrm{Tr}(\xi)$ is in $\mathbb{F}_p$;*
 (ii) *There are elements $\xi \in \mathbb{F}_q$ such that $\mathrm{Tr}(\xi) \neq 0$;*
(iii) *Tr is a linear mapping.*

PROOF.

(i) By definition $(\mathrm{Tr}(\xi))^p = \mathrm{Tr}(\xi)$.
(ii) The equation $x + x^p + \cdots + x^{p^{r-1}} = 0$ cannot have q roots in $\mathbb{F}_q$,
(iii) Since $(\xi + \eta)^p = \xi^p + \eta^p$ and for every $a \in \mathbb{F}_p$ we have $a^p = a$, this is
    obvious.   □

Of course the theorem implies that the trace takes every value $p^{-1}q$ times
and we see that the polynomial $x + x^p + \cdots + x^{p^{r-1}}$ is a product of minimal
polynomials (check this for Example 1.1.23).

Characters

Let $(G, +)$ be a group and let $(T, \ )$ be the group of complex numbers with
absolute value 1 with multiplication as operation. A *character* is a homo-
morphism $\chi: G \to T$, i.e.

(1.1.31) $\forall_{g_1 \in G} \forall_{g_2 \in G} [\chi(g_1 + g_2) = \chi(g_1)\chi(g_2)]$.

From the definition it follows that $\chi(0) = 1$ for every character χ. If $\chi(g) = 1$
for all $g \in G$ then χ is called the *principal character*.

(1.1.32) Lemma. *If χ is a character for $(G, +)$ then*

$$\sum_{g \in G} \chi(g) = \begin{cases} |G|, & \text{if } \chi \text{ is the principal character,} \\ 0, & \text{otherwise.} \end{cases}$$

PROOF. Let $h \in G$. Then

$$\chi(h) \sum_{g \in G} \chi(g) = \sum_{g \in G} \chi(h + g) = \sum_{k \in G} \chi(k).$$

If χ is not the principal character we can choose h such that $\chi(h) \neq 1$.   □

§1.2. Krawtchouk Polynomials

In this section we introduce a sequence of polynomials which play an important role in several parts of coding theory, the so-called *Krawtchouk polynomials*. These polynomials are an example of orthogonal polynomials and
most of the theorems that we mention are special cases of general theorems
that are valid for any sequence of orthogonal polynomials. The reader who
does not know this very elegant part of analysis is recommended to consult
one of the many textbooks about orthogonal polynomials (e.g. G. Szegö [67],
D. Jackson [36], F. G. Tricomi [70]). In fact, for some of the proofs of
theorems that we mention below, we refer the reader to the literature. Because

of the great importance of these polynomials in the sequel, we treat them more extensively than most other subjects in this introduction.

Usually the Krawtchouk polynomials will appear in situations where two parameters n and q have already been fixed. These are usually omitted in the notation for the polynomials.

(1.2.1) Definition. For $k = 0, 1, 2, \ldots$, we define the *Krawtchouk polynomial* $K_k(x)$ by

$$K_k(x; n, q) := K_k(x) := \sum_{j=0}^{k} (-1)^j \binom{x}{j} \binom{n-x}{k-j} (q-1)^{k-j},$$

where

$$\binom{x}{j} := \frac{x(x-1)\cdots(x-j+1)}{j!}, \qquad (x \in \mathbb{R}).$$

Observe that for the special case $q = 2$ we have

$$(1.2.2) \qquad K_k(x) = \sum_{j=0}^{k} (-1)^j \binom{x}{j} \binom{n-x}{k-j} = (-1)^k K_k(n-x).$$

By multiplying the Taylor series for $(1 + (q-1)z)^{n-x}$ and $(1-z)^x$ we find

$$(1.2.3) \qquad \sum_{k=0}^{\infty} K_k(x)z^k = (1 + (q-1)z)^{n-x}(1-z)^x.$$

It is clear from (1.2.1) that $K_k(x)$ is a polynomial of degree k in x with leading coefficient $(-q)^k/k!$ The name orthogonal polynomial is connected with the following "orthogonality relation":

$$(1.2.4) \qquad \sum_{i=0}^{n} \binom{n}{i} (q-1)^i K_k(i) K_l(i) = \delta_{kl} \binom{n}{k} (q-1)^k q^n.$$

The reader can easily prove this relation by multiplying both sides by $x^k y^l$ and summing over k and l (0 to ∞), using (1.2.3). Since the two sums are equal, the assertion is true. From (1.2.1) we find

$$(1.2.5) \qquad (q-1)\binom{n}{i} K_k(i) = (q-1)^k \binom{n}{k} K_i(k),$$

which we substitute in (1.2.4) to find a second kind of orthogonality relation:

$$(1.2.6) \qquad \sum_{i=0}^{n} K_l(i) K_i(k) = \delta_{lk} q^n.$$

We list a few of the Krawtchouk polynomials ($k \leq 2$)

$$(1.2.7) \qquad K_0(n, x) = 1,$$

$$K_1(n, x) = n(q-1) - qx, \qquad (= n - 2x \text{ if } q = 2),$$

$$K_2(n, x) = \tfrac{1}{2}\{q^2 x^2 - q(2qn - q - 2n + 2)x + (q - 1)^2 n(n - 1)\},$$

$$\left(= 2x^2 - 2nx + \binom{n}{2} \text{ if } q = 2\right).$$

In Chapter 7 we shall need the coefficients of x^k, x^{k-1}, x^{k-2}, and x^0 in the expression of $K_k(x)$. If $K_k(x) = \sum_{i=0}^{k} c_i x^i$, then for $q = 2$ we have:

$$c_k = (-2)^k / k!,$$

$$c_{k-1} = (-2)^{k-1} n / (k - 1)!,$$

$$c_{k-2} = \tfrac{1}{6}(-2)^{k-2}\{3n^2 - 3n + 2k - 4\}/(k - 2)!.$$

For several purposes we need certain recurrence relations for the Krawt-chouk polynomials. The most important one is

(1.2.9)
$$(k + 1)K_{k+1}(x)$$
$$= \{k + (q - 1)(n - k) - qx\}K_k(x) - (q - 1)(n - k + 1)K_{k-1}(x).$$

This is easily proved by differentiating both sides of (1.2.3) with respect to z and multiplying the result by $(1 + (q - 1)z)(1 - z)$. Comparison of coefficients yields the result. An even easier exercise is replacing x by $x - 1$ in (1.2.3) to obtain

(1.2.10) $$K_k(i) = K_k(i - 1) - (q - 1)K_{k-1}(i) - K_{k-1}(i - 1),$$

which is an easy way to calculate the numbers $K_k(i)$ recursively.

If $P(x)$ is any polynomial of degree l then there is a unique expansion

(1.2.11) $$P(x) = \sum_{k=0}^{l} \alpha_k K_k(x),$$

which is called the *Krawtchouk expansion* of $P(x)$.

We mention without proof a few properties that we need later. They are special cases of general theorems on orthogonal polynomials. The first is the Christoffel–Darboux formula

(1.2.12) $$\frac{K_{k+1}(x)K_k(y) - K_k(x)K_{k+1}(y)}{y - x} = \frac{2}{k + 1}\binom{n}{k}\sum_{i=0}^{k} \frac{K_i(x)K_i(y)}{\binom{n}{i}}.$$

The recurrence relation (1.2.9) and an induction argument show the very important interlacing property of the zeros of $K_k(x)$:

(1.2.13) $K_k(x)$ has k distinct real zeros on $(0, n)$; if these are
$v_1 < v_2 < \cdots < v_k$ and if $u_1 < u_2 < \cdots < u_{k-1}$ are the
zeros of K_{k-1}, then

$$0 < v_1 < u_1 < v_2 < \cdots < v_{k-1} < u_{k-1} < v_k < n.$$

The following property once again follows from (1.2.3) (where we now take $q = 2$) by multiplying two power series: If $x = 0, 1, 2, \ldots, n$, then

(1.2.14)
$$K_i(x)K_j(x) = \sum_{k=0}^{n} \alpha_k K_k(x),$$

where

$$\alpha_k := \binom{n-k}{(i+j-k)/2}\binom{k}{(i-j+k)/2}.$$

In Chapter 7 we shall need the relation

(1.2.15)
$$\sum_{k=0}^{l} K_k(x) = K_l(x-1; n-1, q).$$

This is easily proved by substituting (1.2.1) on the left-hand side, changing the order of summation and then using $\binom{x}{j} = \binom{x-1}{j-1} + \binom{x-1}{j}$ $(j \geq 1)$. We shall denote $K_l(x-1; n-1, q)$ by $\Psi_l(x)$.

§1.3. Combinatorial Theory

In several chapters we shall make use of notions and results from combinatorial theory. In this section we shall only recall a number of definitions and one theorem. The reader who is not familiar with this area of mathematics is referred to the book *Combinatorial Theory* by M. Hall [32].

(1.3.1) Definition. Let S be a set with v elements and let $\mathscr{B}$ be a collection of subsets of S (which we call *blocks*) such that:

(i) $|B| = k$ for every $B \in \mathscr{B}$,
(ii) for every $T \subset S$ with $|T| = t$ there are exactly λ blocks B such that $T \subset B$.

Then the pair $(S, \mathscr{B})$ is called a *t-design* (notation $t - (v, k, \lambda)$). The elements of S are called the *points* of the design. If $\lambda = 1$ the design is called a *Steiner system*.

A t-design is often represented by its *incidence matrix* A which has $|\mathscr{B}|$ rows and $|S|$ columns and which has the characteristic functions of the blocks as its rows.

(1.3.2) Definition. A *block design* with parameters $(v, k; b, r, \lambda)$ is a $2 - (v, k, \lambda)$ with $|\mathscr{B}| = b$. For every point there are r blocks containing that point. If $b = v$ then the block design is called *symmetric*.

(1.3.3) Definition. A *projective plane* of *order n* is a $2 - (n^2 + n + 1, n + 1, 1)$. In this case the blocks are called the lines of the plane. A projective plane of order n is denoted by PG(2, n).

(1.3.4) Definition. The *affine geometry* of *dimension m* over the field $\mathbb{F}_q$ is the vector space $(\mathbb{F}_q)^m$ (we use the notation AG(m, q) for the geometry). A k-dimensional *affine subspace* or a k-flat is a coset of a k-dimensional linear subspace (considered as a subgroup). If $k = m - 1$ we call the flat a *hyperplane*. The group generated by the linear transformations of $(\mathbb{F}_q)^m$ and the translations of the vector space is called the group of *affine transformations* and denoted by AGL(m, q). The affine permutation group defined in Section 1.1 is the example with $m = 1$. The *projective geometry* of dimension m over $\mathbb{F}_q$ (notation PG(m, q)) consists of the linear subspaces of AG($m + 1$, q). The subspaces of dimension 1 are called *points*, subspaces of dimension 2 are *lines*, etc.

We give one example. Consider AG(3, 3). There are 27 points, $\frac{1}{2}(27 - 1) = 13$ lines through (0, 0, 0) and also 13 planes through (0, 0, 0). These 13 lines are the "points" of PG(2, 3) and the 13 planes in AG(3, 3) are the "lines" of the projective geometry. It is clear that this is a $2 - (13, 4, 1)$. When speaking of the coordinates of a point in PG(m, q) we mean the coordinates of any of the corresponding points different from $(0, 0, \ldots, 0)$ in AG($m + 1$, q). So, in the example of PG(2, 3) the triples (1, 2, 1) and (2, 1, 2) are coordinates for the same point in PG(2, 3).

(1.3.5) Definition. A square matrix H of order n with elements $+1$ and -1, such that $HH^T = nI$, is called a *Hadamard matrix*.

(1.3.6) Definition. A square matrix C of order n with elements 0 on the diagonal and $+1$ or -1 off the diagonal, such that $CC^T = (n - 1)I$, is called a *conference matrix*.

There are several well known ways of constructing Hadamard matrices. One of these is based on the so-called *Kronecker product* of matrices which is defined as follows.

(1.3.7) Definition. If A is an $m \times m$ matrix with entries a_{ij} and B is an $n \times n$ matrix then the Kronecker product $A \otimes B$ is the $mn \times mn$ matrix given by

$$A \otimes B := \begin{bmatrix} a_{11}B & a_{12}B & \ldots & a_{1m}B \\ a_{21}B & a_{22}B & \ldots & a_{2m}B \\ \vdots & \vdots & \ldots & \vdots \\ a_{m1}B & a_{m2}B & \ldots & a_{mm}B \end{bmatrix}.$$

It is not difficult to show that the Kronecker product of Hadamard matrices is again a Hadamard matrix. Starting from $H_2 := \begin{pmatrix} 1 & 1 \\ 1 & -1 \end{pmatrix}$ we can find the sequence $H_2^{\otimes n}$, where $H_2^{\otimes 2} = H_2 \otimes H_2$, etc. These matrices appear in several places in the book (sometimes in disguised form).

One of the best known construction methods is due to R. E. A. C. Paley (cf. Hall [32]). Let q be an odd prime power. We define the function χ on $\mathbb{F}_q$ by $\chi(0) := 0$, $\chi(x) := 1$ if x is a nonzero square, $\chi(x) = -1$ otherwise. Note that χ restricted to the multiplicative group of $\mathbb{F}_q$ is a character. Number the elements of $\mathbb{F}_q$ in any way as $a_0, a_1, \ldots, a_{q-1}$, where $a_0 = 0$.

(1.3.8) Theorem. *The Paley matrix S of order q defined by $S_{ij} := \chi(a_i - a_j)$ has the properties*:

(i) $SJ = JS = 0$,
(ii) $SS^T = qI - J$,
(iii) $S^T = (-1)^{(q-1)/2}S$.

If we take such a matrix S and form the matrix C of order $q + 1$ as follows:

$$C := \begin{bmatrix} 0 & 1 & 1 & \ldots & 1 \\ -1 & & & & \\ -1 & & S & & \\ \vdots & & & & \\ -1 & & & & \end{bmatrix},$$

then C is a conference matrix of order $q + 1$. If $q \equiv 3 \pmod 4$ we can then consider $H := I + C$. Since $C^T = -C$ because -1 is not a square in $\mathbb{F}_q$, we see that H is a Hadamard matrix of order $q + 1$.

§1.4. Probability Theory

Let $\mathbf{x}$ be a random variable which can take a finite number of values $x_1, x_2, \ldots$. As usual, we denote the probability that $\mathbf{x}$ equals x_i, i.e. $P(\mathbf{x} = x_i)$, by p_i. The *mean* or *expected value* of $\mathbf{x}$ is $\mu = \mathscr{E}(\mathbf{x}) := \sum_i p_i x_i$.

If g is a function defined on the set of values of $\mathbf{x}$ then $\mathscr{E}(g(\mathbf{x})) = \sum_i p_i g(x_i)$. We shall use a number of well known facts such as

$$\mathscr{E}(a\mathbf{x} + b\mathbf{y}) = a\mathscr{E}(\mathbf{x}) + b\mathscr{E}(\mathbf{y}).$$

The *standard deviation* σ and the *variance* σ^2 are defined by: $\mu = \mathscr{E}(\mathbf{x})$,

$$\sigma^2 := \sum_i p_i x_i^2 - \mu^2 = \mathscr{E}(\mathbf{x} - \mu)^2, \qquad (\sigma > 0).$$

We also need a few facts about two-dimensional distributions. We use the notation $p_{ij} := P(\mathbf{x} = x_i \wedge \mathbf{y} = y_j)$, $p_{i.} := P(\mathbf{x} = x_i) = \sum_j p_{ij}$ and for the *conditional probability* $P(\mathbf{x} = x_i | \mathbf{y} = y_j) = p_{ij}/p_{.j}$. We say that $\mathbf{x}$ and $\mathbf{y}$ are *independent* if $p_{ij} = p_{i.}p_{.j}$ for all i and j. In that case we have

$$\mathscr{E}(\mathbf{xy}) = \sum_{i,j} p_{ij} x_i y_j = \mathscr{E}(\mathbf{x})\mathscr{E}(\mathbf{y}).$$

All these facts can be found in standard textbooks on probability theory (e.g.

W. Feller [21]). The same is true for the following results that we shall use in
Chapter 2.

(1.4.1) Theorem (Chebyshev's Inequality). *Let* $\mathbf{x}$ *be a random variable with
mean* μ *and variance* σ^2. *Then for any* $k > 0$

$$P(|\mathbf{x} - \mu| \geq k\sigma) < k^{-2}.$$

The probability distribution which will play the most important role in the
next chapter is the *binomial distribution*. Here, $\mathbf{x}$ takes the values $0, 1, \ldots, n$
and $P(\mathbf{x} = i) = \binom{n}{i} p^i q^{n-i}$, where $0 \leq p \leq 1, q := 1 - p$. For this distribution
we have $\mu = np$ and $\sigma^2 = np(1 - p)$. An important tool used when estimating
binomial coefficients is given in the following theorem

(1.4.2) Theorem (Stirling's Formula).

$$\log n! = (n - \tfrac{1}{2}) \log n - n + \tfrac{1}{2}\log(2\pi) + o(1), \qquad (n \to \infty)$$

$$= n \log n - n + O(\log n), \qquad (n \to \infty).$$

Another useful lemma concerning binomial coefficients is Lemma 1.4.3.

(1.4.3) Lemma. *We have*

$$\binom{n}{m} \leq \frac{n^n}{m^m(n - m)^{n-m}}.$$

PROOF.

$$n^n = \{m + (n - m)\}^n \geq \binom{n}{m} m^m(n - m)^{n-m}. \qquad \square$$

We shall now introduce a function that is very important in information
theory. It is known as the *binary entropy* function and usually denoted by H.
In (5.1.5) we generalize this to other q than 2. In the following the logarithms
are to the base 2.

(1.4.4) Definition. The binary entropy function H is defined by

$$H(0) := 0,$$

$$H(x) := -x \log x - (1 - x) \log(1 - x), \qquad (0 < x \leq \tfrac{1}{2}).$$

(1.4.5) Theorem. *Let* $0 \leq \lambda \leq \tfrac{1}{2}$. *Then we have*

(i) $\sum_{0 \leq i \leq \lambda n} \binom{n}{i} \leq 2^{nH(\lambda)}$,

(ii) $\lim_{n \to \infty} n^{-1} \log \sum_{0 \leq i \leq \lambda n} \binom{n}{i} = H(\lambda)$.

PROOF.

$$1 = \{\lambda + (1 - \lambda)\}^n \geq \sum_{0 \leq i \leq \lambda n} \binom{n}{i} \lambda^i (1 - \lambda)^{n-i}$$

$$\geq \sum_{0 \leq i \leq \lambda n} \binom{n}{i} (1 - \lambda)^n \left(\frac{\lambda}{1 - \lambda}\right)^{\lambda n} = 2^{-nH(\lambda)} \sum_{0 \leq i \leq \lambda n} \binom{n}{i}.$$

(iii) Write $m := \lfloor \lambda n \rfloor$. Then $m = \lambda n + O(1)$ for $n \to \infty$. Therefore we find from Theorem 1.4.2:

$$n^{-1} \log \sum_{0 \leq i \leq \lambda n} \binom{n}{i} \geq n^{-1} \log \binom{n}{m}$$

$$= n^{-1}\{n \log n - m \log m - (n - m) \log(n - m) + o(n)\}$$

$$= \log n - \lambda \log(\lambda n) - (1 - \lambda) \log((1 - \lambda)n) + o(1)$$

$$= H(\lambda) + o(1) \qquad \text{for } n \to \infty.$$

The result then follows from part (i). $\qquad\qquad\qquad\qquad\qquad\qquad\qquad$ $\square$

CHAPTER 2

Shannon's Theorem

§2.1. Introduction

This book will present an introduction to the mathematical aspects of the theory of *error-correcting codes*. This theory is applied in many situations which have as a common feature that information coming from some source is transmitted over a noisy communication channel to a receiver. Examples are telephone conversations, storage devices like magnetic tape units which feed some stored information to the computer, telegraph, etc. The following is a typical recent example. Many readers will have seen the excellent pictures which were taken of Mars, Saturn and other planets by satellites such as the Mariners, Voyagers, etc. In order to transmit these pictures to Earth a fine grid is placed on the picture and for each square of the grid the degree of blackness is measured, say in a scale of 0 to 63. These numbers are expressed in the binary system, i.e. each square produces a string of six 0s and 1s. The 0s and 1s are transmitted as two different signals to the receiver station on Earth (the Jet Propulsion Laboratory of the California Institute of Technology in Pasadena). On arrival the signal is very weak and it must be amplified. Due to the effect of thermal noise it happens occasionally that a signal which was transmitted as a 0 is interpreted by the receiver as a 1, and *vice versa*. If the 6-tuples of 0s and 1s that we mentioned above were transmitted as such, then the errors made by the receiver would have great effect on the pictures. In order to prevent this, so-called *redundancy* is built into the signal, i.e. the transmitted sequence consists of more than the necessary information. We are all familiar with the principle of redundancy from everyday language. The words of our language form a small part of all possible strings of letters (symbols). Consequently a misprint in a long(!) word is recognized because the word is changed into something that resembles the correct word more than it resembles any other word we know. This is the essence of the theory to be treated in this book. In the previous example the reader corrects the misprint. A more modest example of coding for noisy channels is the system used on paper tape for computers. In order to represent 32 distinct symbols one can use 5-tuples of 0s and 1s (i.e. the integers 0 to 31 in binary). In practice, one redundant *bit* (= binary digit) is added to the 5-tuple in such a way that the resulting 6-tuple has an even number of 1s. A failure of the machines that use these tapes occurs very rarely but it is possible that an occasional incorrect bit occurs. The result is incorrect parity of the 6-tuple, i.e. it will have an odd number of ones. In this case the machine stops because it detects an error. This is an example of what is called a *single-error-detecting-code*.

We mentioned above that the 6-tuples of 0s and 1s in picture transmission (e.g. Mariner 1969) are replaced by longer strings (which we shall always call *words*). In fact, in the case of Mariner 1969 the words consisted of 32 symbols (see [56]). At this point the reader should be satisfied with the knowledge that some device had been designed which changes the 64 possible information strings (6-tuples of 0s and 1s) into 64 possible *codewords* (32-tuples of 0s and 1s). This device is called the *encoder*. The codewords are transmitted. We consider the random noise, i.e. the *errors* as something that is added to the message (mod 2 addition).

At the receiving end, a device called the *decoder* changes a received 32-tuple, if it is not one of the 64 allowable codewords, into the *most likely* codeword and then determines the corresponding 6-tuple (the blackness of one square of the grid). The code which we have just described has the property that if not more than 7 of the 32 symbols are incorrect, then the decoder makes the right decision. Of course one should realize that we have paid a toll for this possibility of error correction, namely that the time needed for the transmission of a picture is more than five times as long as would have been necessary without coding.

In practice, the situation is more complicated because it is not the transmission time that changes, but the available energy per transmitted bit.

The most spectacular application of the theory of error-correcting codes is the Compact Disc Digital Audio system invented by Philips (Netherlands). Its success depends (among other things) on the use of Reed Solomon codes. These will be treated in Section 6.8. Figure 1 is a model of the situation described above.

In this book our main interest will be in the construction and the analysis of good codes. In a few cases we shall study the mathematical problems of decoding without considering the actual implementation. Even for a fixed code C there are many different ways to design an algorithm for a decoder. A *complete* decoding algorithm decodes every possible received word into some codeword. In some situations an *incomplete* decoding algorithm could be preferable, namely when a decoding error is very undesirable. In that case the algorithm will correct received messages that contain a few errors and for

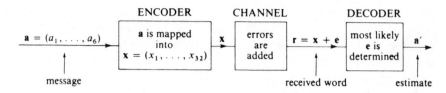

Figure 1

the other possible received messages there will be a decoding failure. In the latter case the receiver either ignores the message or, if possible, asks for a retransmission. Another distinction which is made is the one between so-called *hard decisions* and *soft decisions*. This regards the interpretation of received symbols. Most of them will resemble the signal for 0 or for 1 so much that the receiver has no doubt. In other cases however, this will not be true and then we could prefer putting a ? instead of deciding whether the symbol is 0 or it is 1. This is often referred to as an *erasure*. More complicated systems attach a probability to the symbol.

Introduction to Shannon's Theorem

In order to get a better idea about the origin of coding theory we consider the following experiment.

We are in a room where somebody is tossing a coin at a speed of t tosses per minute. The room is connected with another room by a telegraph wire. Let us assume that we can send two different symbols, which we call 0 and 1, over this communication channel. The channel is noisy and the effect is that there is a probability p that a transmitted 0 (resp. 1) is interpreted by the receiver as a 1 (resp. 0). Such a channel is called a *binary symmetric channel* (B.S.C.) Suppose furthermore that the channel can handle $2t$ symbols per minute and that we can use the channel for T minutes if the coin tossing also takes T minutes. Every time heads comes up we transmit a 0 and if tails comes up we transmit a 1. At the end of the transmission the receiver will have a fraction p of the received information which is incorrect. Now, if we did not have the time limitation specified above, we could achieve arbitrarily small error probability at the receiver as follows. Let N be odd. Instead of a 0 (resp. 1) we transmit N 0s (resp. 1s). The receiver considers a received N-tuple and decodes it into the symbol that occurs most often. The code which we are now using is called a *repetition code* of length N. It consists of two *code-words*, namely $\mathbf{0} = (0, 0, \ldots, 0)$ and $\mathbf{1} = (1, 1, \ldots, 1)$. As an example let us take $p = 0.001$. The probability that the decoder makes an error then is

$$(2.1.1) \qquad \sum_{0 \le k < N/2} \binom{N}{k} q^k p^{N-k} < (0.07)^N, \qquad \text{(here } q := 1 - p),$$

and this probability tends to 0 for $N \to \infty$ (the proof of (2.1.1) is Exercise 2.4.1).

Due to our time limitation we have a serious problem! There is no point in sending each symbol twice instead of once. A most remarkable theorem, due to C. E. Shannon (cf. [62]), states that, in the situation described here, we can still achieve arbitrarily small error probability at the receiver. The proof will be given in the next section. A first idea about the method of proof can be obtained in the following way. We transmit the result of two tosses of the coin as follows:

$$\text{heads, heads} \to 0\ 0\ 0\ 0,$$

$$\text{heads, tails} \to 0\ 1\ 1\ 1,$$

$$\text{tails, heads} \to 1\ 0\ 0\ 1,$$

$$\text{tails, tails} \to 1\ 1\ 1\ 0.$$

Observe that the first two transmitted symbols carry the actual information; the final two symbols are redundant. The decoder uses the following complete decoding algorithm. If a received 4-tuple is not one of the above, then assume that the fourth symbol is correct and that one of the first three symbols is incorrect. Any received 4-tuple can be uniquely decoded. The result is correct if the above assumptions are true. Without coding, the probability that two results are received correctly is $q^2 = 0.998$. With the code described above, this probability is $q^4 + 3q^3 p = 0.999$. The second term on the left is the probability that the received word contains one error, but not in the fourth position. We thus have a nice improvement, achieved in a very easy way. The time requirement is fulfilled. We extend the idea used above by transmitting the coin tossing results three at a time. The information which we wish to transmit is then a 3-tuple of 0s and 1s, say (a_1, a_2, a_3). Instead of this 3-tuple, we transmit the 6-tuple $\mathbf{a} = (a_1, \ldots, a_6)$, where $a_4 := a_2 + a_3$, $a_5 := a_1 + a_3$, $a_6 := a_1 + a_2$ (the addition being addition mod 2). What we have done is to construct a *code* consisting of eight words, each with length 6. As stated before, we consider the noise as something added to the message, i.e. the received word $\mathbf{b}$ is $\mathbf{a} + \mathbf{e}$, where $\mathbf{e} = (e_1, e_2, \ldots, e_6)$ is called the *error pattern* (error vector). We have

$$e_2 + e_3 + e_4 = b_2 + b_3 + b_4 := s_1,$$

$$e_1 + e_3 + e_5 = b_1 + b_3 + b_5 := s_2,$$

$$e_1 + e_2 + e_6 = b_1 + b_2 + b_6 := s_3.$$

Since the receiver knows $\mathbf{b}$, he knows s_1, s_2, s_3. Given s_1, s_2, s_3 the decoder must choose the most likely error pattern $\mathbf{e}$ which satisfies the three equations. The most likely one is the one with the minimal number of symbols 1. One easily sees that if $(s_1, s_2, s_3) \neq (1, 1, 1)$ there is a unique choice for $\mathbf{e}$. If $(s_1, s_2, s_3) = (1, 1, 1)$ the decoder must choose one of the three possibilities (1,

0, 0, 1, 0, 0), (0, 1, 0, 0, 1, 0), (0, 0, 1, 0, 0, 1) for **e**. We see that an error pattern with one error is decoded correctly and among all other error patterns there is one with two errors that is decoded correctly. Hence, the probability that all three symbols a_1, a_2, a_3 are interpreted correctly after the decoding procedure, is

$$q^6 + 6q^5p + q^4p^2 = 0.999986.$$

This is already a tremendous improvement.

Through this introduction the reader will already have some idea of the following important concepts of coding theory.

(2.1.2) Definition. If a code C is used consisting of words of length n, then

$$R := n^{-1} \log|C|$$

is called the *information rate* (or just the rate) of the code.

The concept rate is connected with what was discussed above regarding the time needed for the transmission of information. In our example of the 32 possible words on paper tape the rate is $\frac{5}{6}$. The Mariner 1969 used a code with rate $\frac{6}{32}$, in accordance with our statement that transmission took more than five times as long as without coding. The example given before the definition of rate had $R = \frac{1}{2}$.

We mentioned that the code used by Mariner 1969 had the property that the receiver is able to correct up to seven errors in a received word. The reason that this is possible is the fact that any two distinct codewords differ in at least 16 positions. Therefore a received word with less than eight errors resembles the intended codeword more than it resembles any other codeword. This leads to the following definition:

(2.1.3) Definition. If **x** and **y** are two n-tuples of 0s and 1s, then we shall say that their *Hamming-distance* (usually just distance) is

$$d(\mathbf{x}, \mathbf{y}) := |\{i \,|\, 1 \le i \le n, x_i \ne y_i\}|.$$

(Also see (3.1.1).)

The code C with eight words of length 6 which we treated above has the property that any two distinct codewords have distance at least 3. That is why any error-pattern with one error could be corrected. The code is a *single-error-correcting* code.

Our explanation of decoding rules was based on two assumptions. First of all we assumed that during communication all codewords are equally likely. Furthermore we used the fact that if $n_1 > n_2$ then an error pattern with n_1 errors is less likely than one with n_2 errors.

This means that if **y** is received we try to find a codeword **x** such that $d(\mathbf{x}, \mathbf{y})$ is minimal. This principle is called *maximum-likelihood-decoding*.

§2.2. Shannon's Theorem

We shall now state and prove Shannon's theorem for the case of the example given in Section 2.1. Let us state the problem. We have a binary symmetric channel with probability p that a symbol is received in error (again we write $q := 1 - p$). Suppose we use a code C consisting of M words of length n, each word occurring with equal probability. If $\mathbf{x}_1, \mathbf{x}_2, \ldots, \mathbf{x}_M$ are the codewords and we use maximum-likelihood-decoding, let P_i be the probability of making an incorrect decision given that $\mathbf{x}_i$ is transmitted. In that case the probability of incorrect decoding of a received word is:

$$(2.2.1) \qquad P_C := M^{-1} \sum_{i=1}^{M} P_i.$$

Now consider all possible codes C with the given parameters and define:

$$(2.2.2) \qquad P^*(M, n, p) := \text{minimal value of } P_C.$$

(2.2.3) Theorem (Shannon 1948). *If* $0 < R < 1 + p \log p + q \log q$ *and* $M_n := 2^{\lfloor Rn \rfloor}$ *then* $P^*(M_n, n, p) \to 0$ *if* $n \to \infty$.

(Here all logarithms have base 2.) We remark that in the example of the previous section $p = 0.001$, i.e. $1 + p \log p + q \log q$ is nearly 1. The requirement in the experiment was that the rate should be at least $\frac{1}{2}$. We see that for $\varepsilon > 0$ and n sufficiently large there is a code C of length n, with rate nearly 1 and such that $P_C < \varepsilon$. (Of course long codes cannot be used if T is too small.)

Before giving the proof of Theorem 2.2.3 we treat some technical details to be used later.

The probability of an error pattern with w errors is $p^w q^{n-w}$, i.e. it depends on w only.

The number of errors in a received word is a random variable with expected value np and variance $np(1 - p)$. If $b := (np(1 - p)/(\varepsilon/2))^{1/2}$, then by Chebyshev's inequality (Theorem 1.4.1) we have

$$(2.2.4) \qquad P(w > np + b) \leq \tfrac{1}{2}\varepsilon.$$

Since $p < \frac{1}{2}$, the number $\rho := \lfloor np + b \rfloor$ is less than $\frac{1}{2}n$ for sufficiently large n. Let $B_\rho(\mathbf{x})$ be the set of words $\mathbf{y}$ with $d(\mathbf{x}, \mathbf{y}) \leq \rho$. Then

$$(2.2.5) \qquad |B_\rho(\mathbf{x})| = \sum_{i \leq \rho} \binom{n}{i} < \frac{1}{2} n \binom{n}{\rho} \leq \frac{1}{2} n \cdot \frac{n^n}{\rho^\rho (n - \rho)^{n-\rho}}$$

(cf. Lemma 1.4.3). The set $B_\rho(\mathbf{x})$ is usually called the *sphere* with radius ρ and center $\mathbf{x}$ (although *ball* would have been more appropriate).

We shall use the following estimates:

$$(2.2.6) \qquad \frac{\rho}{n} \log \frac{\rho}{n} = \frac{1}{n} \lfloor np + b \rfloor \log \frac{\lfloor np + b \rfloor}{n} = p \log p + O(n^{-1/2}),$$

$$\left(1 - \frac{\rho}{n}\right) \log\left(1 - \frac{\rho}{n}\right) = q \log q + O(n^{-1/2}), \qquad (n \to \infty).$$

Finally we introduce two functions which play a role in the proof. Let

$$\mathbf{u} \in \{0, 1\}^n, \mathbf{v} \in \{0, 1\}^n.$$

Then

(2.2.7) $$f(\mathbf{u}, \mathbf{v}) := \begin{cases} 0, & \text{if } d(\mathbf{u}, \mathbf{v}) > \rho, \\ 1, & \text{if } d(\mathbf{u}, \mathbf{v}) \leq \rho. \end{cases}$$

If $\mathbf{x}_i \in C$ and $\mathbf{y} \in \{0, 1\}^n$ then

(2.2.8) $$g_i(\mathbf{y}) := 1 - f(\mathbf{y}, \mathbf{x}_i) + \sum_{j \neq i} f(\mathbf{y}, \mathbf{x}_j).$$

Note that if $\mathbf{x}_i$ is the only codeword such that $d(\mathbf{x}_i, \mathbf{y}) \leq \rho$, then $g_i(\mathbf{y}) = 0$ and that otherwise $g_i(\mathbf{y}) \geq 1$.

PROOF OF THEOREM 2.2.3. In the proof of Shannon's theorem we shall pick the codewords $\mathbf{x}_1, \mathbf{x}_2, \ldots, \mathbf{x}_M$ at random (independently). We decode as follows. If $\mathbf{y}$ is received and if there is exactly one codeword $\mathbf{x}_i$ such that $d(\mathbf{x}_i, \mathbf{y}) \leq \rho$, then decode $\mathbf{y}$ as $\mathbf{x}_i$. Otherwise we declare an error (or if we must decode, then we always decode as $\mathbf{x}_1$).

Let P_i be as defined above. We have

$$P_i = \sum_{\mathbf{y} \in \{0,1\}^n} P(\mathbf{y}|\mathbf{x}_i) g_i(\mathbf{y})$$

$$= \sum_{\mathbf{y}} P(\mathbf{y}|\mathbf{x}_i)\{1 - f(\mathbf{y}, \mathbf{x}_i)\} + \sum_{\mathbf{y}} \sum_{j \neq i} P(\mathbf{y}|\mathbf{x}_i) f(\mathbf{y}, \mathbf{x}_j).$$

Here the first term on the right-hand side is the probability that the received word $\mathbf{y}$ is not in $B_\rho(\mathbf{x}_i)$. By (2.2.4) this probability is at most $\frac{1}{2}\varepsilon$.

Hence we have

$$P_C \leq \frac{1}{2}\varepsilon + M^{-1} \sum_{i=1}^{M} \sum_{\mathbf{y}} \sum_{j \neq i} P(\mathbf{y}|\mathbf{x}_i) f(\mathbf{y}, \mathbf{x}_j).$$

The main principle of the proof is the fact that $P^*(M, n, p)$ is less than the expected value of P_C over all possible codes C picked at random. Therefore we have

$$P^*(M, n, p) \leq \frac{1}{2}\varepsilon + M^{-1} \sum_{i=1}^{M} \sum_{\mathbf{y}} \sum_{j \neq i} \mathscr{E}(P(\mathbf{y}|\mathbf{x}_i)) \mathscr{E}(f(\mathbf{y}, \mathbf{x}_j))$$

$$= \frac{1}{2}\varepsilon + M^{-1} \sum_{i=1}^{M} \sum_{\mathbf{y}} \sum_{j \neq i} \mathscr{E}(P(\mathbf{y}|\mathbf{x}_i)) \cdot \frac{|B_\rho|}{2^n}$$

$$= \frac{1}{2}\varepsilon + (M - 1)2^{-n}|B_\rho|.$$

We now take logarithms, apply (2.2.5) and (2.2.6), and then we divide by n.

The result is

$$n^{-1} \log(P^*(M, n, p) - \tfrac{1}{2}\varepsilon)$$

$$\leq n^{-1} \log M - (1 + p \log p + q \log q) + O(n^{-1/2}).$$

Substituting $M = M_n$ on the right-hand side we find, using the restriction on R,

$$n^{-1} \log(P^*(M_n, n, p) - \tfrac{1}{2}\varepsilon) < -\beta < 0,$$

for $n > n_0$, i.e. $P^*(M, n, p) < \tfrac{1}{2}\varepsilon + 2^{-\beta n}$.

   This proves the theorem.   □

§2.3. Comments

C. E. Shannon's paper on the "Mathematical theory of communication"
(1948) [62] marks the beginning of coding theory. Since the theorem shows
that good codes exist, it was natural that one started to try to construct such
codes. Since these codes had to be used with the aid of often very small
electronic apparatus one was especially interested in codes with a lot of
structure which would allow relatively simple decoding algorithms. In the
following chapters we shall see that it is very difficult to obtain highly regular
codes without losing the property promised by Theorem 2.2.3. We remark
that one of the important areas where coding theory is applied is telephone
communication. Many of the names which the reader will encounter in this
book are names of (former) members of the staff of Bell Telephone
Laboratories. Besides Shannon we mention Berlekamp, Gilbert, Hamming,
Lloyd, MacWilliams, Slepian and Sloane. It is not surprising that much of the
early literature on coding theory can be found in the *Bell System Technical
Journal*. The author gratefully acknowledges that he acquired a large part of
his knowledge of coding theory during his many visits to Bell Laboratories.
The reader interested in more details about the code used in the Mariner 1969
is referred to reference [56]. For the coding in Compact Disc see [77], [78].

   By consulting the references the reader can see that for many years now
the most important results on coding theory have been published in *IEEE
Transactions on Information Theory*.

§2.4. Problems

2.4.1. Prove (2.1.1).

2.4.2. Consider the code of length 6 which was described in the coin-tossing experi-
        ment in Section 2.2. We showed that the probability that a received word is
        decoded correctly is $q^6 + 6q^5 p + q^4 p^2$. Now suppose that after decoding we

retain only the first three symbols of every decoded word (i.e. the information concerning the coin-tossing experiment). Determine the probability that a symbol in this sequence is incorrect; (this is called the *symbol error probability*, which without coding would be p).

2.4.3. Construct a code consisting of eight words of length 7 such that any two distinct codewords have distance at least 4. Determine for a B.S.C. with error probability p which is the probability that a received word is decoded correctly.

2.4.4. A binary channel has a probability $q = 0.9$ that a transmitted symbol is received correctly and a probability $p = 0.1$ that an erasure occurs (i.e. we receive ?). On this channel we wish to use a code with rate $\frac{1}{2}$. Does the probability of correct interpretation increase if we repeat each transmitted symbol ? Is it possible to construct a code with eight words of length 6 such that two erasures can do no harm? Compare the probabilities of correct interpretation for these two codes. (Assume that the receiver does not change the erasures by guessing a symbol.)

CHAPTER 3

Linear Codes

§3.1. Block Codes

In this chapter we assume that information is coded using an *alphabet* Q with q distinct symbols. A code is called a *block code* if the coded information can be divided into blocks of n symbols which can be decoded independently. These blocks are the *codewords* and n is called the *block length* or *word length* (or just length). The examples in Chapter 2 were all block codes. In Chapter 11 we shall briefly discuss a completely different system, called *convolutional coding*, where an infinite sequence of information symbols $i_0, i_1, i_2, \ldots$ is coded into an infinite sequence of message symbols. For example, for rate $\frac{1}{2}$ one could have $i_0, i_1, i_2, \ldots \to i_0, i_0', i_1, i_1', \ldots$, where i_n' is a function of $i_0, i_1, \ldots, i_n$. For block codes we generalize (2.1.3) to arbitrary alphabets.

(3.1.1.) Definition. If $\mathbf{x} \in Q^n$, $\mathbf{y} \in Q^n$, then the *distance* $d(\mathbf{x}, \mathbf{y})$ of $\mathbf{x}$ and $\mathbf{y}$ is defined by

$$d(\mathbf{x}, \mathbf{y}) := |\{i \mid 1 \leq i \leq n, x_i \neq y_i\}|.$$

The *weight* $w(\mathbf{x})$ of $\mathbf{x}$ is defined by

$$w(\mathbf{x}) := d(\mathbf{x}, \mathbf{0}).$$

(We always denote $(0, 0, \ldots, 0)$ by $\mathbf{0}$ and $(1, 1, \ldots, 1)$ by $\mathbf{1}$.)

The distance defined in (3.1.1), again called *Hamming-distance*, is indeed a metric on Q^n. If we are using a channel with the property that an error in position i does not influence other positions and a symbol in error can be each of the remaining $q - 1$ symbols with equal probability, then Hamming-distance is a good way to measure the error content of a received message. In

Chapter 10 we shall see that in other situations a different distance function is preferable.

In the following a *code C* is a nonempty proper subset of Q''. If $|C| = 1$ we call the code *trivial*. If $q = 2$ the code is called a *binary* code, for $q = 3$ a *ternary* code, etc. The following concepts play an essential rôle in this book (cf. Chapter 2).

(3.1.2) Definition. The *minimum distance* of a nontrivial code C is

$$\min\{d(\mathbf{x}, \mathbf{y}) | \mathbf{x} \in C, \mathbf{y} \in C, \mathbf{x} \neq \mathbf{y}\}.$$

The *minimum weight* of C is

$$\min\{w(\mathbf{x}) | \mathbf{x} \in C, \mathbf{x} \neq 0\}.$$

We also generalize the concept of rate.

(3.1.3) Definition. If $|Q| = q$ and $C \subset Q''$ then

$$R := n^{-1} \log_q |C|$$

is called (*information-*) *rate* of C.

Sometimes we shall be interested in knowing how far a received word can be from the closest codeword. For this purpose we introduce a counterpart of minimum distance.

(3.1.4) Definition. If $C \subset Q^n$ then the *covering radius* $\rho(C)$ of C is

$$\max\{\min\{d(\mathbf{x}, \mathbf{c}) | \mathbf{c} \in C\} | \mathbf{x} \in Q^n\}.$$

We remind the reader that in Chapter 2 the *sphere* $B_\rho(\mathbf{x})$ with radius ρ and center $\mathbf{x}$ was defined to be the set $\{\mathbf{y} \in Q^n | d(\mathbf{x}, \mathbf{y}) \leq \rho\}$. If ρ is the largest integer such that the spheres $B_\rho(\mathbf{c})$ with $\mathbf{c} \in C$ are disjoint, then $d = 2\rho + 1$ or $d = 2\rho + 2$. The covering radius is the smallest ρ such that the spheres $B_\rho(\mathbf{c})$ with $\mathbf{c} \in C$ cover the set Q^n. If these numbers are equal, then the code C is called *perfect*. This can be stated as follows.

(3.1.5) Definition. A code $C \subset Q^n$ with minimum distance $2e + 1$ is called a *perfect code* if every $\mathbf{x} \in Q^n$ has distance $\leq e$ to exactly one codeword.

The fact that the minimum distance is $2e + 1$ means that the code is e-error-correcting. The following is obvious.

(3.1.6) Sphere-packing Condition
If $C \subset Q^n$ is a perfect e-error-correcting code, then

$$|C| \sum_{i=0}^{e} \binom{n}{i} (q - 1)^i = q^n.$$

Of course a trivial code is perfect even though one cannot speak of minimum distance for such a code. A simple example of a perfect code was treated in Chapter 2, namely the binary repetition code of odd length n consisting of the two words $\mathbf{0}$ and $\mathbf{1}$.

§3.2. Linear Codes

We now turn to the problem of constructing codes which have some algebraic structure. The first idea is to take a group Q as alphabet and to take a subgroup C of Q^n as code. This is called a *group code*. In this section (in fact in most of this book) we shall require (a lot) more structure. In the following Q is the field $\mathbb{F}_q$, where $q = p^r$ (p prime). Then Q^n is an n-dimensional vector space, namely $\mathbb{F}_q^n$ (sometimes denoted by $\mathscr{R}$). In later chapters we sometimes use the fact that Q^n is isomorphic to the additive group of $\mathbb{F}_{q^n}$ (cf. Section 1.1).

(3.2.1) Definition. A *q-ary linear code* C is a linear subspace of $\mathbb{F}_q^n$. If C has dimension k then C is called an $[n, k]$ code.

From now on we shall use $[n, k, d]$ code as the notation for a k-dimensional linear code of length n with minimum distance d. An (n, M, d) code is any code with word length n, M codewords, and minimum distance d.

(3.2.2) Definition. A *generator matrix* G for a linear code C is a k by n matrix for which the rows are a basis of C.

If G is a generator matrix for C, then $C = \{\mathbf{a}G | \mathbf{a} \in Q^k\}$. We shall say that G is in *standard form* (often called reduced echelon form) if $G = (I_k \quad P)$, where I_k is the k by k identity matrix. The $(6, 8, 3)$ code which we used in the example of Section 2.1 is a linear code with $G = (I \quad J - I)$. If G is in standard form, then the first k symbols of a codeword are called *information symbols*. These can be chosen arbitrarily and then the remaining symbols, which are called *parity check symbols*, are determined. The code used on paper tape mentioned in the Introduction has one parity check bit (responsible for the name) and generator matrix $G = (I_5 \quad \mathbf{1}^T)$.

As far as error-correcting capability is concerned, two codes C_1 and C_2 are equally good if C_2 is obtained by applying a fixed permutation of the symbols to all the codewords of C_1. We call such codes *equivalent*. Sometimes the definition of equivalence is extended by also allowing a permutation of the symbols of Q (for each position). It is well known from linear algebra that every linear code is equivalent to a code with a generator matrix in standard form.

In general a code C is called *systematic* on k positions (and the symbols in these positions are called information symbols) if $|C| = q^k$ and there is exactly eword for every possible choice of coordinates in the k positions. So we saw above that an $[n, k]$ code is systematic on at least one k-tuple of positions. Since one can separate information symbols and redundant symbols, these codes are also called *separable*. By (3.1.3) an $[n, k]$ code has rate k/n, in accordance with the fact that k out of n symbols carry information.

The reader will have realized that if a code C has minimum distance $d = 2e + 1$, then it corrects up to e errors in a received word. If $d = 2e$ then an error pattern of weight e is always detected. In general if C has M words one must check $\binom{M}{2}$ pairs of codewords to find d. For linear codes the work is easier.

(3.2.3) Theorem. *For a linear code C the minimum distance is equal to the minimum weight.*

PROOF. $d(\mathbf{x}, \mathbf{y}) = d(\mathbf{x} - \mathbf{y}, \mathbf{0}) = w(\mathbf{x} - \mathbf{y})$ and if $\mathbf{x} \in C$, $\mathbf{y} \in C$ then $\mathbf{x} - \mathbf{y} \in C$.

□

(3.2.4) Definition. If C is an $[n, k]$ code we define the *dual code* $C^{\perp}$ by

$$C^{\perp} := \{\mathbf{y} \in \mathcal{R} | \forall_{\mathbf{x} \in C}[\langle \mathbf{x}, \mathbf{y} \rangle = 0]\}.$$

The dual code $C^{\perp}$ is clearly a linear code, namely an $[n, n - k]$ code. The reader should be careful not to think of $C^{\perp}$ as an orthogonal complement in the sense of vector spaces over $\mathbb{R}$. In the case of a finite field Q, the subspaces C and $C^{\perp}$ can have an intersection larger than $\{\mathbf{0}\}$ and in fact they can even be equal. If $C = C^{\perp}$ then C is called a *self-dual* code.

If $G = (I_k \quad P)$ is a generator matrix in standard form of the code C, then $H = (-P^{\top} \quad I_{n-k})$ is a generator matrix for $C^{\perp}$. This follows from the fact that H has the right size and rank and that $GH^{\top} = 0$ implies that every codeword $\mathbf{a}G$ has inner product 0 with every row of H. In other words we have

(3.2.5) $\mathbf{x} \in C \Leftrightarrow \mathbf{x}H^{\top} = \mathbf{0}.$

In (3.2.5) we have $n - k$ linear equations which every codeword must satisfy.

If $\mathbf{y} \in C^{\perp}$ then the equation $\langle \mathbf{x}, \mathbf{y} \rangle = 0$ which holds for every $\mathbf{x} \in C$, is called a *parity check* (equation). H is called a *parity check matrix* of C. For the $[6, 3]$ code used in Section 2.1 the equation $a_4 = a_2 + a_3$ is one of the parity checks.

(3.2.6) Definition. If C is a linear code with parity check matrix H then for every $\mathbf{x} \in Q^n$ we call $\mathbf{x}H^{\top}$ the *syndrome* of $\mathbf{x}$. Observe that the covering radius $\rho(C)$ of an $[n, k]$ code (cf. (3.14)) is the smallest integer ρ such that any (column-)vector in Q^{n-k} can be written as the sum of at most ρ columns of H.

In (3.2.5) we saw that codewords are characterized by syndrome $\mathbf{0}$. The syndrome is an important aid in decoding received vectors $\mathbf{x}$. Once again this idea was introduced using the [6, 3] code in Section 2.1. Since C is a subgroup of Q^n we can partition Q^n into cosets of C. Two vectors $\mathbf{x}$ and $\mathbf{y}$ are in the same coset iff they have the same syndrome ($\mathbf{x}H^\top = \mathbf{y}H^\top \Leftrightarrow \mathbf{x} - \mathbf{y} \in C$). Therefore if a vector $\mathbf{x}$ is received for which the error pattern is $\mathbf{e}$ then $\mathbf{x}$ and $\mathbf{e}$ have the same syndrome. It follows that for maximum likelihood decoding of $\mathbf{x}$ one must choose a vector $\mathbf{e}$ of minimal weight in the coset which contains $\mathbf{x}$ and then decode $\mathbf{x}$ as $\mathbf{x} - \mathbf{e}$. The vector $\mathbf{e}$ is called the *coset leader*. How this works in practice was demonstrated in Section 2.1 for the [6, 3]-code. For seven of the eight cosets there was a unique coset leader. Only for the syndrome (s_1, s_2, s_3) = (1, 1, 1) did we have to pick one out of three possible coset leaders.

Here we see the first great advantage of introducing algebraic structure. For an $[n, k]$ code over $\mathbb{F}_q$ there are q^k codewords and q^n possible received messages. Let us assume that the rate is reasonably high. The receiver needs to know the q^{n-k} coset leaders corresponding to all possible syndromes. Now q^{n-k} is much smaller than q^n. If the code had no structure, then for every possible received word $\mathbf{x}$ we would have to list the most likely transmitted word.

It is clear that if C has minimum distance $d = 2e + 1$, then every error pattern of weight $\leq e$ is the unique coset leader of some coset because two vectors with weight $\leq e$ have distance $\leq 2e$ and are therefore in different cosets. If C is perfect then there are no other coset leaders. If a code C has minimum distance $2e + 1$ and all coset leaders have weight $\leq e + 1$ then the code is called *quasi-perfect*. The [6, 3] code of Section 2.1 is an example. The covering radius is the weight of a coset leader with maximum weight.

We give one other example of a very simple decoding procedure (cf. [3]). Let C be a $[2k, k]$ binary self-dual code with generator matrix $G = (I_k \quad P)$. The decoding algorithm works if C can correct 3 errors and if the probability that more than 3 errors occur in a received vector is very small. We have the parity check matrix $H = (P^\top \quad I_k)$ but G is also a parity check matrix because C is self-dual. Let $\mathbf{y} = \mathbf{c} + \mathbf{e}$ be the received vector. We write $\mathbf{e}$ as $(\mathbf{e}_1; \mathbf{e}_2)$ where $\mathbf{e}_1$ corresponds to the first k places, $\mathbf{e}_2$ to the last k places. We calculate the two syndromes

$$\mathbf{s}^{(1)} := \mathbf{y}H^\top = \mathbf{e}_1 P + \mathbf{e}_2,$$

$$\mathbf{s}^{(2)} := \mathbf{y}G^\top = \mathbf{e}_1 + \mathbf{e}_2 P^\top.$$

If the $t \leq 3$ errors all occur in the first or last half of $\mathbf{y}$, i.e. $\mathbf{e}_1 = \mathbf{0}$ or $\mathbf{e}_2 = \mathbf{0}$, then one of the syndromes will have weight ≤ 3 and we immediately have $\mathbf{e}$. If this is not the case then the assumption $t \leq 3$ implies that $\mathbf{e}_1$ or $\mathbf{e}_2$ has weight 1. We consider $2k$ vectors $\mathbf{y}^{(i)}$ obtained by changing the ith coordinate of $\mathbf{y}$ ($1 \leq i \leq 2k$). For each of these vectors we calculate $\mathbf{s}_1$ (for $i \leq k$) resp. $\mathbf{s}_2$ (if $i > k$). If we find a syndrome with weight ≤ 2, we can correct the remaining errors. If we find a syndrome with weight 3, we have detected four errors if C is a code with distance 8 and if C has distance ≥ 10 we can correct this pattern of four errors.

It will often turn out to be useful to adjoin one extra symbol to every codeword of a code C according to some natural rule. The most common of these is given in the following definition.

(3.2.7) Definition. If C is a code of length n over the alphabet $\mathbb{F}_q$ we define the *extended code* $\bar{C}$ by

$$\bar{C} := \left\{ (c_1, c_2, \ldots, c_n, c_{n+1}) | (c_1, \ldots, c_n) \in C, \sum_{i=1}^{n+1} c_i = 0 \right\}.$$

If C is a linear code with generator matrix G and parity check matrix H then $\bar{C}$ has generator matrix $\bar{G}$ and parity check matrix $\bar{H}$, where $\bar{G}$ is obtained by adding a column to G in such a way that the sum of the columns of $\bar{G}$ is 0 and where

$$\bar{H} := \begin{bmatrix} 1 & 1 & 1 \ldots & 1 \\ & & & 0 \\ & H & & 0 \\ & & & \vdots \\ & & & 0 \end{bmatrix}.$$

If C is a binary code with an odd minimum distance d, then $\bar{C}$ has minimum distance $d + 1$ since all weights and distances for $\bar{C}$ are even.

§3.3. Hamming Codes

Let G be the k by n generator matrix of an $[n, k]$ code C over $\mathbb{F}_q$. If any two columns of G are linearly independent, i.e. the columns represent distinct points of $PG(k - 1, q)$, then C is called a *projective code*. The dual code $C^{\perp}$ has G as parity check matrix. If $\mathbf{c} \in C^{\perp}$ and if $\mathbf{e}$ is an error vector of weight 1, then the syndrome $(\mathbf{c} + \mathbf{e})G^{\top}$ is a multiple of a column of G. Since this uniquely determines the column of G it follows that $C^{\perp}$ is a code which corrects at least one error. We now look at the case in which n is maximal (given k).

(3.3.1) Definition. Let $n := (q^k - 1)/(q - 1)$. The $[n, n - k]$ *Hamming code* over $\mathbb{F}_q$ is a code for which the parity check matrix has columns that are pairwise linearly independent (over $\mathbb{F}_q$), i.e. the columns are a maximal set of pairwise linearly independent vectors.

Here we obviously do not distinguish between equivalent codes. Clearly the minimum distance of a Hamming code is equal to 3.

(3.3.2) Theorem. *Hamming codes are perfect codes.*

PROOF. Let C be the $[n, n - k]$ Hamming code over $\mathbb{F}_q$, where $n = (q^k - 1)/(q - 1)$. If $\mathbf{x} \in C$ then

$$|B_1(\mathbf{x})| = 1 + n(q - 1) = q^k.$$

Therefore the q^{n-k} disjoint spheres of radius 1 around the codewords of C contain $|C| \cdot q^k = q^n$ words, i.e. all possible words. Hence C is perfect (cf. (3.1.5) and (3.1.6)). $\qquad \blacksquare$

(3.3.3) EXAMPLE. The $[7, 4]$ binary Hamming code C has parity check matrix

$$H = \begin{bmatrix} 0 & 0 & 0 & 1 & 1 & 1 & 1 \\ 0 & 1 & 1 & 0 & 0 & 1 & 1 \\ 1 & 0 & 1 & 0 & 1 & 0 & 1 \end{bmatrix}.$$

If we consider two columns of H and the sum of these two (e.g. the first three columns of H), then there is a word of weight 3 in C with 1s in the positions corresponding to these columns (e.g. (1110000)). Therefore C has seven words of weight 3 which, when listed as rows of a matrix, form PG(2, 2). The words of even weight in C are a solution to Problem 2.4.3. By inspection of H we see that the extended code $\overline{C}$ is self-dual.

§3.4. Majority Logic Decoding

In this section we shall briefly sketch a decoding method which is used with many linear codes. Generalizations will occur in later chapters. The method is simple and it has the advantage that in some cases more errors are corrected than one expects.

(3.4.1) **Definition.** A system of parity check equations $\langle \mathbf{x}, \mathbf{y}^{(v)} \rangle = 0$ $(1 \le v \le r)$, is said to be *orthogonal with respect to position i* (for the code C; $\mathbf{y}^{(v)} \in C^{\perp}$) if

(i) $y_i^{(v)} = 1 \ (1 \le v \le r)$,
(ii) if $j \ne i$ then $y_j^{(v)} \ne 0$ for at most one value of v.

Now suppose $\mathbf{x}$ is a received word that contains t errors, where $t \le \frac{1}{2}r$. Then

$$\langle \mathbf{x}, \mathbf{y}^{(v)} \rangle \ne 0 \quad \text{for} \begin{cases} \le t \text{ values of } v, & \text{if } x_i \text{ is correct,} \\ \ge r - (t - 1) \text{ values of } v, & \text{if } x_i \text{ is incorrect.} \end{cases}$$

Since $r - (t - 1) > t$, the majority of the values of $\langle \mathbf{x}, \mathbf{y}^{(v)} \rangle$ (i.e. 0, resp. not 0) decides for us whether x_i is correct or not. In the case of a binary code we can subsequently correct the error. If we have such orthogonal check sets for every i, we can correct the different positions one by one.

As an example we consider the dual of the $[7, 4]$ Hamming code (cf. (3.3.3)). The parity check equations

$$x_1 + x_2 + x_3 = 0,$$

$$x_1 + x_4 + x_5 = 0,$$

$$x_1 + x_6 + x_7 = 0,$$

are othogonal with respect to position 1. If $\mathbf{x}$ contains one error, then the three equations yield 1, 1, 1 if x_1 is incorrect, respectively two 0s and one 1 if x_1 is correct. If two outcomes are 1, we see that more than one error has been made (the code is two-error detecting).

§3.5. Weight Enumerators

The minimum distance of a linear code tells us how many errors a received word may contain and still be decoded correctly. Often it is necessary to have more detailed information about the distances in the code. For this purpose we introduce the so-called *weight enumerator* of the code.

(3.5.1) Definition. Let C be a linear code of length n and let A_i be the number of codewords of weight i.
  Then

$$A(z) := \sum_{i=0}^{n} A_i z^i$$

is called the *weight enumerator* of C. The sequence $(A_i)_{i=0}^{n}$ is called the *weight distribution* of C.

As an example we calculate the weight enumerator of the binary Hamming code of length n. Consider $i - 1$ columns of the parity check matrix of this code. There are three possibilities:

  (i) the sum of these columns is $\mathbf{0}$;
  (ii) the sum of these columns is one of the chosen columns;
  (iii) the sum of these columns is one of the remaining columns.

We can choose the $i - 1$ columns in $\binom{n}{i-1}$ ways. Possibility (i) occurs A_{i-1} times, possibility (ii) occurs $(n - (i - 2))A_{i-2}$ times, and possibility (iii) occurs iA_i times. Therefore

$$iA_i = \binom{n}{i-1} - A_{i-1} - (n - i + 2)A_{i-2},$$

which is trivially correct if $i > n + 1$. If we multiply both sides by z^{i-1} and then sum over i we find

$$A'(z) = (1 + z)^n - A(z) - nzA(z) + z^2 A'(z).$$

Since $A(0) = 1$, this differential equation has the unique solution

(3.5.2) $\qquad A(z) = \dfrac{1}{n+1}(1+z)^n + \dfrac{n}{n+1}(1+z)^{(n-1)/2}(1-z)^{(n+1)/2}.$

One of the most fundamental results in coding theory is a theorem due to F. J. MacWilliams (1963) which gives a relation between the weight enumerators of a linear code and its dual.

(3.5.3) Theorem. *Let C be an $[n, k]$ code over $\mathbb{F}_q$ with weight enumerator $A(z)$ and let $B(z)$ be the weight enumerator of $C^{\perp}$. Then*

$$B(z) = q^{-k}(1 + (q-1)z)^n A\left(\frac{1-z}{1+(q-1)z}\right).$$

PROOF. Let χ be any nontrivial character of $(\mathbb{F}_q, +)$. As usual let $\mathcal{R} = \mathbb{F}_q^n$. We define

$$g(\mathbf{u}) := \sum_{\mathbf{v} \in \mathcal{R}} \chi(\langle \mathbf{u}, \mathbf{v} \rangle)z^{w(\mathbf{v})}.$$

Then we have

$$\sum_{\mathbf{u} \in C} g(\mathbf{u}) = \sum_{\mathbf{u} \in C} \sum_{\mathbf{v} \in \mathcal{R}} \chi(\langle \mathbf{u}, \mathbf{v} \rangle)z^{w(\mathbf{v})} = \sum_{\mathbf{v} \in \mathcal{R}} z^{w(\mathbf{v})} \sum_{\mathbf{u} \in C} \chi(\langle \mathbf{u}, \mathbf{v} \rangle).$$

Here, if $\mathbf{v} \in C^{\perp}$ the inner sum is $|C|$. If $\mathbf{v} \notin C^{\perp}$ then in the inner sum $\langle \mathbf{u}, \mathbf{v} \rangle$ takes every value in $\mathbb{F}_q$ the same number of times, i.e. the inner sum is 0. Therefore

(3.5.4) $\qquad\qquad \sum_{\mathbf{u} \in C} g(\mathbf{u}) = |C| \cdot B(z).$

Extend the weight function to $\mathbb{F}_q$ by writing $w(v) = 0$ if $v = 0$ and $w(v) = 1$ otherwise. Then, writing $\mathbf{u} = (u_1, u_2, \ldots, u_n)$ and $\mathbf{v} = (v_1, v_2, \ldots, v_n)$, we have from the definition of $g(\mathbf{u})$:

$$g(\mathbf{u}) = \sum_{(v_1, v_2, \ldots, v_n) \in \mathcal{R}} z^{w(v_1) + \cdots + w(v_n)} \chi(u_1 v_1 + \cdots + u_n v_n)$$

$$= \sum_{(v_1, v_2, \ldots, v_n) \in \mathcal{R}} z^{w(v_1)} \chi(u_1 v_1) z^{w(v_2)} \chi(u_2 v_2) \cdots z^{w(v_n)} \chi(u_n v_n)$$

$$= \prod_{i=1}^{n} \sum_{v \in \mathbb{F}_q} z^{w(v)} \chi(u_i v).$$

In the last expression the inner sum is equal to $1 + (q-1)z$ if $u_i = 0$ and it is equal to

$$1 + z \sum_{\alpha \in \mathbb{F}_q \setminus \{0\}} \chi(\alpha) = 1 - z, \qquad \text{if } u_i \neq 0.$$

Therefore

(3.5.5) $\qquad\qquad g(\mathbf{u}) = (1-z)^{w(\mathbf{u})}(1 + (q-1)z)^{n - w(\mathbf{u})}.$

Since $|C| = q^k$ the theorem now follows by substituting (3.5.5) in (3.5.4). $\qquad \square$

For a generalization we refer to Section 7.2.

§3.6. Comments

The subject of linear codes was greatly influenced by papers by D. E. Slepian and R. W. Hamming written in the 1950s. The reader interested in knowing more about majority logic decoding should consult the book by J. L. Massey [47]. There are several generalizations of MacWilliams' theorem even to nonlinear codes. An extensive treatment can be found in Chapter 5 of [46]. For an application of (3.5.2) see Chapter 2 of [42].

§3.7. Problems

3.7.1. Let C be a binary perfect code of length n with minimum distance 7. Show that $n = 7$ or $n = 23$.

3.7.2. Let C be an $[n, k]$ code over $\mathbb{F}_q$ which is systematic on any set of k positions. Show that C has minimum distance $d = n - k + 1$.

3.7.3. Let C be a $[2k + 1, k]$ binary code such that $C \subset C^{\perp}$. Describe $C^{\perp} \backslash C$.

3.7.4. Let $\mathcal{R} = \mathbb{F}_2^6$ and let $\mathbf{x} \in \mathcal{R}$. Determine $|B_1(\mathbf{x})|$. Is it possible to find a set $C \subset \mathcal{R}$ with $|C| = 9$ such that for all $\mathbf{x} \in C, \mathbf{y} \in C, \mathbf{x} \neq \mathbf{y}$ the distance $d(\mathbf{x}, \mathbf{y})$ is at least 3?

3.7.5. Let C be an $[n, k]$ code over $\mathbb{F}_q$ with generator matrix G. If G does not have a column of 0s then the sum of the weights of the codewords of C is $n(q - 1)q^{k-1}$. Prove this.

3.7.6. Let C be a binary $[n, k]$ code. If C has word of odd weight then the words of even weight in C form an $[n, k - 1]$ code. Prove this.

3.7.7. Let C be a binary code with generator matrix

$$\begin{bmatrix} 1 & 0 & 0 & 0 & 1 & 0 & 1 \\ 0 & 1 & 0 & 0 & 1 & 0 & 1 \\ 0 & 0 & 1 & 0 & 0 & 1 & 1 \\ 0 & 0 & 0 & 1 & 0 & 1 & 1 \end{bmatrix}.$$

Decode the following received words:

(a) $(1 \quad 1 \quad 0 \quad 1 \quad 0 \quad 1 \quad 1)$;
(b) $(0 \quad 1 \quad 1 \quad 0 \quad 1 \quad 1 \quad 1)$;
(c) $(0 \quad 1 \quad 1 \quad 1 \quad 0 \quad 0 \quad 0)$.

3.7.8. Let p be a prime. Is there an $[8, 4]$ self-dual code over $\mathbb{F}_p$?

3.7.9. For $q = 2$ let R_k denote the rate of the Hamming code defined in (3.3.1). Determine $\lim_{k \to \infty} R_k$.

3.7.10. Let C be a binary code with weight enumerator $A(z)$. What is the weight enumerator of $\bar{C}$? What is the weight enumerator of the dual of the extended binary Hamming code of length 2^k?

3.7.11. Let C be a binary $[n, k]$ code with weight enumerator $A(z)$. We use C on a binary symmetric channel with error probability p. Our purpose is error detection only. What is the probability that an incorrect word is received and the error is not detected?

3.7.12. The n_1 by n_2 matrices over $\mathbb{F}_2$ clearly form a vector space $\mathscr{R}$ of dimension $n_1 n_2$. Let C_i be an $[n_i, k_i]$ binary code with minimum distance d_i $(i = 1, 2)$. Let C be the subset of $\mathscr{R}$ consisting of those matrices for which every column, respectively row, is a codeword in C_1, respectively C_2. Show that C is an $[n_1 n_2, k_1 k_2]$ code with minimum distance $d_1 d_2$. This code is called *direct product* of C_1 and C_2.

3.7.13. Let C be the binary $[10, 5]$ code with generator matrix

$$G = \begin{bmatrix} 1 & 0 & 0 & 0 & 0 & 0 & 0 & 0 & 1 & 1 \\ 0 & 1 & 0 & 0 & 0 & 0 & 1 & 1 & 0 & 0 \\ 0 & 0 & 1 & 0 & 0 & 1 & 0 & 1 & 0 & 0 \\ 0 & 0 & 0 & 1 & 0 & 1 & 1 & 0 & 0 & 0 \\ 0 & 0 & 0 & 0 & 1 & 1 & 1 & 1 & 0 & 0 \end{bmatrix}.$$

Show that C is *uniquely decodable* in the following sense: For every received word $\mathbf{x}$ there is a unique code word $\mathbf{c}$ such that $d(\mathbf{x}, \mathbf{c})$ is minimal.

3.7.14. Let us define *lexicographically least binary codes* with distance d as follows. The word length is not specified at first. Start with $\mathbf{c}_0 = \mathbf{0}$ and $\mathbf{c}_1 = (1, 1, \ldots, 1, 0, 0, 0, \ldots, 0)$ of weight d. If $\mathbf{c}_0, \mathbf{c}_1, \ldots, \mathbf{c}_{l-1}$ have been chosen then $\mathbf{c}_l$ is chosen as the word which comes first in the lexicographic ordering (with 1s as far to the left as possible) such that $d(\mathbf{c}_i, \mathbf{c}_l) \geq d (0 \leq i \leq l - 1)$. After l steps the length of the code is defined to be the length of the part where coordinates 1 occur.

(i) Show that after 2^k vectors have been chosen the lexicographically least code is linear!

(ii) For $d = 3$ the Hamming codes occur among the lexicographically least codes. Prove this.

CHAPTER 4

Some Good Codes

§4.1. Hadamard Codes and Generalizations

Let H_n be a Hadamard matrix of order n (see (1.3.5)). In H_n and $-H_n$ we replace -1 by 0. In this way we find $2n$ rows which are words in $\mathbb{F}_2^n$. Since any two rows of a Hadamard matrix differ in half of the positions we have constructed an $(n, 2n, \frac{1}{2}n)$ code. For $n = 8$ this is an extended Hamming code. For $n = 32$ the code is the one used by Mariner 1969 which was mentioned in Section 2.1. In general these codes are called *Hadamard codes*.

A similar construction starts from a Paley matrix S of order n (see (1.3.8)). We construct a code C with codewords $\mathbf{0}$, $\mathbf{1}$, the rows of $\frac{1}{2}(S + I + J)$ and $\frac{1}{2}(-S + I + J)$. From Theorem 1.3.8 it follows that C is an $(n, 2(n + 1), d)$ code, where $d = \frac{1}{2}(n - 1)$ if $n \equiv 1 \pmod 4$ and $d = \frac{1}{2}(n - 3)$ if $n \equiv 3 \pmod 4$. In the case $n = 9$ the code consists of the rows of the matrix

$$
(4.1.1) \qquad
\begin{bmatrix}
0\ 0\ 0 & 0\ 0\ 0 & 0\ 0\ 0 \\
J & P^2 & P \\
P & J & P^2 \\
P^2 & P & J \\
I & J - P^2 & J - P \\
J - P & I & J - P^2 \\
J - P^2 & J - P & I \\
1\ 1\ 1 & 1\ 1\ 1 & 1\ 1\ 1
\end{bmatrix}
$$

where I and J are 3 by 3 and

$$
P = \begin{bmatrix} 0 & 1 & 0 \\ 0 & 0 & 1 \\ 1 & 0 & 0 \end{bmatrix}
$$

§4.2. The Binary Golay Code

The most famous of all (binary) codes is the so-called binary *Golay code* $\mathcal{G}_{23}$. There are very many constructions of this code, some of them quite elegant and with short proofs of the properties of this code. We shall prove that $\mathcal{G}_{24}$, the extended binary Golay code, is unique and treat a few constructions. From these it follows that the automorphism group of the extended code is transitive and hence $\mathcal{G}_{23}$ is also unique.

We consider the incidence matrix N of a 2-(11, 6, 3) design. It is easy to show (by hand) that this design is unique. We have $NN^\top = 3I + 3J$. Consider N as a matrix with entries in $\mathbb{F}_2$. Then $NN^\top = I + J$. So N has rank 10 and the only vector $\mathbf{x}$ with $\mathbf{x}N = \mathbf{0}$ is $\mathbf{1}$. The design properties imply trivially that the rows of N all have weight 6, and that the sum of any two distinct rows of N also has weight 6. Furthermore, we know that the sum of three or four rows of N is not $\mathbf{0}$.

Next, let G be the 12 by 24 matrix (over $\mathbb{F}_2$) given by $G := (I_{12}P)$, where

(4.2.1)
$$
P := \begin{pmatrix} 0 & 1 & \cdots & 1 \\ 1 & & & \\ \vdots & & N & \\ 1 & & & \end{pmatrix}.
$$

Every row of G has a weight $\equiv 0 \pmod 4$. Any two rows of G have inner product 0. This implies that the weight of any linear combination of the rows of G is $\equiv 0 \pmod 4$ (proof by induction). The observations made about N then show that a linear combination of any number of rows of G has weight at least 8. Consider the binary code generated by G and call it $\mathcal{G}_{24}$. Delete any coordinate to find a binary [23, 12] code with minimum distance at least 7. The distance cannot be larger, since (3.1.6) is satisfied with $e = 3$, which shows that in fact this [23, 12, 7] code is a *perfect code*! We denote this code by $\mathcal{G}_{23}$; (as mentioned above, we shall prove its uniqueness, justifying the notation).

(4.2.2) Theorem. *The codewords of weight 8 in $\mathcal{G}_{24}$ form a 5-(24, 8, 1) design.*

PROOF. By an easy counting argument, one can show that the weight enumerator of a perfect code containing $\mathbf{0}$ is uniquely determined. In fact, we have $A_0 = A_{23} = 1, A_7 = A_{16} = 253, A_8 = A_{15} = 506, A_{11} = A_{12} = 1288$. So, $\mathcal{G}_{24}$ has 759 words of weight 8, no two overlapping in more than four positions. Hence, these words together cover $759 \cdot \binom{8}{5} = \binom{24}{5}$ fivetuples. □

(4.2.3) Theorem. *If C is a binary code of length 24, with $|C| = 2^{12}$, minimum distance 8, and if $\mathbf{0} \in C$, then C is equivalent to $\mathcal{G}_{24}$.*

PROOF. (i) The difficult part of the proof is to show that C must be a *linear* code. To see this, observe that deleting any coordinate produces a code C' of length 23 and distance 7 with $|C'| = 2^{12}$. So, this code is perfect and its weight enumerator is as in the proof of the previous theorem. From the fact that this is the case, no matter which of the 24 positions is deleted, it follows that all codewords in C have weight 0, 8, 12, 16, or 24. Furthermore, a change of origin, obtained by adding a fixed codeword of C to all the words of C, shows that we can conclude that the distance of any two words of C is also 0, 8, 12, 16, or 24. Since all weights and all distances are $\equiv 0 \pmod 4$, any two codewords have inner product 0. Therefore the codewords of C span a linear code that is selforthogonal. This span clearly has dimension at most 12, i.e. at most 2^{12} codewords. It follows that this span must be C itself. In other words, C is a selfdual linear code! (ii) We form a generator matrix G of C, taking as first row any word of weight 12. After a permutation of positions we have

$$G = \begin{pmatrix} 1 & \cdots & 1 & 0 & \cdots & 0 \\ & A & & & B & \end{pmatrix}.$$

We know that any linear combination of the rows of B must have even weight $\neq 0$. So, B has rank 11. This implies that the code generated by B is the $[12, 11, 2]$ even weight code. We may therefore assume that B is the matrix I_{11} bordered by a column of 1's. A second permutation of the columns of G yields a generator matrix G' of the form $(I_{12} P)$, where P has the same form as in (4.2.1). What do we know about the matrix N in this case? Clearly any row of N must have weight 6 (look at the first row of G'). In the same way we see that the sum of any two rows of N has weight 6. This implies that N is the incidence matrix of the (unique!) 2-(11, 6, 3) design. Hence C is equivalent to $\mathscr{G}_{24}$. $\square$

The following construction of $\mathscr{G}_{24}$ is due to R. J. Turyn. We consider the $[7, 4]$ Hamming code H in the following representation. Take $\mathbf{0}$ and the seven cyclic shifts of $(1\ 1\ 0\ 1\ 0\ 0\ 0)$; (note that these seven vectors form the incidence matrix of $PG(2, 2)$). Then take the eight complements of these words. Together these form H. Let H^* be obtained by reversing the order of the symbols in the words of H. By inspection we see that $\overline{H}$ and $\overline{H^*}$ are $[8, 4]$ codes with the property $\overline{H} \cap \overline{H^*} = \{\mathbf{0}, \mathbf{1}\}$. We know that both $\overline{H}$ and $\overline{H^*}$ are selfdual codes with minimum distance 4.

We now form a code C with word length 24 by concatenating as follows:

$$C := \{(\mathbf{a} + \mathbf{x}, \mathbf{b} + \mathbf{x}, \mathbf{a} + \mathbf{b} + \mathbf{x}) | \mathbf{a} \in \overline{H}, \mathbf{b} \in \overline{H}, \mathbf{x} \in \overline{H^*}\}.$$

By letting $\mathbf{a}$ and $\mathbf{b}$ run through a basis of $\overline{H}$ and $\mathbf{x}$ run through a basis of $\overline{H^*}$, we see that the words $(\mathbf{a}, \mathbf{0}, \mathbf{a})$, $(\mathbf{0}, \mathbf{b}, \mathbf{b})$, $(\mathbf{x}, \mathbf{x}, \mathbf{x})$ form a basis for the code C. Hence C is a $[24, 12]$ code. Any two (not necessarily distinct) basis vectors of C are orthogonal, i. e. C is selfdual. Since all the basis vectors have a weight divisible by 4, this holds for every word in C. Can a word $\mathbf{c} \in C$ have weight less than 8? Since the three components $\mathbf{a} + \mathbf{x}$, $\mathbf{b} + \mathbf{x}$, $\mathbf{a} + \mathbf{b} + \mathbf{x}$ all obviously have even weight, one of them must be $\mathbf{0}$. Our observation on the intersection of $\overline{H}$ and $\overline{H^*}$ then leads to the conclusion that $\mathbf{x} = \mathbf{0}$ or $\mathbf{1}$. Without loss of generality we assume that $\mathbf{x} = \mathbf{0}$. Since the words of H have weight 0, 4, or 8, it follows that $\mathbf{c} = \mathbf{0}$.

We have shown that C is a $[24, 12, 8]$ code; hence $C = \mathscr{G}_{24}$.

The next construction is due to J. H. Conway. Let $\mathbb{F}_4 = \{0, 1, \omega, \overline{\omega}\}$. Let C be the $[6, 3]$ code over $\mathbb{F}_4$ with codewords $(a, b, c, f(1), f(\omega), f(\overline{\omega}))$, where $f(x) := ax^2 + bx + c$. It is an easy exercise to show that C has minimum weight 4 and no words of weight 5. C is known as the *hexacode*.

Now, let G be the binary code of length 24 for which the words are represented as 4 by 6 binary matrices A. Denote the four rows of such a matrix A by $\mathbf{a}_0$, $\mathbf{a}_1$, $\mathbf{a}_\omega$, and $\mathbf{a}_{\overline{\omega}}$. A matrix A belongs to G iff the following two conditions are satisfied

(1) Every column of A has the same parity as its first row $\mathbf{a}_0$;
(2) $\mathbf{a}_1 + \omega\mathbf{a}_\omega + \overline{\omega}\mathbf{a}_{\overline{\omega}} \in C$.

These conditions obviously define a linear code.

If the first row of A has even parity and the codeword in (2) is not $\mathbf{0}$, then A has at least four columns of weight ≥ 2, i. e. weight ≥ 8. If, on the other hand, the codeword in (2) is $\mathbf{0}$, then either A is the zero word or A has at least two columns of weight 4, again a total weight at least 8. If A has a first row of odd parity, then all the columns of A have odd weight. These weights cannot all be 1, because this would imply that the word of C in condition (2) has odd weight. We have shown that G has minimum distance 8. We leave it as an exercise for the reader to show that conditions (1) and (2) and the fact that C has dimension 3 imply that G has dimension 12. Therefore, the matrices A form $\mathscr{G}_{24}$.

In Section 6.9 we shall find yet another construction of $\mathscr{G}_{23}$ as a cyclic code, i. e. a code with an automorphism of order 23. All these constructions together show that the automorphism group of $\mathscr{G}_{24}$ is transitive (in fact 5-transitive; it is the *Mathieu group* M_{24}). Therefore $\mathscr{G}_{23}$ is also unique.

We mention that the construction of Exercise 3.7.14 with $d = 8$ and $k = 12$ also produces the extended binary Golay code $\mathscr{G}_{24}$.

The following decoding algorithm for $\mathscr{G}_{24}$ is a generalization of Section 3.4 based on Theorem 4.2.1. Let $\mathbf{y}_i$ $(1 \leq i \leq 253)$ be the 253 code words of weight 8 of $\mathscr{G}_{24}$ with a 1 in a given position, say position 1. Consider the parity checks $\langle \mathbf{x}, \mathbf{y}_i \rangle$ $(1 \leq i \leq 253)$; here we use the fact that $\mathscr{G}_{24}$ is self-dual. Suppose $\mathbf{x}$ is received and contains $t \leq 4$ errors. Theorem 4.2.1 implies that the number of parity checks which fail is given by the following table.

	x_1 correct	x_1 incorrect
$t = 1$	77	253
2	112	176
3	125	141
4	128	128

So in case $t \leq 3$ we can correct the symbol x_1. The line corresponding to $t = 4$ demonstrates that $\mathscr{G}_{24}$ is 4-error-detecting but not 4-error-correcting.

We remark that the procedure for self-dual codes that we described in Section 3.2, when applied to the extended binary Golay code, involves the calculation of at most $26 \times 12 = 312$ parity checks and produces all the coordinates of the error vector (if $t \leq 3$).

§4.3. The Ternary Golay Code

Let S_5 be the Paley matrix of size 5 defined in (1.3.8), i.e.

$$
S_5 = \begin{bmatrix}
0 & + & - & - & + \\
+ & 0 & + & - & - \\
- & + & 0 & + & - \\
- & - & + & 0 & + \\
+ & - & - & + & 0
\end{bmatrix}.
$$

Consider the [11, 6] ternary code C defined by the generator matrix

$$
G = \begin{bmatrix}
 & & & 1\ 1\ 1\ 1\ 1 \\
 & I_6 & & \boxed{\ \ S_5\ \ } \\
\end{bmatrix}
$$

The code C is an [11, 6] code. From (1.3.8) it follows that $\bar{C}$ is self-dual. Therefore all the words of $\bar{C}$ have weight divisible by 3. The generator $\bar{G}$ for $\bar{C}$ is obtained by adding the column $(0, -1, -1, -1, -1, -1)^T$ to G. Every row of $\bar{G}$ has weight 6. A linear combination of two rows of $\bar{G}$ has weight at least $2 + 2$, hence it has weight 6. Therefore a linear combination of two rows of $\bar{G}$ has exactly two zeros in the last six positions and this implies that a linear combination of three rows of $\bar{G}$ has weight at least $3 + 1$, i.e. weight at least 6. Therefore $\bar{C}$ has minimum distance 6. It follows that C is an $(11, 3^6, 5)$ code. From $|B_2(\mathbf{x})| = \sum_{i=0}^{2} \binom{11}{i} 2^i = 3^5$ it then follows that C is a perfect code. This code is known as the *ternary Golay code*. It has been shown that any $(11, 3^6, 5)$ code is equivalent to C (cf. [46]). A simple uniqueness proof such as we gave for the binary Golay code has not been found yet.

§4.4. Constructing Codes from Other Codes

Many good codes have been constructed by modifying (in various ways) previously constructed codes. In this section we shall give several examples. The first method was introduced in (3.2.7), namely *extending* a code by adding an extra symbol called the overall parity check. The inverse process, which we used in Section 4.2 to obtain the binary Golay code from its extension is called *puncturing* a code. If we consider as another example the (9, 20, 4) code of (4.1.1) and puncture it, i.e. delete the last symbol in every word, we obtain an (8, 20, 3) code. In the next chapter we shall see that this is indeed a good code. We remark that an equivalent code can also be obtained by taking all cyclic permutations of the words (1 1 0 1 0 0 0 0), (1 1 1 0 0 1 0 0), and (1 0 1 0 1 0 1 0) together with **0** and **1**.

A third procedure is *shortening* a code C. Here, one takes all codewords in C that end in the same symbol and subsequently deletes this symbol. This procedure decreases the length and the number of codewords but it does not lower the minimum distance. Note that if the deleted symbol is not 0, this procedure changes a linear code to a nonlinear code (generally).

Let us now look at a slightly more complicated method. From one of the constructions of the extended binary Golay code $\mathscr{G}_{24}$ in Section 4.2 one immediately sees that $\mathscr{G}_{24}$ has a subcode consisting of 32 words with 0 in the first eight positions. Similarly, if we take $c_8 = 1$ and exactly one of the symbols c_1 to c_7 equal to 1, then we find a subcode of 32 words $(c_1, c_2, \ldots, c_{24})$. Doing this in all possible ways, we have a subset of 256 words of $\mathscr{G}_{24}$ with the property that any two of them differ in at most two positions among the first eight. Now we delete the first eight symbols from these words. The result is a binary (16, 256, 6) code which is nonlinear. This code is called the *Nordstrom-Robinson code*. This code is the first one in an infinite sequence that we discuss in Section 7.4. If we shorten this code twice and then puncture once the result is a (13, 64, 5) code, which we denote by Y. This will be an important example in the next chapter. It is known that Y is unique and that if we shorten Y there are two possible results (J.-M. Goethals 1977; cf. [26]). The two codes are: a code known as the *Nadler code* and the code of Problem 4.7.7.

A construction similar to our construction of the extended binary Golay code is known as the $(\mathbf{u}, \mathbf{u} + \mathbf{v})$-construction. Let C_i be an (n, M_i, d_i) binary code ($i = 1, 2$). Define

(4.4.1) $$C := \{(\mathbf{u}, \mathbf{u} + \mathbf{v}) | \mathbf{u} \in C_1, \mathbf{v} \in C_2\}.$$

Then C is a $(2n, M_1 M_2, d)$ code, where $d := \min\{2d_1, d_2\}$. To show this we consider two codewords $(\mathbf{u}_1, \mathbf{u}_1 + \mathbf{v}_1)$ and $(\mathbf{u}_2, \mathbf{u}_2 + \mathbf{v}_2)$. If $\mathbf{v}_1 = \mathbf{v}_2$ and $\mathbf{u}_1 \neq \mathbf{u}_2$, their distance is at least $2d_1$. If $\mathbf{v}_1 \neq \mathbf{v}_2$ the distance is $w(\mathbf{u}_1 - \mathbf{u}_2) + w(\mathbf{u}_1 - \mathbf{u}_2 + \mathbf{v}_1 - \mathbf{v}_2)$ which clearly exceeds $w(\mathbf{v}_1 - \mathbf{v}_2)$, i.e. it is at least d_2. As an example we take for C_2 the (8, 20, 3) code constructed above, and for C_1 we take the [8, 7] even weight code. The construction yields a $(16, 5 \cdot 2^9, 3)$ code. There is no $(16, M, 3)$ code known at present with $M > 5 \cdot 2^9$.

Many good codes were constructed using the following idea due to H. J. Helgert and R. D. Stinaff (1973; cf. [34]). Let C be an $[n, k]$ binary code with minimum distance d. We may assume that C has a generator matrix G with a word of weight d as its first row, say

$$G = \begin{bmatrix} 1 & 1 & \dots & 1 & & 0 & 0 & \dots & 0 \\ & & G_1 & & & & & G_2 & \end{bmatrix}.$$

Let d' be the minimum distance of the $[n - d, k - 1]$ code generated by G_2 which we call the *residual code* w.r.t. the first row of G. From G we see that to each codeword of the residual code there correspond two codewords of C, at least one of which has weight $\leq \frac{1}{2}d$ on the first d positions. Hence $d' \geq \frac{1}{2}d$. To illustrate this method we now show that a linear code with the parameters of the Nadler code does not exist. If there were such a code it would have a generator matrix G as above where G_2 generates a $[7, 4]$ code with distance $d' \geq 3$. Therefore the residual code is a Hamming code. W.l.o.g. we can take G_2 to have four rows of weight 3 and then G_1 must have (w.l.o.g.) four rows of weight 2. There are only a few possibilities to try and these do not yield a code with $d = 5$. Even for small parameter values it is often quite difficult to find good codes. For example, a rather complicated construction (cf. [46], Chapter 2, Section 7) produced a $(10, M, 4)$ code with $M = 38$ and for a long time it was believed that this could not be improved. M. R. Best (1978; cf. [8]) found a $(10, 40, 4)$ code which we describe below. In the next chapter we shall see that for $n = 10, d = 4$ this is indeed the *Best code*! Consider the $[5, 3]$ code C_1 with generator $\begin{bmatrix} 1 & 0 & 0 & 0 & 1 \\ 0 & 1 & 0 & 1 & 1 \\ 0 & 0 & 1 & 1 & 0 \end{bmatrix}$. By doubling all the codewords we have a $[10, 3]$ code C_2 with minimum distance $d = 4$. Now add $(10000 \quad 00100)$ to all the words of C_2. The new code is no longer linear and does not contain $\mathbf{0}$. Numbering the positions from 1 to 10 we subsequently permute the positions of the codewords by elements of the subgroup of S_{10} generated by $(1 \quad 2 \quad 3 \quad 4 \quad 5)(6 \quad 7 \quad 8 \quad 9 \quad 10)$. This yields 40 codewords which turn out to have minimum distance 4.

§4.5. Reed–Muller Codes

We shall now describe a class of binary codes connected with finite geometries. The codes were first treated by D. E. Muller (1954) and I. S. Reed (1954). The codes are not as good as some of the codes that will be treated in later chapters but in practice they have the advantage that they are easy to decode. The method is a generalization of majority logic decoding (see Section 3.4).

There are several ways of representing the codewords of a Reed–Muller code. We shall try to give a unified treatment which shows how the different points of view are related. As preparation we need a theorem from number theory that is a century old (Lucas (1878)).

(4.5.1) Theorem. *Let p be a prime and let*

$$n = \sum_{i=0}^{l} n_i p^i \qquad and \qquad k = \sum_{i=0}^{l} k_i p^i$$

be representations of n and k in base p (i.e. $0 \leq n_i \leq p - 1$, $0 \leq k_i \leq p - 1$). Then

$$\binom{n}{k} \equiv \prod_{i=0}^{l} \binom{n_i}{k_i} \pmod{p}.$$

PROOF. We use the fact that $(1 + x)^p \equiv 1 + x^p \pmod{p}$. If $0 \leq r < p$ then

$$(1 + x)^{ap+r} \equiv (1 + x^p)^a (1 + x)^r \pmod{p}.$$

Comparing coefficients of x^{bp+s} (where $0 \leq s < p$) on both sides yields

$$\binom{ap + r}{bp + s} \equiv \binom{a}{b}\binom{r}{s} \pmod{p}.$$

The result now follows by induction.   □

The following theorem on weights of polynomials is also a preparation. Let $q = 2^r$. For a polynomial $P(x) \in \mathbb{F}_q[x]$ we define the Hamming weight $w(P(x))$ to be the number of nonzero coefficients in the expansion of $P(x)$. Let $c \in \mathbb{F}_q$, $c \neq 0$. The polynomials $(x + c)^i$, $i \geq 0$, are a basis of $\mathbb{F}_q[x]$.

(4.5.2) Theorem (Massey *et al.* 1973; cf. [49]). *Let $P(x) = \sum_{i=0}^{l} b_i(x + c)^i$, where $b_l \neq 0$ and let i_0 be the smallest index i for which $b_i \neq 0$. Then*

$$w(P(x)) \geq w((x + c)^{i_0}).$$

PROOF. For $l = 0$ the assertion is obvious. We use induction. Assume the theorem is true for $l < 2^n$. Now let $2^n \leq l < 2^{n+1}$. Then we have

$$P(x) = \sum_{i=0}^{2^n-1} b_i(x + c)^i + \sum_{i=2^n}^{l} b_i(x + c)^i$$

$$= P_1(x) + (x + c)^{2^n} P_2(x) = (P_1(x) + c^{2^n} P_2(x)) + x^{2^n} P_2(x),$$

where $P_1(x)$ and $P_2(x)$ are polynomials for which the theorem holds. We distinguish two cases.

(i) If $P_1(x) = 0$ then $w(P(x)) = 2w(P_2(x))$ and since $i_0 \geq 2^n$

$$w((x + c)^{i_0}) = w((x^{2^n} + c^{2^n})(x + c)^{i_0 - 2^n}) = 2w((x + c)^{i_0 - 2^n}),$$

from which the assertion follows.

(ii) If $P_1(x) \neq 0$ then for every term in $c^{2^n} P_2(x)$ that cancels a term in $P_1(x)$ we have a term in $x^{2^n} P_2(x)$ that does not cancel. Hence $w(P(x)) \geq w(P_1(x))$ and the result follows from the induction hypothesis.   □

The three representations of codewords in Reed–Muller codes which we now introduce are: (i) characteristic functions of subsets in AG(m, 2); (ii) coefficients of binary expansions of polynomials; and (iii) lists of values which are taken by a Boolean function on $\mathbb{F}_2^m$.

First some notations and definitions. We consider the points of AG(m, 2), i.e. $\mathbb{F}_2^m$ as column vectors and denote the standard basis by $\mathbf{u}_0, \mathbf{u}_1, \ldots, \mathbf{u}_{m-1}$. Let the binary representation of j be $j = \sum_{i=0}^{m-1} \xi_{ij} 2^i$ $(0 \leq j < 2^m)$.

We define $\mathbf{x}_j := \sum_{i=0}^{m-1} \xi_{ij} \mathbf{u}_i$. This represents a point of AG(m, 2) and all points are obtained in this way. Let E be the matrix with columns $\mathbf{x}_j$ $(0 \leq j < 2^m)$. Write $n := 2^m$. The m by n matrix E is a list of the points of AG(m, 2), written as column vectors.

(4.5.3) Definitions.

(i) $A_i := \{\mathbf{x}_j \in \text{AG}(m, 2) | \xi_{ij} = 1\}$, i.e. A_i is an $(m - 1)$-dimensional affine subspace (a hyperplane), for $0 \leq i < m$;

(ii) $\mathbf{v}_i :=$ the ith row of E, i.e. the characteristic function of A_i. The vector $\mathbf{v}_i$ is a word in $\mathbb{F}_2^n$; as usual we write $\mathbf{1} := (1, 1, \ldots, 1)$ for the characteristic function of AG(m, 2);

(iii) if $\mathbf{a} = (a_0, a_1, \ldots, a_{n-1})$ and $\mathbf{b} = (b_0, b_1, \ldots, b_{n-1})$ are words in $\mathbb{F}_2^n$, we define

$$\mathbf{ab} := (a_0 b_0, a_1 b_1, \ldots, a_{n-1} b_{n-1});$$

(iv) if $S \subset \{0, 1, \ldots, m - 1\}$ we define

$$C(S) := \left\{ j = \sum_{i=0}^{m-1} \xi_{ij} 2^i \,\middle|\, i \notin S \Rightarrow \xi_{ij} = 0 \; (0 \leq i < m) \right\}.$$

(4.5.4) Lemma. *Let* $l = \sum_{i=0}^{m-1} \xi_{il} 2^i$ *and let* $i_1, \ldots, i_s$ *be the values of* i *for which* $\xi_{il} = 0$. *If*

$$\mathbf{v}_{i_1} \mathbf{v}_{i_2} \ldots \mathbf{v}_{i_s} = (a_{l,0}, a_{l,1}, \ldots, a_{l,n-1}),$$

then

$$(x + 1)^l = \sum_{j=0}^{n-1} a_{l,j} x^{n-1-j}.$$

(Here, as usual, a product with no factors ($s = 0$) is defined to be **1**.)

PROOF. By Theorem 4.5.1 the binomial coefficient $\binom{l}{n-1-j}$ is 1 iff $\xi_{ij} = 1$ for every i for which $\xi_{il} = 0$. By (4.5.3) (i), (ii) and (iii) we also have $a_{l,j} = 1$ iff $\xi_{ij} = 1$ for $i = i_1, \ldots, i_s$.   □

The following shows how to interpret the products $\mathbf{v}_{i_1} \ldots \mathbf{v}_{i_s}$ geometrically.

(4.5.5) Lemma. *If* $i_1, i_2, \ldots, i_s$ *are different then*

(i) $\mathbf{v}_{i_1} \mathbf{v}_{i_2} \ldots \mathbf{v}_{i_s}$ *is the characteristic function of the* $(m - s)$-*flat*

$$A_{i_1} \cap A_{i_2} \cap \cdots \cap A_{i_s},$$

(ii) *the weight* $w(\mathbf{v}_{i_1} \dots \mathbf{v}_{i_s})$ *of the vector* $\mathbf{v}_{i_1} \dots \mathbf{v}_{i_s}$ *in* $\mathbb{F}_2^n$ *is* 2^{m-s},

(iii) *the characteristic function of* $\{\mathbf{x}_j\}$, *i.e. the jth basis vector of* $\mathbb{F}_2^n$ *is*

$$\mathbf{e}_j = \prod_{i=0}^{m-1} \{\mathbf{v}_i + (1 + \xi_{ij})\mathbf{1}\},$$

(iv) *the products* $\mathbf{v}_{i_1} \dots \mathbf{v}_{i_s}$ $(0 \le s \le m)$ *are a basis of* $\mathbb{F}_2^n$.

PROOF.

(i) This is a consequence of (4.5.3)(i)–(iii).

(ii) By (i) the weight is the cardinality of an $(m - s)$-flat.

(iii) Consider the matrix E. For every i such that $\xi_{ij} = 0$ we replace the ith row of E, i.e. $\mathbf{v}_i$, by its complement $\mathbf{1} + \mathbf{v}_i$. If we then multiply the rows of the new matrix, the product vector will have entry 1 only in position j, since all possible columns occur only once. As an example consider $\{\mathbf{x}_{14}\}$ in the following table. Since $14 = 0 + 2 + 2^2 + 2^3$ we see that $1 + \xi_{ij} = 1$ only if $i = 0$ (here $j = 14$). So in the table we complement the row corresponding to $\mathbf{v}_0$ and then multiply to find $(\mathbf{v}_0 + \mathbf{1}) \mathbf{v}_1 \mathbf{v}_2 \mathbf{v}_3$ which is a row vector which has a 1 only in the fourteenth position.

(iv) There are $\sum_{s=0}^{m} \binom{m}{s} = 2^m = n$ products $\mathbf{v}_{i_1} \dots \mathbf{v}_{i_s}$. The result follows from (iii). Since the polynomials $(x + 1)^l$ are independent we could also have used Lemma 4.5.4. □

The following table illustrates Lemmas 4.5.4 and 4.5.5. For example, $\mathbf{v}_0$ $\mathbf{v}_2$ corresponds to $l = 15 - 2^0 - 2^2 = 10$ and hence $(x + 1)^{10} = x^{10} + x^8 + x^2 + 1$.

$\mathbf{v}_{i_1}\mathbf{v}_{i_2}\dots\mathbf{v}_{i_s}$	Coordinates = coefficients of $(x + 1)^l$	$l = n - 1 - \sum 2^{i_s}$
$\mathbf{1}$	1 1 1 1 1 1 1 1 1 1 1 1 1 1 1 1	$15 = 1111$
$\mathbf{v}_0$	0 1 0 1 0 1 0 1 0 1 0 1 0 1 0 1	$14 = 1110$
$\mathbf{v}_1$	0 0 1 1 0 0 1 1 0 0 1 1 0 0 1 1	$13 = 1101$
$\mathbf{v}_2$	0 0 0 0 1 1 1 1 0 0 0 0 1 1 1 1	$11 = 1011$
$\mathbf{v}_3$	0 0 0 0 0 0 0 0 1 1 1 1 1 1 1 1	$7 = 0111$
$\mathbf{v}_0\ \mathbf{v}_1$	0 0 0 1 0 0 0 1 0 0 0 1 0 0 0 1	$12 = 1100$
$\mathbf{v}_0\ \mathbf{v}_2$	0 0 0 0 0 1 0 1 0 0 0 0 0 1 0 1	$10 = 1010$
$\mathbf{v}_0\ \mathbf{v}_3$	0 0 0 0 0 0 0 0 0 1 0 1 0 1 0 1	$6 = 0110$
$\mathbf{v}_1\ \mathbf{v}_2$	0 0 0 0 0 0 1 1 0 0 0 0 0 0 1 1	$9 = 1001$
$\mathbf{v}_1\ \mathbf{v}_3$	0 0 0 0 0 0 0 0 0 0 1 1 0 0 1 1	$5 = 0101$
$\mathbf{v}_2\ \mathbf{v}_3$	0 0 0 0 0 0 0 0 0 0 0 0 1 1 1 1	$3 = 0011$
$\mathbf{v}_0\ \mathbf{v}_1\ \mathbf{v}_2$	0 0 0 0 0 0 0 1 0 0 0 0 0 0 0 1	$8 = 1000$
$\mathbf{v}_0\ \mathbf{v}_1\ \mathbf{v}_3$	0 0 0 0 0 0 0 0 0 0 0 1 0 0 0 1	$4 = 0100$
$\mathbf{v}_0\ \mathbf{v}_2\ \mathbf{v}_3$	0 0 0 0 0 0 0 0 0 0 0 0 0 1 0 1	$2 = 0010$
$\mathbf{v}_1\ \mathbf{v}_2\ \mathbf{v}_3$	0 0 0 0 0 0 0 0 0 0 0 0 0 0 1 1	$1 = 0001$
$\mathbf{v}_0\ \mathbf{v}_1\ \mathbf{v}_2\ \mathbf{v}_3$	0 0 0 0 0 0 0 0 0 0 0 0 0 0 0 1	$0 = 0000$

(4.5.6) Definition. Let $0 \leq r < m$. The linear code of length $n = 2^m$ which has the products $\mathbf{v}_{i_1} \ldots \mathbf{v}_{i_s}$ with $s \leq r$ factors as basis is called the rth *order binary Reed–Muller code* (RM code; notation $\mathcal{R}(r, m)$).

The special case $\mathcal{R}(0, m)$ is the repetition code. From Lemma 4.5.5(i) we see that the Boolean function $x_{i_1} x_{i_2} \ldots x_{i_s}$ where $\mathbf{x} = (x_0, \ldots, x_{m-1})$ runs through $\mathbb{F}_2^m$ has value 1 iff $\mathbf{x} \in A_{i_1} \cap \cdots \cap A_{i_s}$. Hence $\mathcal{R}(r, m)$ consists of the sequences of values taken by polynomials in $x_0, \ldots, x_{m-1}$ of degree at most r.

(4.5.7) Theorem. $\mathcal{R}(r, m)$ *has minimum distance* 2^{m-r}.

PROOF. By the definition and Lemma 4.5.5(ii) the minimum distance is at most 2^{m-r} and by Lemma 4.5.4 and Theorem 4.5.2 it is at least 2^{m-r}. (Also see Problem 4.7.9.)   □

(4.5.8) Theorem. *The dual of* $\mathcal{R}(r, m)$ *is* $\mathcal{R}(m - r - 1, m)$.

PROOF.

(a) By the definition and the independence of the products $\mathbf{v}_{i_1} \ldots \mathbf{v}_{i_s}$ the dimension of $\mathcal{R}(r, m)$ is $1 + \binom{m}{1} + \cdots + \binom{m}{r}$. So dim $\mathcal{R}(r, m) +$ dim $\mathcal{R}(m - r - 1, m) = n$.

(b) Let $\mathbf{v}_{i_1} \ldots \mathbf{v}_{i_s}$ and $\mathbf{v}_{j_1} \ldots \mathbf{v}_{j_t}$ be basis vectors of $\mathcal{R}(r, m)$ and $\mathcal{R}(m - r - 1, m)$ respectively. Then $s + t < m$. Hence the product of these two basis vectors has the form $\mathbf{v}_{k_1} \ldots \mathbf{v}_{k_u}$ where $u < m$. By Lemma 4.5.5(ii) this product has even weight, i.e. the original two basis vectors are orthogonal.   □

Corollary. $\mathcal{R}(m - 2, m)$ is the $[n, n - m - 1]$ extended Hamming code.

We have chosen the characteristic functions of certain flats as basis for an RM-code. We shall now show that for every flat of suitable dimension the characteristic function is in certain RM codes.

(4.5.9) Theorem. *Let* $C = \mathcal{R}(m - l, m)$ *and let* A *be an* l-*flat in* AG$(m, 2)$. *Then the characteristic function of* A *is in* C.

PROOF. Let $\mathbf{f} = \sum_{j=0}^{n-1} f_j \mathbf{e}_j$ be the characteristic function of A. By Definition 4.5.3(iv) and Lemma 4.5.5(iii) we have

$$\mathbf{e}_j = \sum_{s=0}^{m} \sum_{\substack{(i_1, \ldots, i_s) \\ j \in C(i_1, \ldots, i_s)}} \mathbf{v}_{i_1} \mathbf{v}_{i_2} \ldots \mathbf{v}_{i_s}$$

and therefore

$$\mathbf{f} = \sum_{s=0}^{m} \sum_{(i_1, \ldots, i_s)} \left(\sum_{j \in C(i_1, \ldots, i_s)} f_j \right) \mathbf{v}_{i_1} \ldots \mathbf{v}_{i_s}.$$

Here the inner sum counts the number of points in the intersection of A and the s-flat

$$L = \{\mathbf{x}_j \in AG(m, 2) | j \in C(i_i, \ldots, i_s)\}.$$

If $s > m - l$ then $L \cap A$ is either empty or an affine subspace of positive dimension. In both cases $|L \cap A|$ is even, i.e. the inner sum is 0.   □

This theorem and the definition show that a word is in $\mathscr{R}(r, m)$ iff it is the sum of characteristic functions of affine subspaces of dimension $\geq m - r$. In the terminology of Boolean functions $\mathscr{R}(r, m)$ is the set of polynomials in x_0, $x_1, \ldots, x_{m-1}$ of degree $\leq r$.

In Section 3.2 we defined the notion of equivalence of codes using permutations acting on the positions of the codewords. Let us now consider a code C of length n and the permutations $\pi \in S_n$ which map every word in C to a word in C. These permutations form a group, called the *automorphism group* of C (Notation: Aut(C)). For example, if C is the repetition code then Aut(C) = S_n.

(4.5.10) Theorem. $AGL(m, 2) \subset \text{Aut}(\mathscr{R}(r, m))$.

PROOF. This is an immediate consequence of Theorem 4.5.9 and the fact that $AGL(m, 2)$ maps a k-flat onto a k-flat (for every k).   □

Remark. The reader should realize that we consider $AGL(m, 2)$ acting on $AG(m, 2)$ as a group of permutations of the n positions, which have been numbered by the elements of $AG(m, 2)$.

Without going into details we briefly describe a decoding procedure for RM codes which is a generalization of majority decoding. Let $C = \mathscr{R}(r, m)$. By Theorems 4.5.8 and 4.5.9 the characteristic function of any $(r + 1)$-flat in $AG(m, 2)$ is a parity check vector for C. Given an r-flat A there are $2^{m-r} - 1$ distinct $(r + 1)$-flats which contain A. A point not in A is in exactly one of these $(r + 1)$-flats. Each of these $(r + 1)$-flats contains the points of A and exactly as many points not in A.

Now let us look at the result of the parity checks. Let a received word contain less than 2^{m-r-1} errors (see Theorem 4.5.7). Let t parity checks fail. These are two possible explanations:

(i) This was caused by an odd number of errors in the positions of A, compensated $2^{m-r} - 1 - t$ times by an odd number of errors in the remaining positions of the check set.

(ii) The number of errors in the positions of A is even but in t of the parity check equations there is an odd number of errors in the remaining positions.

By maximum likelihood (ii) is more probable than (i) if $t < 2^{m-r-1}$ and otherwise (i) is more probable. This means that it is possible to determine the parity of the number of errors in the positions of any r-flat. Then, using a similar procedure, the same thing is done for $(r-1)$-flats, etc. After $r+1$ steps the errors have been located. This procedure is called *multistep majority decoding*.

§4.6. Kerdock Codes

We shall briefly discuss a class of nonlinear codes known as *Kerdock codes*, (cf. [75], [11]). A Kerdock code is a subcode of a second order Reed-Muller code consisting of a number of cosets of the corresponding first order Reed-Muller code. Note that $\mathcal{R}(2, m)$ is itself a union of cosets of $\mathcal{R}(1, m)$, each coset corresponding to some quadratic form

$$(4.6.1) \qquad\qquad Q(\mathbf{v}) := \sum_{0 \le i < j < m} q_{ij} v_i v_j.$$

Corresponding to Q, there is an alternating bilinear form B defined by

$$B(\mathbf{v}, \mathbf{w}) := Q(\mathbf{v} + \mathbf{w}) - Q(\mathbf{v}) - Q(\mathbf{w}) = \mathbf{v} B \mathbf{w}^\top,$$

where B is a symplectic matrix (zero on the diagonal and $B = -B^\top$). By an easy induction proof one can show that, by a suitable affine transformation, Q can be put into the form

$$(4.6.2) \qquad\qquad \sum_{i=0}^{h-1} v_{2i} v_{2i+1} + L(\mathbf{v}),$$

where L is linear and $2h$ is the rank of B. In fact, one can see to it that $L(\mathbf{v}) = 0$, 1 or v_{2h}.

(4.6.3) Lemma. *The number of points* $(x_0, x_1, \ldots, x_{2h-1}) \in \mathbb{F}_2^{2h}$ *for which* $\sum_{i=0}^{h-1} x_{2i} x_{2i+1} = 0$ *is* $2^{2h-1} + 2^{h-1}$.

PROOF. If $x_0 = x_2 = \cdots = x_{2h-2} = 0$, then there are 2^h choices for $(x_1, \ldots, x_{2h-1})$. Otherwise there are 2^{h-1} choices. So, the number of zeros is $2^h + (2^h - 1)2^{h-1}$. □

From (4.6.2) and (4.6.3) we find the following lemma.

(4.6.4) Lemma. *Let m be even. If $Q(\mathbf{v})$ is a quadratic form corresponding to a symplectic form of rank m, then the coset of $\mathcal{R}(1, m)$ determined by $Q(\mathbf{v})$ has 2^m words of weight $2^{m-1} - 2^{m/2-1}$ and 2^m words of weight $2^{m-1} + 2^{m/2-1}$.*

(Note that this implies that if Q has rank smaller than m, the corresponding coset has smaller minimum weight).

Clearly, a union of cosets of $\mathcal{R}(1, m)$ will be a code with minimum distance at most $2^{m-1} - 2^{m/2-1}$. We wish to form a code C by taking the union of cosets corresponding to certain quadratic forms $Q_1, \ldots, Q_l$ (with associated symplectic forms $B_1, \ldots, B_l$). To find the minimum distance of this code, we must consider codes corresponding to cosets defined by the forms $Q_i - Q_j$ ($i \neq j$) and find their minimum weight. The best that we can achieve is that each difference $Q_i - Q_j$ corresponds to a symplectic form of maximal rank, that is a *nonsingular* symplectic form. Since the symplectic forms correspond to skew-symmetric matrices with zero diagonal and no two of these can have the same first row, it follows that $l \leq 2^{m-1}$ if the minimum distance d of C is to be $2^{m-1} - 2^{m/2-1}$.

(4.6.5) Definition. Let m be even. A set of 2^{m-1} symplectic matrices of size m such that the difference of any two distinct elements is nonsingular, is called a *Kerdock set*.

(4.6.6) Definition. Let m be even. Let $l = 2^{m-1}$ and let $Q_1, \ldots, Q_l$ be a Kerdock set. The nonlinear code $\mathcal{K}(m)$ of length $n = 2^m$ consisting of cosets of $\mathcal{R}(1, m)$, corresponding to the forms Q_i ($1 \leq i \leq l$), is called a *Kerdock code*.

To show that such codes actually exist is a nontrivial problem related to the geometry of $\mathbb{F}_2^m$ (cf. [11]). We only give one example. Let $m = 4$. If Q is a quadratic form $\sum_{i=0}^{3} q_{ij} x_i x_j$, we represent Q by a graph on the vertices $x_0, \ldots, x_3$ with an edge $\{x_i, x_j\}$ if and only if $q_{ij} = 1$.

If Q corresponds to a nonsingular sympletic form, then the graph must be isomorphic to one of the following graphs:

| (1) | (2) | (3) | (4) |

Order the partitions (12)(34), (13)(24), and (14)(23) cyclically. Form six graphs of type (2) by taking two sides from one pair of these partitions and one from the following one. It is easily seen that these six graphs, the empty graph and the graph of type (4) have the property that the sum (or difference) of any two corresponds to a nonsingular symplectic form. In this way we find the $8 \cdot 2^5 = 2^8$ words of a $(16, 2^8, 6)$ code, which is in fact the Nordstrom-Robinson code of §4.4.

In the general case $\mathcal{K}(m)$ is a $(2^m, 2^{2m}, 2^{m-1} - 2^{m/2-1})$ code. So, the number of words is considerably larger than for $\mathcal{R}(1, m)$ although the minimum distance is only slightly smaller.

§4.7. Comments

For details about the application of Hadamard codes in the Mariner expeditions we refer to reference [56].

The Golay codes were constructed by M. J. E. Golay in 1949 in a different way from our treatment. For more about these codes and several connections to combinatorial theory we refer to a book by P. J. Cameron and J. H. van Lint [11] or to [46]; also see [19].

The reader who is interested in more material related to Section 4.4 is referred to references [64] and [65]. For more about encoding and decoding of RM codes see [2] or [46].

§4.8. Problems

4.8.1. Let $n = 2^m$. Show that the Reed-Muller code $\mathcal{R}(1, m)$ is a Hadamard code of length n.

4.8.2. Show that the ternary Golay code has 132 words of weight 5. For each pair $\{\mathbf{x}, 2\mathbf{x}\}$ of codewords of weight 5 consider the subset of positions where $x_i \neq 0$. Show that these 66 sets form a $4 - (11, 5, 1)$ design.

4.8.3. Let S be the Paley matrix of order 11 and $A = \frac{1}{2}(S + I + J)$. Consider the rows of A, all 55 sums of two distinct rows of A, and the complements of these vectors. Show that this is an $(11, 132, 3)$ code.

4.8.4. Construct a $(17, 36, 8)$ code.

4.8.5. Consider Conway's construction of $\mathscr{G}_{24}$. Then consider the subcode consisting of the matrices A that have the form (B, B, B), where each B is a 4 by 2 matrix. Show that the matrices B are the words of a code equivalent to the $[8, 4]$ extended Hamming code.

4.8.6. Show that if there is a binary (n, M, d) code with d even then there exists an (n, M, d) code in which all codewords have even weight.

4.8.7. Consider I, J, and P of size 3 as in (4.1.1). Define

$$
A := \begin{bmatrix} J-I & I & I & I \\ I & J-I & I & I \\ I & I & J-I & I \\ I & I & I & J-I \end{bmatrix}, \quad
B := \begin{bmatrix} J & P & I & P^2 \\ P & J & P^2 & I \\ I & P^2 & J & P \\ P^2 & I & P & J \end{bmatrix},
$$

$$
C := (J-I \quad J-I \quad J-I \quad J-I), \quad
D := \begin{bmatrix} 000 & 111 & 111 & 111 \\ 111 & 000 & 111 & 111 \\ 111 & 111 & 000 & 111 \\ 111 & 111 & 111 & 000 \end{bmatrix}.
$$

Show that $\mathbf{0}$ and the rows of A, B, C and D are the words of a $(12, 32, 5)$ code.

4.8.8. Let H be the Hadamard matrix H_{12} of (1.3.9) and let $A := H - I$, $G := (I \quad A)$. Show that G is the generator matrix of a ternary $[24, 12]$ code with minimum distance 9.

4.8.9. Show that the $(\mathbf{u}, \mathbf{u} + \mathbf{v})$-construction of (4.4.1) with $C_1 = \mathcal{R}(r + 1, m)$, $C_2 = \mathcal{R}(r, m)$ yields $C = \mathcal{R}(r + 1, m + 1)$. Use this to give a second proof of Theorem 4.5.7.

4.8.10. (i) Let $n = 2^m$. For $\mathbf{x} \in \mathbb{F}_2^n$ we define $\mathbf{x}^* \in \{1, -1\}^n$ as the vector obtained by replacing the 0s in $\mathbf{x}$ by -1. In Problem 4.7.1 we saw that this mapping applied to $\mathcal{R}(1, m)$ yields vectors $\pm\mathbf{a}_1, \pm\mathbf{a}_2, \ldots, \pm\mathbf{a}_n$ where the $\mathbf{a}_i$ are the rows of a Hadamard matrix. By using this show that if $\mathbf{x} \in \mathbb{F}_2^n$ then there exists a codeword $\mathbf{c} \in \mathcal{R}(1, m)$ such that $d(\mathbf{x}, \mathbf{c}) \leq (n - \sqrt{n})/2$.

If $m = 2k$ and $\mathbf{x}$ is the word $\in \mathcal{R}(2, m)$ corresponding to the Boolean function $x_1 x_2 + x_3 x_4 + \cdots + x_{2k-1} x_{2k}$ show that $d(\mathbf{x}, \mathbf{c}) \geq (n - \sqrt{n})/2$ for all $\mathbf{c} \in \mathcal{R}(1, m)$. (In other words: the covering radius of $(1, 2k)$ is $2^{2k-1} - 2^{k-1}$.)

4.8.11. Let H be a parity check matrix for the $[4, 2]$ ternary Hamming code and let I and J be the 4 by 4 identity resp. all one matrix. Show that

$$G := \begin{bmatrix} J + I & I & I \\ 0 & H & -H \end{bmatrix}$$

generates a $[12, 6]$ code C with $d = 6$, i.e. a code equivalent to the extended ternary Golay code.

CHAPTER 5

Bounds on Codes

§5.1. Introduction; The Gilbert Bound

In this chapter we shall be interested in codes that have as many codewords
as possible, given their length and minimum distance. We shall not be interested in questions like usefulness in practice, encoding or decoding of such
codes. We again consider as alphabet a set Q of q symbols and we define
$\theta := (q - 1)/q$. Notation is as in Section 3.1. We assume q has been chosen
and then define an $(n, *, d)$ code as a code with length n and minimum
distance d. We are interested in the maximal number of codewords (i.e. the
largest M which can be put in place of the $*$). An (n, M, d) code which is not
contained in any $(n, M + 1, d)$ code is called *maximal*.

(5.1.1) Definition. $A(n, d) := \max\{M \mid \text{an } (n, M, d) \text{ code exists}\}$. A code C such
that $|C| = A(n, d)$ is called *optimal*.

Some authors use the term "optimal" for $[n, k]$ codes with $d = n - k + 1$
(see Problem 3.7.2). Such codes are optimal in the sense of (5.1.1) (cf. (5.2.2)).
Usually $[n, k, n - k + 1]$ codes are called *maximum distance separable* codes
(MDS codes).
   The study of the numbers $A(n, d)$ is considered to be the central problem
in combinatorial coding theory. In Chapter 2 we learned that good codes are
long, or more precisely, given a channel with a certain error probability p, we
can reduce the probability of error by looking at a sequence of codes with
increasing length n. Clearly the average number of errors in a received word
is np and hence d must grow at least as fast as $2np$ if we wish to correct these
errors. This explains the importance of the number $\alpha(\delta)$ which we define as
follows.

(5.1.2) Definition.

$$\alpha(\delta) := \limsup_{n \to \infty} n^{-1} \log_q A(n, \delta n).$$

In Chapter 2 we studied good codes with a given rate R. In that case we should ask how large d/n is (as a function of n). By (5.1.2) this means that we are interested in the inverse function $\overleftarrow{\alpha}(R)$.

The functions A and α are not known in general. We shall study upper and lower bounds for both of them and special values of $A(n, d)$. The techniques of extending, shortening, or puncturing (see Section 4.4) will often come in handy. These immediately yield the following theorem.

(5.1.3) Theorem. *For binary codes we have*

$$A(n, 2l - 1) = A(n + 1, 2l).$$

We remind the reader of the definition of a sphere $B_r(\mathbf{x})$, given in Section 3.1 and we define

(5.1.4) $V_q(n, r) := |B_r(\mathbf{x})| = \sum_{i=0}^{r} \binom{n}{i}(q - 1)^i$

(cf. (3.1.6)).

In order to study the function α, we need a generalization of the entropy function defined in (1.4.4). We define the *entropy function* H_q on $[0, \theta]$, where $\theta := (q - 1)/q$, by

(5.1.5) $H_q(0) := 0,$

$$H_q(x) := x \log_q(q - 1) - x \log_q x - (1 - x) \log_q(1 - x)$$

$$\text{for } 0 < x \le \theta.$$

Note that $H_q(x)$ increases from 0 to 1 as x runs from 0 to θ.

(5.1.6) Lemma. *Let* $0 \le \lambda \le \theta, q \ge 2$. *Then*

$$\lim_{n \to \infty} n^{-1} \log_q V_q(n, \lfloor \lambda n \rfloor) = H_q(\lambda).$$

PROOF. For $r = \lfloor \lambda n \rfloor$ the last term of the sum of the right-hand side of (5.1.4) is the largest. Hence

$$\binom{n}{\lfloor \lambda n \rfloor}(q - 1)^{\lfloor \lambda n \rfloor} \le V_q(n, \lfloor \lambda n \rfloor) \le (1 + \lfloor \lambda n \rfloor)\binom{n}{\lfloor \lambda n \rfloor}(q - 1)^{\lfloor \lambda n \rfloor}.$$

By taking logarithms, dividing by n, and then proceeding as in the proof of Theorem 1.4.5 the result follows.   □

To finish this section we discuss a lower found for $A(n, d)$ and the corresponding bound for $\alpha(\delta)$. Although the result is nearly trivial, it was thought for a long time that $\alpha(\delta)$ would be equal to this lower bound. In 1982, Tsfasman, Vlădut and Zink [81] improved the lower bound (for $q \geq 49$) using methods from algebraic geometry.

(5.1.7) Theorem. *For $n \in \mathbb{N}, d \in \mathbb{N}, d \leq n$, we have*

$$A(n, d) \geq q^n/V_q(n, d - 1).$$

PROOF. Let the (n, M, d) code C be maximal. This implies that there is no word in Q^n with distance d or more to all the words of C. In other words: the spheres $B_{d-1}(\mathbf{c})$, with $\mathbf{c} \in C$, cover Q^n. Therefore the sum of their "volumes", i.e. $|C| V_q(n, d - 1)$ exceeds $q^n = |Q|^n$. $\qquad\square$

The proof shows that a code which has at least $q^n/V_q(n, d - 1)$ codewords can be constructed by simply starting with any word $\mathbf{c}_0$ and then consecutively adding new words that have distance at least d to the words which have been chosen before, until the code is maximal. Such a code has no structure. Surprisingly enough, the requirement that C is linear is not an essential restriction as the following theorem shows.

(5.1.8) Theorem. *If $n \in \mathbb{N}. d \in \mathbb{N}, k \in \mathbb{N}$ satisfy $V_q(n, d - 1) < q^{n-k+1}$ then an $[n, k, d]$ code exists.*

PROOF. For $k = 0$ this is trivial. Let C_{k-1} be an $[n, k - 1, d]$ code. Since $|C_{k-1}| V_q(n, d - 1) < q^n$, this code is not maximal. Hence there is a word $\mathbf{x} \in Q^n$ with distance $\geq d$ to all words of C_{k-1}. Let C_k be the code spanned by C_{k-1} and $\{\mathbf{x}\}$. Let $\mathbf{z} = a\mathbf{x} + \mathbf{y}$ (where $0 \neq a \in Q$, $\mathbf{y} \in C_{k-1}$) be a codeword in C_k. Then

$$w(\mathbf{z}) = w(a^{-1}\mathbf{z}) = w(\mathbf{x} + a^{-1}\mathbf{y}) = d(\mathbf{x}, -a^{-1}\mathbf{y}) \geq d. \qquad\square$$

The codes of Problem 3.7.14 are an example of Theorem 5.1.8.

EXAMPLE. Let $q = 2, n = 13, d = 5$. Then from (5.1.4) we find $V_2(13, 4) = 1093$ and hence $A(13, 5) \geq \lfloor 8192/1093 \rfloor = 8$. In fact Theorem 5.1.8 guarantees the existence of a $[13, 3, 5]$ code. Clearly this is not a very good code since by Theorem 4.5.7 puncturing $\mathcal{R}(1, 4)$ three times yields a $[13, 5, 5]$ code and in fact the code Y of Section 4.4 is an even better nonlinear code, namely a $(13, 64, 5)$ code. This example shows one way of finding bounds for $A(n, d)$, namely by constructing good codes. We know that $A(13, 5) \geq 64$.

The bound of Theorem 5.1.7 is known as the *Gilbert bound* (or *Gilbert-Varshamov* bound). Let us now look at the corresponding bound for α.

(5.1.9) Theorem (Asymptotic Gilbert Bound). *If $0 \leq \delta \leq \theta$ then*

$$\alpha(\delta) \geq 1 - H_q(\delta).$$

PROOF. By (5.1.7) and (5.1.6) we have

$$\alpha(\delta) = \limsup_{n \to \infty} n^{-1} \log_q A(n, \delta n) \geq \lim_{n \to \infty} \{1 - n^{-1} \log_q V_q(n, \delta n)\}$$

$$= 1 - H_q(\delta). \qquad \square$$

§5.2. Upper Bounds

In this section we treat a number of upper bounds for $A(n, d)$ that are fairly easy to derive. In the past few years more complicated methods have produced better bounds, which we shall discuss in Section 5.3.

By puncturing an (n, M, d) code $d - 1$ times we obtain an $(n - d + 1, M, 1)$ code, i.e. the M punctured words are different. Hence $M \leq q^{n-d+1}$. We have proved the following theorem, known as the *Singleton bound*.

(5.2.1) Theorem. *For $q, n, d \in \mathbb{N}$, $q \geq 2$ we have*

$$A(n, d) \leq q^{n-d+1}.$$

(5.2.2) Corollary. *For an $[n, k]$ code over $\mathbb{F}_q$ we have $k \leq n - d + 1$.*

A code achieving this bound is called an MDS code (see Problem 3.7.2).

EXAMPLE. Let $q = 2$, $n = 13$, $d = 5$. Then we have $A(13, 5) \leq 512$.
The asymptotic form of Theorem 5.2.1 is as follows.

(5.2.3) Theorem. *For $0 \leq \delta \leq 1$ we have $\alpha(\delta) \leq 1 - \delta$.*

Our next bound is obtained by calculating the maximal possible value of the average distance between two distinct codewords. Suppose C is an (n, M, d) code. We make a list of words of C. Consider a column in this list. Let the jth symbol of Q $(0 \leq j \leq q - 1)$ occur m_j times in this column. The contribution of this column to the sum of the distances between all ordered pairs of distinct codewords is $\sum_{j=0}^{q-1} m_j(M - m_j)$. Since $\sum_{j=0}^{q-1} m_j = M$ we have from the Cauchy-Schwarz inequality

$$\sum_{j=0}^{q-1} m_j(M - m_j) = M^2 - \sum_{j=0}^{q-1} m_j^2 \leq M^2 - q^{-1}\left(\sum_{j=0}^{q-1} m_j\right)^2 = \theta M^2.$$

Since our list has n columns and since there are $M(M - 1)$ ordered pairs of codewords, we find

$$M(M - 1)d \leq n\theta M^2.$$

We have proved the so-called *Plotkin bound*.

(5.2.4) Theorem. *For $q, n, d \in \mathbb{N}, q \geq 2, \theta = 1 - q^{-1}$ we have*

$$A(n, d) \leq \frac{d}{d - \theta n}, \qquad if \ d > \theta n.$$

EXAMPLES. (a) Let $q = 2$, $n = 13$, $d = 5$. Then $\theta = \frac{1}{2}$. In order to be able to apply Theorem 5.2.4 we consider a $(13, M, 5)$ code and shorten it four times to obtain a $(9, M', 5)$ code with $M' \geq 2^{-4}M$. By the Plotkin bound $M' \leq 5/(5 - 4\frac{1}{2}) = 10$. So $M \leq 160$, i.e. $A(13, 5) \leq 160$. A better bound can be obtained by first applying Theorem 5.1.3 to get $A(13, 5) = A(14, 6)$ and then repeating the above argument to get $A(14, 6) \leq 2^3 \cdot 6/(6 - 5\frac{1}{2}) = 96$.

(b) Let $q = 3$, $n = 13$, $d = 9$. Then $\theta = \frac{2}{3}$ and the Plotkin bound yields $A(13, 9) \leq 27$ for ternary codes. Consider the dual of the ternary Hamming code (see (3.3.1)). This code has generator matrix

$$G = \begin{bmatrix} 0 & 0 & 0 & 0 & 1 & 1 & 1 & 1 & 1 & 1 & 1 & 1 & 1 \\ 0 & 1 & 1 & 1 & 0 & 0 & 0 & 1 & 1 & 1 & 2 & 2 & 2 \\ 1 & 0 & 1 & 2 & 0 & 1 & 2 & 0 & 1 & 2 & 0 & 1 & 2 \end{bmatrix}.$$

This matrix has the points of $PG(2, 3)$ as columns. The positions where $(a_1, a_2, a_3)G$ has a zero correspond to the points of $PG(2, 3)$ on the projective line with equation $a_1 x_1 + a_2 x_2 + a_3 x_3 = 0$, i.e. if $\mathbf{a} \neq \mathbf{0}$ there are exactly four such positions. Hence every codeword $\neq \mathbf{0}$ has weight 9 and hence any two distinct codewords have distance 9. So this is a linear code satisfying Theorem 5.2.4 with equality.

From the proof of Theorem 5.2.4 we can see that equality is possible only if all pairs of distinct codewords indeed have the same distance. Such a code is called an *equidistant code*.

Again we derive an asymptotic result.

(5.2.5) Theorem (Asymptotic Plotkin Bound). *We have*

$$\alpha(\delta) = 0, \qquad if \ \theta \leq \delta \leq 1,$$
$$\alpha(\delta) \leq 1 - \delta/\theta, \qquad if \ 0 \leq \delta < \theta.$$

PROOF. The first assertion is a trivial consequence of Theorem 5.2.4. For the second assertion we define $n' := \lfloor (d - 1)/\theta \rfloor$. Then $1 \leq d - \theta n' \leq 1 + \theta$. Shorten an (n, M, d) code to an (n', M', d) code. Then $M' \geq q^{n'-n}M$ and by Theorem 5.2.4 we have $M' \leq d/(d - \theta n') \leq d$. So $M \leq dq^{n-n'}$. From this and $n'/n \to \delta/\theta$ if $n \to \infty$ and $d = \delta n$ we find $\alpha(\delta) \leq 1 - \delta/\theta$. $\qquad\square$

The following bound, found by J. H. Griesmer (1960), is a bound for linear codes which is asymptotically equivalent to the Plotkin bound but in some cases is better. Even though the proof is elementary, it turns out that the bound is sharp quite often. The proof is based on the same ideas as the method of Helgert and Stinaff treated in Section 4.4. Let G be the generator matrix of an $[n, k, d]$ code. We may assume that the first row of G has weight d, in fact we may assume w.l.o.g. that it is $(111 \cdots 10 \cdots 0)$ with d ones. Every other row has at least $\lceil d/q \rceil$ coordinates in the first d positions that are the same. Therefore the residual code with respect to the first row is an $[n - d, k - 1, d']$ code with $d' \geq \lceil d/q \rceil$. Using induction we then find the following theorem.

(5.2.6) Theorem (Griesmer Bound). *For an $[n, k, d]$ code over $\mathbb{F}_q$ we have*

$$n \geq \sum_{i=0}^{k-1} \lceil d/q^i \rceil.$$

EXAMPLES. (a) Let $q = 2$, $n = 13$, $d = 5$. Since $\sum_{i=0}^{5} \lceil 5/2^i \rceil = 13$ we see that a $[13, k, 5]$ code must have $k \leq 6$. The code Y of Section 4.4 has 64 words but it is not linear. In fact a $[13, 6, 5]$ code cannot exist because it would imply the existence of a $[12, 5, 5]$ code contradicting the analysis given in Section 4.4. So in this case the Griesmer bound is not sharp.

(b) Let $q = 3$, $n = 14$, $d = 9$. From $\sum_{i=0}^{3} \lceil 9/3^i \rceil = 14$ it follows that a $[14, k, 9]$ ternary code has $k \leq 4$. A shortened version of such a code would be like Example (b) following Theorem 5.2.4. Suppose such a code exists. As before we can assume w.l.o.g. that $(11 \ldots 100000)$ of weight 9 is the first row of the generator matrix. Then, as in the proof of the Griesmer bound, the residual code is a $[5, 3, 3]$ ternary code. W.l.o.g. the generator of such a code would be

$$G = \begin{bmatrix} 1 & 0 & 0 & 1 & 1 \\ 0 & 1 & 0 & a & b \\ 0 & 0 & 1 & c & d \end{bmatrix}, \qquad \text{where } a, b, c, d \text{ are not } 0.$$

Clearly $a \neq b$ and $c \neq d$ and hence there is a combination of rows 2 and 3 with weight 2. Again the Griesmer bound is not sharp.

One of the easiest bounds to understand generalizes (3.1.6). It is known as the *Hamming bound* or *sphere packing bound*.

(5.2.7) Theorem. *If $q, n, e \in \mathbb{N}$, $q \geq 2$, $d = 2e + 1$, then*

$$A(n, d) \leq q^n / V_q(n, e).$$

PROOF. The spheres $B_e(\mathbf{c})$, where $\mathbf{c}$ runs through an $(n, M, 2e + 1)$ code, are disjoint. Therefore $M \cdot V_q(n, e) \leq q^n$.   □

EXAMPLE. Let $q = 2$, $n = 13$, $d = 5$. Then from $V_2(13, 2) = 1 + 13 + 78 = 92$ we find $A(13, 5) \leq \lfloor 2^{13}/92 \rfloor = 89$.

We have defined a perfect code to be a code that satisfies (5.2.7) with equality. We return to this question in Chapter 7.

(5.2.8) Theorem (Asymptotic Hamming Bound). *We have*

$$\alpha(\delta) \leq 1 - H_q(\tfrac{1}{2}\delta).$$

PROOF. $A(n, \lceil \delta n \rceil) \leq A(n, 2\lceil \tfrac{1}{2}\delta n \rceil - 1) \leq q^n / V_q(n, \lceil \tfrac{1}{2}\delta n \rceil - 1)$.

The result follows from Lemma 5.1.6.   □

We now come to an upper bound which is somewhat more difficult to prove. For a long time it was the best known upper bound. From the proof of the Plotkin bound it should be clear that that bound cannot be good if the distances between codewords are not all close to the average distance. The following idea, due to P. Elias, gives a stronger result. Apply the method of proof of the Plotkin bound to the set of codewords in a suitably chosen sphere in Q^n. The following lemma shows how to choose the sphere. W.l.o.g. we take $Q = \mathbb{Z}/q\mathbb{Z}$.

(5.2.9) Lemma. *If A and C are subsets of Q^n then there is an $\mathbf{x} \in Q^n$ such that*

$$\frac{|(\mathbf{x} + A) \cap C|}{|A|} \geq \frac{|C|}{q^n}.$$

PROOF. Choose $\mathbf{x}_0$ such that $|(\mathbf{x}_0 + A) \cap C|$ is maximal. Then

$$|(\mathbf{x}_0 + A) \cap C| \geq q^{-n} \sum_{\mathbf{x} \in Q^n} |(\mathbf{x} + A) \cap C|$$

$$= q^{-n} \sum_{\mathbf{x} \in Q^n} \sum_{\mathbf{a} \in A} \sum_{\mathbf{c} \in C} |\{\mathbf{x} + \mathbf{a}\} \cap \{\mathbf{c}\}|$$

$$= q^{-n} \sum_{\mathbf{a} \in A} \sum_{\mathbf{c} \in C} 1 = q^{-n} |A| \cdot |C|. \qquad \square$$

Now let C be an (n, M, d) code and let A be $B_r(\mathbf{0})$. We may assume w.l.o.g. that the point $\mathbf{x}_0$ of the lemma is $\mathbf{0}$. Consider the code $A \cap C$. This is an (n, K, d) code with $K \geq MV_q(n, r)/q^n$. We list the words of this code as rows of a K by n matrix. Let m_{ij} denote the number of occurrences of the symbol j in the ith column of this matrix. We know

(i) $\sum_{j=0}^{q-1} m_{ij} = K$

and

(ii) $\sum_{i=1}^{n} m_{i0} =: S \geq K(n - r)$

because every row of the matrix has weight at most r.

Therefore:

(iii) $\sum_{j=1}^{q-1} m_{ij}^2 \geq (q - 1)^{-1} (\sum_{j=1}^{q-1} m_{ij})^2 = (q - 1)^{-1} (K - m_{i0})^2$

and

(iv) $\sum_{i=1}^{n} m_{i0}^2 \geq n^{-1} (\sum_{i=1}^{n} m_{i0})^2 = n^{-1} S^2$.

We again calculate the sum of the distances of all ordered pairs of rows of the matrix. We find from (i) to (iv):

$$\sum_{i=1}^{n} \sum_{j=0}^{q-1} m_{ij}(K - m_{ij}) = nK^2 - \sum_{i=1}^{n} \left(m_{i0}^2 + \sum_{j=1}^{q-1} m_{ij}^2 \right)$$

$$\leq nK^2 - (q-1)^{-1} \sum_{i=1}^{n} (qm_{i0}^2 + K^2 - 2Km_{i0})$$

$$\leq nK^2 - (q-1)^{-1}(qn^{-1}S^2 + nK^2 - 2KS).$$

In this inequality, we substitute $S \geq K(n - r)$, where we now pick $r \leq \theta n$, and hence $S \geq q^{-1}nK$. We find $\sum_{i=1}^{n} \sum_{j=0}^{q-1} m_{ij}(K - m_{ij}) \leq K^2 r(2 - (r/\theta n))$. Since the number of pairs of rows is $K(K - 1)$, we have

$$K(K - 1)d \leq K^2 r(2 - r\theta^{-1}n^{-1}).$$

Therefore we have proved the following lemma.

(5.2.10) Lemma. *If the words of an (n, K, d) code all have weight $\leq r \leq \theta n$, then*

$$d \leq \frac{Kr}{K - 1}\left(2 - \frac{r}{\theta n}\right).$$

(5.2.11) Theorem (Elias Bound). *Let $q, n, d, r \in \mathbb{N}$, $q \geq 2$, $\theta = 1 - q^{-1}$ and assume that $r \leq \theta n$ and $r^2 - 2\theta nr + \theta nd > 0$. Then*

$$A(n, d) \leq \frac{\theta nd}{r^2 - 2\theta nr + \theta nd} \cdot \frac{q^n}{V_q(n, r)}.$$

PROOF. From Lemma 5.2.9 we saw that an (n, M, d) code has a subcode with $K \geq MV_q(n, r)/q^n$ words which are all in some $B_r(\mathbf{x})$. So we may apply Lemma 5.2.10. This yields

$$q^{-n}MV_q(n, r) \leq K \leq \frac{\theta nd}{r^2 - 2\theta nr + \theta nd}. \qquad \square$$

Note that $r = \theta n$, $d > \theta n$ yields the Plotkin bound.

EXAMPLE. Let $q = 2$, $n = 13$, $d = 5$. Then $\theta = \frac{1}{2}$. The best result is obtained if we estimate $A(14, 6)$ in (5.2.11). The result is

$$A(13, 5) = A(14, 6) \leq \frac{42}{r^2 - 14r + 42} \cdot \frac{2^{14}}{\displaystyle\sum_{i \leq r} \binom{14}{i}}$$

and then the best choice is $r = 3$ which yields $A(13, 5) \leq 162$.

The result in the example is not as good as earlier estimates. However, asymptotically the Elias bound is the best result of this section.

(5.2.12) Theorem (Asymptotic Elias Bound). *We have*

$$\alpha(\delta) \leq 1 - H_q(\theta - \sqrt{\theta(\theta - \delta)}), \qquad \text{if } 0 \leq \delta < \theta,$$

$$\alpha(\delta) = 0, \qquad\qquad\qquad\qquad \text{if } \theta \leq \delta < 1.$$

PROOF. The second part follows from Theorem 5.2.5. So let $0 < \delta \leq \theta$. Choose $0 \leq \lambda < \theta - \sqrt{\theta(\theta - \delta)}$ and take $r = \lfloor \lambda n \rfloor$. Then $\theta\delta - 2\theta\lambda + \lambda^2 > 0$. From Theorem 5.2.11 we find, with $d = \lfloor \delta n \rfloor$

$$n^{-1} \log_q A(n, \delta n) \leq n^{-1} \log_q \left(\frac{\theta n d}{r^2 - 2\theta nr + \theta n d} \cdot \frac{q^n}{V_q(n, r)} \right)$$

$$\sim n^{-1} \left\{ \log_q \left(\frac{\theta\delta}{\lambda^2 - 2\theta\lambda + \theta\delta} \right) + n - n H_q(\lambda) \right\}$$

$$\sim 1 - H_q(\lambda), \qquad (n \to \infty).$$

Therefore $\alpha(\delta) \leq 1 - H_q(\lambda)$. Since this is true for every λ with $\lambda < \theta - \sqrt{\theta(\theta - \delta)}$ the result follows. $\qquad\qquad\qquad\qquad\qquad\qquad\qquad\qquad\square$

The next bound is also based on the idea of looking at a subset of the codewords. In this case we consider codewords with a fixed weight w.

We must first study certain numbers similar to $A(n, d)$. We restrict ourselves to the case $q = 2$.

(5.2.13) Definition. We denote by $A(n, d, w)$ the maximal number of codewords in a binary code of length n and minimum distance $\geq d$ for which all codewords have weight w.

(5.2.14) Lemma. *We have*

$$A(n, 2k - 1, w) = A(n, 2k, w) \leq \left\lfloor \frac{n}{w} \left\lfloor \frac{n-1}{w-1} \cdots \left\lfloor \frac{n-w+k}{k} \right\rfloor \cdots \right\rfloor \right\rfloor.$$

PROOF. Since words with the same weight have even distance $A(n, 2k - 1, w) = A(n, 2k, w)$. Suppose we have a code C with $|C| = K$ satisfying our conditions. Write the words of C as rows of a matrix. Every column of this matrix has at most $A(n - 1, 2k, w - 1)$ ones. Hence $Kw \leq nA(n - 1, 2k, w - 1)$, i.e.

$$A(n, 2k, w) \leq \left\lfloor \frac{n}{w} A(n - 1, 2k, w - 1) \right\rfloor.$$

Since $A(n, 2k, k - 1) = 1$ the result follows by induction. $\qquad\qquad\qquad\square$

This lemma shows how to estimate the numbers $A(n, d, w)$. The numbers can be used to estimate $A(n, d)$ as is done in the following generalization of the Hamming bound, which is known as the *Johnson bound*.

(5.2.15) Theorem. *Let* $q = 2$, $n, e \in \mathbb{N}$, $d = 2e + 1$. *Then*

$$A(n, d) \leq \cfrac{2^n}{\displaystyle\sum_{i=0}^{e} \binom{n}{i} + \cfrac{\dbinom{n}{e+1} - \dbinom{d}{e} A(n, d, d)}{\left\lfloor \dfrac{n}{e+1} \right\rfloor}}.$$

PROOF. The idea is the same as the proof of the Hamming bound. Let there be N_{e+1} words in $\{0, 1\}^n$ which have distance $e + 1$ to the (n, M, d) code C. Then

$$M \sum_{i=0}^{e} \binom{n}{i} + N_{e+1} \leq 2^n.$$

In order to estimate N_{e+1} we consider an arbitrary codeword **c** which we can take to be **0** (w.l.o.g.). Then the number of words in C with weight d is clearly at most $A(n, d, d)$. Each of these words has distance e to $\binom{d}{e}$ words of weight $e + 1$. Since there are $\binom{n}{e+1}$ words of weight $e + 1$ there must be at least $\binom{n}{e+1} - \binom{d}{e} A(n, d, d)$ among them that have distance $e + 1$ to C. By varying **c** we thus count $M \left\{ \binom{n}{e+1} - \binom{d}{e} A(n, d, d) \right\}$ words in $\{0, 1\}^n$ that have distance $e + 1$ to the code. How often has each of these words been counted? Take one of them, again w.l.o.g. we call it **0**. The codewords with distance $e + 1$ to **0** have mutual distances $\geq 2e + 1$ iff they have 1s in different positions. Hence there are at most $\lfloor n/(e + 1) \rfloor$ such codewords. This gives us the desired estimate for N_{e+1}. □

From Lemma 5.2.14 we find, taking $k = e + 1$, $w = 2e + 1$

$$\binom{d}{e} A(n, d, d) \leq \binom{n}{e} \left\lfloor \frac{n - e}{e + 1} \right\rfloor.$$

Substitution in Theorem 5.2.15 shows that a code C satisfies

$$|C| \left\{ \sum_{i=0}^{e} \binom{n}{i} + \cfrac{\dbinom{n}{e}}{\left\lfloor \dfrac{n}{e+1} \right\rfloor} \left(\frac{n-e}{e+1} - \left\lfloor \frac{n-e}{e+1} \right\rfloor \right) \right\} \leq 2^n,$$

which is the original form of the Johnson bound.

EXAMPLE. Let $q = 2$, $n = 13$, $d = 5$ (i.e. $e = 2$). Then $A(13, 5, 5) \leq \lfloor \frac{13}{5} \lfloor \frac{12}{4} \lfloor \frac{11}{3} \rfloor \rfloor \rfloor = 23$ and the Johnson bound yields

$$A(13, 5) \le \left\lfloor \frac{2^{13}}{1 + 13 + 78 + \frac{286 - 10 \cdot 23}{4}} \right\rfloor = 77.$$

For $n = 13$, $q = 2$, $d = 5$ this is the best result up to now. Only the powerful methods of the next section are enough to produce the true value of $A(13, 5)$.

§5.3. The Linear Programming Bound

Many of the best known bounds for the numbers $A(n, d)$ known at present are based on a method which was developed by P. Delsarte (1973). The idea is to derive inequalities that have a close connection to the MacWilliams identity (Theorem 3.5.3) and then to use linear programming techniques to analyze these inequalities. In this section we shall have to rely heavily on properties of the so-called *Krawtchouk polynomials*.

In order to avoid cumbersome notation, we assume that q and n have been chosen and are fixed. Then we define

$$K_k(x) := \sum_{j=0}^{k} (-1)^j \binom{x}{j} \binom{n - x}{k - j} (q - 1)^{k-j},$$

where

$$\binom{x}{j} := \frac{x(x - 1) \cdots (x - j + 1)}{j!}, \qquad (x \in \mathbb{R}).$$

For a discussion of these polynomials and the properties which we need, we refer to Section 1.2.

In the following we assume that the alphabet Q is the ring $\mathbb{Z}/q\mathbb{Z}$ (which we may do w.l.o.g). Then $\langle \mathbf{x}, \mathbf{y} \rangle$ denotes the usual inner product $\sum_{i=1}^{n} x_i y_i$ for $\mathbf{x}$, $\mathbf{y} \in Q^n$.

(5.3.1) Lemma. *Let ω be a primitive qth root of unity in $\mathbb{C}$ and let $\mathbf{x} \in Q^n$ be a fixed word of weight i. Then*

$$\sum_{\substack{\mathbf{y} \in Q^n \\ w(\mathbf{y})=k}} \omega^{\langle \mathbf{x}, \mathbf{y} \rangle} = K_k(i).$$

PROOF. We may assume that $\mathbf{x} = (x_1, x_2, \ldots, x_i, 0, 0, \ldots, 0)$ where the co-ordinates x_1 to x_i are not 0. Choose k positions, $h_1, h_2, \ldots, h_k$ such that $0 < h_1 < h_2 < \cdots < h_j \le i < h_{j+1} < \cdots < h_k \le n$. Let D be the set of all words (of weight k) that have their nonzero coordinates in these positions. Then by Lemma 1.1.32

$$\sum_{\mathbf{y} \in D} \omega^{\langle \mathbf{x}, \mathbf{y} \rangle} = \sum_{y_{h_1} \in Q \setminus \{0\}} \cdots \sum_{y_{h_k} \in Q \setminus \{0\}} \omega^{x_{h_1} y_{h_1} + \cdots + x_{h_k} y_{h_k}}$$

$$= (q-1)^{k-j} \prod_{i=1}^{j} \sum_{y \in Q \setminus \{0\}} \omega^{x_{h_i} y} = (-1)^{j} (q-1)^{k-j}.$$

Since there are $\binom{i}{j}\binom{n-i}{k-j}$ choices for D the result follows. $\square$

In order to be able to treat arbitrary (i.e. not necessarily linear) codes we generalize (3.5.1).

(5.3.2) Definition. Let $C \subseteq Q^n$ be a code with M words. We define

$$A_i := M^{-1} |\{(\mathbf{x}, \mathbf{y}) \,|\, \mathbf{x} \in C, \mathbf{y} \in C, d(\mathbf{x}, \mathbf{y}) = i\}|.$$

The sequence $(A_i)_{i=0}^{n}$ is called the *distance distribution* or *inner distribution* of C.

Note that if C is linear the distance distribution is the weight distribution.

The following lemma is the basis of the *linear programming bound* (Theorem 5.3.4).

(5.3.3) Lemma. *Let $(A_i)_{i=0}^{n}$ be the distance distribution of a code $C \subseteq Q^n$. Then*

$$\sum_{i=0}^{n} A_i K_k(i) \geq 0,$$

for $k \in \{0, 1, \ldots, n\}$.

PROOF. By Lemma 5.3.1 we have

$$M \sum_{i=0}^{n} A_i K_k(i) = \sum_{i=0}^{n} \sum_{\substack{(\mathbf{x}, \mathbf{y}) \in C^2 \\ d(\mathbf{x}, \mathbf{y}) = i}} \sum_{\substack{\mathbf{z} \in Q^n \\ w(\mathbf{z}) = k}} \omega^{\langle \mathbf{x} - \mathbf{y}, \mathbf{z} \rangle}$$

$$= \sum_{\substack{\mathbf{z} \in Q^n \\ w(\mathbf{z}) = k}} \left| \sum_{\mathbf{x} \in C} \omega^{\langle \mathbf{x}, \mathbf{z} \rangle} \right|^2 \geq 0. \qquad \square$$

(5.3.4) Theorem. *Let $q, n, d \in \mathbb{N}$, $q \geq 2$. Then*

$$A(n, d) \leq \max \left\{ \sum_{i=0}^{n} A_i \,\middle|\, A_0 = 1, A_i = 0 \text{ for } 1 \leq i < d, \right.$$

$$\left. A_i \geq 0, \sum_{i=0}^{n} A_i K_k(i) \geq 0 \text{ for } k \in \{0, 1, \ldots, n\} \right\}.$$

If $q = 2$ and d is even we may take $A_i = 0$ for i odd.

PROOF. By Lemma 5.3.3, the distance distribution of an (n, M, d) code satisfies the inequalities $\sum_{i=0}^{n} A_i K_k(i) \geq 0$. Clearly the A_i are nonnegative and $A_0 = 1$, $A_i = 0$ for $1 \leq i < d$. Furthermore by (5.3.2) we have $\sum_{i=0}^{n} A_i = M^{-1}|C^2| = M$. The final assertion is Problem 4.8.6. $\square$

EXAMPLE. As in several previous examples we wish to estimate $A(13, 5) = A(14, 6)$ for $q = 2$. For the distance distribution of a $(14, M, 6)$ code we may assume

$$A_0 = 1, A_1 = A_2 = A_3 = A_4 = A_5 = A_7 = A_9 = A_{11} = A_{13} = 0,$$

$$A_6 \geq 0, A_8 \geq 0, A_{10} \geq 0, A_{12} \geq 0, A_{14} \geq 0.$$

For these we have the following inequalities from Lemma 5.3.3. (The values of $K_k(i)$ are found by using (1.2.10).)

$$14 + 2A_6 - 2A_8 - 6A_{10} - 10A_{12} - 14A_{14} \geq 0,$$

$$91 - 5A_6 - 5A_8 + 11A_{10} + 43A_{12} + 91A_{14} \geq 0,$$

$$364 - 12A_6 + 12A_8 + 4A_{10} - 100A_{12} - 364A_{14} \geq 0,$$

$$1001 + 9A_6 + 9A_8 - 39A_{10} + 121A_{12} + 1001A_{14} \geq 0,$$

$$2002 + 30A_6 - 30A_8 + 38A_{10} - 22A_{12} - 2002A_{14} \geq 0,$$

$$3003 - 5A_6 - 5A_8 + 27A_{10} - 165A_{12} + 3003A_{14} \geq 0,$$

$$3432 - 40A_6 + 40A_8 - 72A_{10} + 264A_{12} - 3432A_{14} \geq 0.$$

We must find an upper bound for $M = 1 + A_6 + A_8 + A_{10} + A_{12} + A_{14}$. This linear programming problem turns out to have a unique solution, namely

$$A_6 = 42, A_8 = 7, A_{10} = 14, A_{12} = A_{14} = 0.$$

Hence $M \leq 64$. In Section 4.4 we constructed a $(13, 64, 5)$ code Y. Therefore we have now proved that $A(13, 5) = 64$.

We shall now put Theorem 5.3.4 into another form which often has advantages over the original form. The reader familiar with linear programming will realize that we are applying the duality theorem (cf. [32]).

(5.3.5) Theorem. Let $\beta(x) = 1 + \sum_{k=1}^{n} \beta_k K_k(x)$ be any polynomial with $\beta_k \geq 0$ $(1 \leq k \leq n)$ such that $\beta(j) \leq 0$ for $j = d, d + 1, \ldots, n$. Then $A(n, d) \leq \beta(0)$.

PROOF. Suppose $A_0, A_1, \ldots, A_n$ satisfy the conditions of Theorem 5.3.4, i.e. $K_k(0) + \sum_{i=d}^{n} A_i K_k(i) \geq 0$ $(k = 0, 1, \ldots, n; A_i \geq 0$ for $i = d, d + 1, \ldots, n)$. Then the condition on β yields $\sum_{i=d}^{n} A_i \beta(i) \leq 0$ i.e.

$$-\sum_{i=d}^{n} A_i \geq \sum_{k=1}^{n} \beta_k \sum_{i=d}^{n} A_i K_k(i) \geq -\sum_{k=1}^{n} \beta_k K_k(0) = 1 - \beta(0)$$

and hence

$$1 + \sum_{i=d}^{n} A_i \le \beta(0). \qquad \square$$

The advantage of Theorem 5.3.5 is that any polynomial β satisfying the conditions of the theorem yields a bound for $A(n, d)$ whereas in Theorem 5.3.4 one has to find the optimal solution to the system of inequalities.

EXAMPLE. Let $q = 2, n = 2l + 1, d = l + 1$. We try to find a bound for $A(n, d)$ by taking $\beta(x) = 1 + \beta_1 K_1(x) + \beta_2 K_2(x) = 1 + \beta_1(n - 2x) + \beta_2(2x^2 - 2nx + \frac{1}{2}n(n - 1))$. Choose β_1 and β_2 in such a way that $\beta(d) = \beta(n) = 0$. We find $\beta_1 = (n + 1)/2n, \beta_2 = 1/n$ and hence the conditions of Theorem 5.3.5 are satisfied. So we have $A(2l + 1, l + 1) \le \beta(0) = 1 + \beta_1 n + \beta_2 \binom{n}{2} = 2l + 2$.

This is the same as the Plotkin bound (5.2.4).

The best bound for $\alpha(\delta)$ that is known at present is due to R. J. McEliece, E. R. Rodemich, H. C. Rumsey and L. R. Welch (1977; cf. [50]). We shall not treat this best bound but we give a slightly weaker result (actually equal for $\delta > 0.273$), also due to these authors. It is based on an application of Theorem 5.3.5.

(5.3.6) Theorem. Let $q = 2$. Then

$$\alpha(\delta) \le H_2(\tfrac{1}{2} - \sqrt{\delta(1 - \delta)}).$$

PROOF. We consider an integer t with $1 \le t \le \frac{1}{2}n$ and a real number a in the interval $[0, n]$. Define the polynomial $\alpha(x)$ by

$$\alpha(x) := (a - x)^{-1}\{K_t(a)K_{t+1}(x) - K_{t+1}(a)K_t(x)\}^2.$$

By applying (1.2.12) we find

$$(5.3.7) \quad \alpha(x) = \frac{2}{t + 1}\binom{n}{t}\{K_t(a)K_{t+1}(x) - K_{t+1}(a)K_t(x)\} \sum_{k=0}^{t} \frac{K_k(a)K_k(x)}{\binom{n}{k}}.$$

Let $\alpha(x) = \sum_{k=0}^{2t+1} \alpha_k K_k(x)$ be the Krawtchouk expansion of $\alpha(x)$. We wish to choose a and t in such a way that $\beta(x) := \alpha(x)/\alpha_0$ satisfies the conditions of Theorem 5.3.5. If we take $a \le d$ then the only thing we have to check is whether $\alpha_i \ge 0 \,(i = 1, \ldots, n), \alpha_0 > 0$. If $x_1^{(k)}$ denotes the smallest zero of K_k then we know that $0 < x_1^{(t+1)} < x_1^{(t)}$ (cf. (1.2.13)).

In order to simplify the following calculations, we choose t in such a way that $x_1^{(t)} < d$ and then choose a between $x_1^{(t+1)}$ and $x_1^{(t)}$ in such a way that $K_t(a) = -K_{t+1}(a) > 0$. It follows that (5.3.7) expresses $\alpha(x)$ in the form $\sum c_{kl} K_k(x)K_l(x)$, where all coefficients c_{kl} are nonnegative. Then it follows from (1.2.14) that all α_i are nonnegative. Furthermore, $\alpha_0 = -[2/(t + 1)] \times$

$\binom{n}{t} K_t(a)K_{t+1}(a) > 0$. Hence we can indeed apply Theorem 5.3.5. We find

$$(5.3.8) \qquad\qquad A(n, d) \le \beta(0) = \frac{\alpha(0)}{\alpha_0} = \frac{(n+1)^2}{2a(t+1)}\binom{n}{t}.$$

To finish the proof, we need to know more about the location of the zero $x_1^{(t)}$.
It is known that if $0 < \tau < \frac{1}{2}$, $n \to \infty$ and $t/n \to \tau$ then $x_1^{(t)}/n \to \frac{1}{2} - \sqrt{\tau(1 - \tau)}$.
It follows that we can apply (5.3.8) to the situation $n \to \infty$, $d/n \to \delta$ with a
sequence of values of t such that $t/n \to \frac{1}{2} - \sqrt{\delta(1 - \delta)}$. Taking logarithms in
(5.3.8) and dividing by n, the assertion of the theorem follows. (For a proof of
the statement about $x_1^{(t)}$, we refer the reader to one of the references on
orthogonal polynomials or [46] or [50].) $\square$

§5.4. Comments

For a treatment of the codes defined using algebraic geometry, and for the
improvement of the Gilbert bound, we refer to [73]. For an example see §6.8.
    In Figure 2 we compare the asymptotic bounds derived in this chapter. We

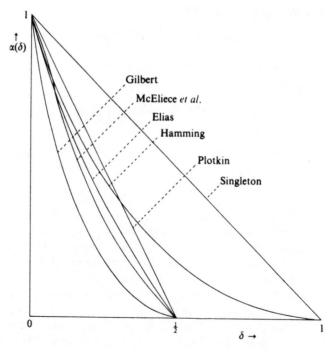

Figure 2

have not included bounds given by V. I. Levenshtein (1975; cf. [40]) and V. M. Sidelnikov (1975; cf. [63]) because these are not as good as the results by McEliece et al. [50] and rather difficult to derive. The best known bound mentioned above is

(5.4.1) $\alpha(\delta) \leq \min\{1 + g(u^2) - g(u^2 + 2\delta u + 2\delta)|0 \leq u \leq 1 - 2\delta\}$,

where

$$g(x) := H_2\left(\frac{1 - \sqrt{1-x}}{2}\right).$$

For a proof we refer to [50] or [52]. For very small values of δ, the Elias bound is better than (5.3.6) but not as good as (5.4.1).

In a paper by M. R. Best et al. (1977; cf. [6]) (5.3.3) and (5.3.4) are generalized:

(i) by observing that if $|C|$ is odd, then the inequalities of (5.3.3) are much stronger; and
(ii) by adding inequalities (such as the obvious inequality $A_{n-1} + A_n \leq 1$) to (5.3.4). This yields several very good bounds (see Problem 5.5.12).

§5.5. Problems

5.5.1. Use the fact that a linear code can be defined by its parity check matrix to show that an $[n, k, d]$ code over $\mathbb{F}_q$ exists if $V_q(n - 1, d - 2) < q^{n-k}$. Compare this with Theorem 5.1.8.

5.5.2. Determine $A(10, 5)$ for $q = 2$.

5.5.3. Let $q = 2$. Show that if in Theorem 5.2.4 the right-hand side is an odd integer l then $A(n, d) \leq l - 1$.

5.5.4. Determine bounds for $A(17, 8)$ if $q = 2$.

5.5.5. Consider a generator matrix for the $[31, 5]$ dual binary Hamming code. Show that it is possible to leave out a number of columns of this matrix in such a way that the resulting code has $d = 10$ and meets the Griesmer bound.

5.5.6. Let C be a binary code of length n with minimum distance $d = 2k$ and let all codewords of C have weight w. Suppose $|C| = [n(n - 1)/w(w - 1)] \times A(n - 2, 2k, w - 2)$. Show that the words of C are the blocks of a 2-design.

5.5.7. Show that a shortened binary Hamming code is optimal.

5.5.8. Let $w \in \mathbb{N}$, $w > 4$. Let C_l be the binary code of length n defined by

$$C_l := \left\{(c_0, c_1, \ldots, c_{n-1}) \left| \sum_{i=0}^{n-1} c_i = w, \sum_{i=0}^{n} ic_i \equiv l \pmod{n}\right.\right\},$$

where the summations are in $\mathbb{Z}$. Show that

$$A(n, 4, w) \sim \frac{n^{w-1}}{w!}, \qquad (n \to \infty).$$

5.5.9. Let $q = 2$. Show that $\binom{n}{w} A(n, 2k) \leq 2^n A(n, 2k, w)$.

5.5.10. (i) Show that $A(n, 2k, w) \leq \left(1 - \frac{w}{k}\left(1 - \frac{w}{n}\right)\right)^{-1}$, if the right-hand side is positive.

(ii) Using this and Problem 5.5.9 derive the Elias bound.

5.5.11. Let C be a binary (n, M, d) code with $n - \sqrt{n} < 2d \leq n$. Suppose C has the property that if $\mathbf{x} \in C$ then also $\mathbf{x} + \mathbf{1} \in C$. Show that $k = 2$ in (5.3.3) yields the bound

$$M \leq \frac{8d(n - d)}{n - (n - 2d)^2}.$$

(This is known as the *Grey bound*.)

5.5.12. Show that the $(8, 20, 3)$ code of Section 4.4 is optimal. (This is difficult. See Section 5.4.)

CHAPTER 6

Cyclic Codes

§6.1. Definitions

In Section 4.5 we defined the automorphism group Aut(C) of a code C. Corresponding to this group there is a group of permutation matrices. Sometimes the definition of Aut(C) is extended by replacing permutation matrices by monomial matrices, i.e. matrices for which the nonzero entries correspond to a permutation matrix. In both cases we are interested in the group of permutations. In this chapter we shall study linear codes for which the automorphism group contains the cyclic group of order n, where n is the word length.

(6.1.1) Definition. A linear code C is called *cyclic* if

$$\forall_{(c_0, c_1, \ldots, c_{n-1}) \in C}[(c_{n-1}, c_0, c_1, \ldots, c_{n-2}) \in C].$$

This definition is extended by using monomial matrices instead of permutations as follows. If for every codeword $(c_0, c_1, \ldots, c_{n-1})$, the word $(\lambda c_{n-1}, c_0, c_1, \ldots, c_{n-2})$ is also in C (here λ is fixed), the code is called *constacyclic* (and *negacyclic* if $\lambda = -1$). We shall present the theory for cyclic codes; the generalization to constacyclic codes is an easy exercise for the reader.

The most important tool in our description of cyclic codes is the following isomorphism between $\mathbb{F}_q^n$ and a group of polynomials. The multiples of $x^n - 1$ form a principal ideal in the polynomial ring $\mathbb{F}_q[x]$. The residue class ring $\mathbb{F}_q[x]/(x^n - 1)$ has the set of polynomials

$$\{a_0 + a_1 x + \cdots + a_{n-1} x^{n-1} \mid a_i \in \mathbb{F}_q, 0 \le i < n\}$$

as a system of representatives. Clearly $\mathbb{F}_q^n$ is isomorphic to this ring (considered only as an additive group). In the following we shall also use the multiplicative structure which we have now introduced, namely multiplication of polynomials $\mod(x^n - 1)$. From now on we make the following identification:

(6.1.2) $(a_0, a_1, \ldots, a_{n-1}) \in \mathbb{F}_q^n \rightleftarrows a_0 + a_1 x + \cdots + a_{n-1} x^{n-1} \in \mathbb{F}_q[x]/(x^n - 1)$

and we shall often speak of a codeword $\mathbf{c}$ as the codeword $c(x)$, using (6.1.2). Extending this, we interpret a linear code as a subset of $\mathbb{F}_q[x]/(x^n - 1)$.

(6.1.3) Theorem. *A linear code C in $\mathbb{F}_q^n$ is cyclic if and only if C is an ideal in $\mathbb{F}_q[x]/(x^n - 1)$.*

PROOF.

(i) If C is an ideal in $\mathbb{F}_q[x]/(x^n - 1)$ and $c(x) = c_0 + c_1 x + \cdots + c_{n-1} x^{n-1}$ is any codeword, then $xc(x)$ is also a codeword, i.e.

$$(c_{n-1}, c_0, c_1, \ldots, c_{n-2}) \in C.$$

(ii) Conversely, if C is cyclic, then for every codeword $c(x)$ the word $xc(x)$ is also in C. Therefore $x^i c(x)$ is in C for every i, and since C is linear $a(x)c(x)$ is in C for every polynomial $a(x)$. Hence C is an ideal. $\square$

(6.1.4) Convention. From now on we only consider cyclic codes of length n over $\mathbb{F}_q$ with $(n, q) = 1$. For some theory of binary cyclic codes with even length see §6.10.

Since $\mathbb{F}_q[x]/(x^n - 1)$ is a principal ideal ring every cyclic code C consists of the multiples of a polynomial $g(x)$ which is the monic polynomial of lowest degree (i.e. not the zero polynomial) in the ideal (cf. Section 1.1).

This polynomial $g(x)$ is called the *generator polynomial* of the cyclic code. The generator polynomial is a divisor of $x^n - 1$ (since otherwise the g.c.d. of $x^n - 1$ and $g(x)$ would be a polynomial in C of degree lower than the degree of $g(x)$). Let $x^n - 1 = f_1(x)f_2(x) \ldots f_t(x)$ be the decomposition of $x^n - 1$ into irreducible factors. Because of (6.1.4), these factors are different. We can now find all cyclic codes of length n by picking (in all possible ways) one of the 2^t factors of $x^n - 1$ as generator polynomial $g(x)$ and defining the corresponding code to be the set of multiples of $g(x) \mod(x^n - 1)$.

(6.1.5) Example. Over $\mathbb{F}_2$ we have

$$x^7 - 1 = (x - 1)(x^3 + x + 1)(x^3 + x^2 + 1).$$

There are altogether eight cyclic codes of length 7. One of these has $\mathbf{0}$ as the only codeword and one contains all possible words. The code with generator $x - 1$ contains all words of even weight. The [7, 1] cyclic code has $\mathbf{0}$ and $\mathbf{1}$ as codewords. The remaining four codes have dimension 3, 3, 4, and 4 respectively. For example, taking $g(x) := (x - 1)(x^3 + x + 1) = x^4 + x^3 + x^2 + 1$, we find a [7, 3] cyclic code. This code is an example of the irreducible cyclic codes defined below.

(6.1.6) Definition. The cyclic code generated by $f_i(x)$ is called a *maximal cyclic code* (since it is a maximal ideal) and denoted by M_i^+. The code generated by $(x^n - 1)/f_i(x)$ is called a *minimal cyclic code* and denoted by M_i^-. Minimal cyclic codes are also called *irreducible* cyclic codes.

Our definition (6.1.1) guarantees that the automorphism group of a cyclic code C contains the cyclic group generated by the permutation

$$i \mapsto i + 1 \ (\mathrm{mod}\ n).$$

However, since $a(x^q) = a(x)^q$ is in the same cyclic codes as $a(x)$, we see that the permutation π_q defined by $\pi_q(i) = qi \ (\mathrm{mod}\ n)$ (i.e. $x \mapsto x^q$) also maps a cyclic code onto itself. If m is the order of $q \ (\mathrm{mod}\ n)$ then the two permutations $i \mapsto i + 1$ and π_q generate a group of order nm contained in $\mathrm{Aut}(C)$.

§6.2. Generator Matrix and Check Polynomial

Let $g(x)$ be the generator polynomial of a cyclic code C of length n. If $g(x)$ has degree $n - k$, then the codewords $g(x), xg(x), \ldots, x^{k-1}g(x)$ clearly form a basis for C, i.e. C is an $[n, k]$ code. Hence, if $g(x) = g_0 + g_1 x + \cdots + g_{n-k}x^{n-k}$, then

$$G = \begin{bmatrix} g_0 & g_1 & \cdots & g_{n-k} & 0 & 0 & \cdots & 0 \\ 0 & g_0 & \cdots & g_{n-k-1} & g_{n-k} & 0 & \cdots & 0 \\ 0 & 0 & \cdots & & & & \cdots & 0 \\ 0 & 0 & \cdots & & g_0 & g_1 & \cdots & g_{n-k} \end{bmatrix}$$

is a generator matrix for C. This means that we encode an information sequence $(a_0, a_1, \ldots, a_{k-1})$ as $\mathbf{a}G$ which is the polynomial

$$(a_0 + a_1 x + \cdots + a_{k-1}x^{k-1})g(x).$$

A more convenient form of the generator matrix is obtained by defining (for $i \geq n - k$), $x^i = g(x)q_i(x) + r_i(x)$, where $r_i(x)$ is a polynomial of degree $< n - k$. The polynomials $x^i - r_i(x)$ are codewords of C and form a basis for the code, which yields a generator matrix of C in standard form (with I_k in back). In this case $(a_0, a_1, \ldots, a_{k-1})$ is encoded as follows: divide $(a_0 + a_1 x + \cdots + a_{k-1}x^{k-1})x^{n-k}$ by $g(x)$ and subtract the remainder from $(a_0 + a_1 x + \cdots + a_{k-1}x^{k-1})x^{n-k}$, thus obtaining a codeword.

Technically this is a very easy way to encode information because the division by a fixed polynomial can be realized by a simple shift register (for a definition see Chapter 11).

Since $g(x)$ is a divisor of $x^n - 1$, there is a polynomial $h(x) = h_0 + h_1 x + \cdots + h_k x^k$ such that $g(x)h(x) = x^n - 1$ (in $\mathbb{F}_q[x]$). In the ring $\mathbb{F}_q[x]/(x^n - 1)$ we

have $g(x)h(x) = 0$, i.e. $g_0 h_i + g_1 h_{i-1} + \cdots + g_{n-k} h_{i-n+k} = 0$ for $i = 0, 1, \ldots,$
$n - 1$. It follows that

$$
\begin{bmatrix}
0 & 0 & \ldots & 0 & h_k & \ldots & h_1 & h_0 \\
0 & 0 & \ldots & h_k & \ldots & h_1 & h_0 & 0 \\
\vdots & & & & & & & \vdots \\
h_k & \ldots & h_1 & h_0 & 0 & \ldots & & 0
\end{bmatrix}
$$

is a parity check matrix for the code C. We call $h(x)$ the *check polynomial* of
C. The code C consists of all $c(x)$ such that $c(x)h(x) = 0$. By comparing G and
H we see that the code with generator polynomial $h(x)$ is equivalent to the
dual of C (obtained by reversing the order of the symbols). Very often this
code is simply called the dual of C (which causes a lot of confusion since it is
not equal to $C^\perp$). Notice that in this sense, the "dual" of a maximal cyclic code
M_i^+ is the minimal cyclic code M_i^-.

Consider the minimal cyclic code M_i^- with generator $g(x) = (x^n - 1)/f_i(x)$
where $f_i(x)$ has degree k. If $a(x)$ and $b(x)$ are two codewords in M_i^- such that
$a(x)b(x) = 0$, then one of them must be divisible by $f_i(x)$ and it is therefore 0.
Since M_i^- has no zero divisors, it is a field, i.e. it is isomorphic to $\mathbb{F}_q^k$. A
particularly interesting example is obtained if we take $n = 2^k - 1$ and $f_i(x)$ a
primitive polynomial of degree k. In that case the n cyclic shifts of the
generator polynomial $g(x)$ are apparently all the nonzero codewords of M_i^-.
This means that the code is equidistant (cf. Section 5.2) and therefore this
distance is 2^{k-1} (by 3.7.5)). As a consequence we see that for every primitive
divisor $f(x)$ of $x^n - 1$ (where $n = 2^k - 1$) the polynomial $(x^n - 1)/f(x)$ has
exactly 2^{k-1} coefficients equal to 1. An example with $k = 3$ was given in (6.1.5).

§6.3. Zeros of a Cyclic Code

Let $x^n - 1 = f_1(x) \ldots f_t(x)$ and let β_i be a zero of $f_i(x)$ in some extension field
of $\mathbb{F}_q$. Then $f_i(x)$ is the minimal polynomial of β_i and therefore the maximal
code M_i^+ is nothing but the set of polynomials $c(x)$ for which $c(\beta_i) = 0$. So in
general a cyclic code can be specified by requiring that all codewords have
certain prescribed zeros. In fact, it is sufficient to take one zero β_i of each
irreducible factor f_i of the generator polynomial $g(x)$ and require that all
codewords have these points as zeros (all in a suitable extension field of $\mathbb{F}_q$). If
we start with any set $\alpha_1, \alpha_2, \ldots, \alpha_s$ and define a code C by $c(x) \in C$ iff $c(\alpha_i) = 0$
for $i = 1, 2, \ldots, s$, then C is cyclic and the generator polynomial of C is the
least common multiple of the minimal polynomials of $\alpha_1, \alpha_2, \ldots, \alpha_s$. Suppose
that all these zeros lie in $\mathbb{F}_{q^m}$ (which we can represent as a vector space $\mathbb{F}_q^m$).
For every i we can consider the m by n matrix with the vector representations
of $1, \alpha_i, \alpha_i^2, \ldots, (\alpha_i)^{n-1}$ as columns and put all these together to form the
sm by n matrix H which has its entries in $\mathbb{F}_q$. Clearly $\mathbf{c}H^T = \mathbf{0}$, where $\mathbf{c} = (c_0, c_1, \ldots, c_{n-1})$, means the same thing as $c(\alpha_i) = 0$ for $i = 1, 2, \ldots, s$. The

rows of H are not necessarily independent. We may obtain a parity check matrix from H by deleting some of the rows. As an illustration of this way of describing cyclic codes, we shall prove that binary (and many other) Hamming codes (cf. (3.3.1)) are (equivalent to) cyclic codes.

(6.3.1) Theorem. *Let $n := (q^m - 1)/(q - 1)$ and let β be a primitive nth root of unity in q^m. Furthermore, let $(m, q - 1) = 1$. The cyclic code*

$$C := \{c(x) | c(\beta) = 0\}$$

is equivalent to the $[n, n - m]$ Hamming code over $\mathbb{F}_q$.

PROOF. Since

$$n = (q - 1)(q^{m-2} + 2q^{m-3} + \cdots + m - 1) + m,$$

we have $(n, q - 1) = (m, q - 1) = 1$. Therefore $\beta^{i(q-1)} \neq 1$ for $i = 1, 2, \ldots,$ $n - 1$, i.e. $\beta^i \notin \mathbb{F}_q$ for $i = 1, 2, \ldots, n - 1$. It follows that the columns of the matrix H, which are the representations of $1, \beta, \beta^2, \ldots, \beta^{n-1}$ as vectors in $\mathbb{F}_q^m$, are pairwise linearly independent over $\mathbb{F}_q$. So H is the parity check matrix of an $[n, n - m]$ Hamming code. □

We illustrate what we have learned so far by constructing binary cyclic codes of length 9.

(6.3.2) EXAMPLE. The smallest extension field of $\mathbb{F}_2$ which contains a primitive 9th root of unity is $\mathbb{F}_{2^6}$. If α is a primitive element of the field, then $\alpha^{63} = 1$ and $\beta := \alpha^7$ is a primitive 9th root of unity. By Theorem 1.1.22, the minimal polynomial of β has the zeros $\beta, \beta^2, \beta^4, \beta^8, \beta^{16} = \beta^7, \beta^{14} = \beta^5$. This polynomial must be $(x^9 - 1)/(x^3 - 1) = x^6 + x^3 + 1$ (cf. (1.1.28)). So

$$(x^9 - 1) = (x - 1)(x^2 + x + 1)(x^6 + x^3 + 1) = f_1(x)f_2(x)f_3(x).$$

The code M_3^+ has pairwise independent columns in H, i.e. minimum distance ≥ 3. Since M_3^+ clearly consists of the codewords

$$(c_0 \, c_1 \, c_2 \quad c_0 \, c_1 \, c_2 \quad c_0 \, c_1 \, c_2)$$

we immediately see that $d = 3$. The code M_3^- has check polynomial $x^6 + x^3 + 1$, so it is a $[9, 6]$ code. Since $x^3 - 1$ is a codeword, the distance is 2. If we construct $\mathbb{F}_{2^6}$ with $x^6 + x + 1$ and then form the 12 by 9 matrix H for M_3^- in the way described before (6.3.1) it will have six rows of 0s only, the all one row, the row $(110 \quad 110 \quad 110)$ and four rows $(011 \quad 011 \quad 011)$. So from this we find a 3 by 9 parity check matrix. Of course from $x^6 + x^3 + 1$ we find a parity check matrix equivalent to $(I \quad I \quad I)$. The reader can work out less trivial examples in a similar way.

(6.3.3) Example. We consider $x^8 - 1$ over $\mathbb{F}_3$. If β is an 8th root of unity in $\mathbb{F}_{3^2}$, then $\beta^9 = \beta$. Therefore $x^8 - 1$ must be the product of $(x - 1), (x + 1)$, and three irreducible polynomials of degree 2. By substituting $x = 0$, 1, or 2 in $x^2 + ax + b$, we see that the only irreducible polynomials of degree 2 in $\mathbb{F}_3[x]$ are $x^2 + 1$, $x^2 + x + 2$, and $x^2 + 2x + 2$. So we know the factorization of $x^8 - 1$. The cyclic code with generator $g(x) := (x^2 + 1)(x^2 + x + 2)$ has minimum distance ≤ 4 since $g(x)$ has weight 4. In §6.6 we demonstrate an easy way to prove that 4 is the minimum distance of this code.

§6.4. The Idempotent of a Cyclic Code

In many applications it turns out to be advantageous to replace the generator polynomial of a cyclic code by a polynomial $c(x)$ called the *idempotent*. The definition is included in the following theorem.

(6.4.1) Theorem. *Let C be a cyclic code. Then there is a unique codeword $c(x)$ which is an identity element for C.*

PROOF. Let $g(x)$ be the generator polynomial of C and $h(x)$ the check polynomial, i.e. $g(x)h(x) = x^n - 1$ in $\mathbb{F}_q[x]$. Since $x^n - 1$ has no multiple zeros we have $(g(x), h(x)) = 1$ and hence there exist polynomials $a(x)$ and $b(x)$ such that $a(x)g(x) + b(x)h(x) = 1$. Now define

$$c(x) := a(x)g(x) = 1 - b(x)h(x).$$

Clearly $c(x)$ is a codeword in C. Furthermore if $p(x)g(x)$ is any codeword in C, then

$$c(x)p(x)g(x) = p(x)g(x) - b(x)h(x)p(x)g(x)$$
$$\equiv p(x)g(x) \quad (\mathrm{mod}(x^n - 1)).$$

So $c(x)$ is an identity element for C, and hence it is unique.   □

Since $c^2(x) = c(x)$, this codeword is called the *idempotent*. Of course, there can be other elements in C that are equal to their squares, but only one of these is an identity for the code. Since every codeword $v(x)$ can be written as $v(x)c(x)$, i.e. as a multiple of $c(x)$, we see that $c(x)$ generates the ideal C.

Let us consider the factorization $x^n - 1 = f_1(x)\ldots f_t(x)$ once more. We now take $q = 2$. From Theorem 1.1.22 we know that these factors correspond to the decomposition of $\{0, 1, \ldots, n - 1\}$ into so-called *cyclotomic cosets*: $\{0\}$, $\{1, 2, 4, \ldots, 2^r\}$, $\ldots$, $\{a, 2a, \ldots, 2^s a\}$, where s is the minimal exponent such that $a(2^{s+1} - 1) \equiv 0 \,(\mathrm{mod}\, n)$. In Example 6.3.2 this decomposition was $\{0\}$, $\{1, 2, 4, 8, 7, 5\}$, $\{3, 6\}$, with $n = 9$. On the other hand, it is obvious that if an idempotent $c(x)$ contains the term x^i, it also contains the term x^{2i}. Therefore an idempotent must be a sum of idempotents of the form $x^a + x^{2a} + \cdots + x^{2^s a}$, where $\{a, 2a, \ldots, 2^s a\}$ is one of the cyclotomic cosets. Since there are exactly 2^t such sums, we see that it is very easy to find all possible idempotents and hence generate all binary cyclic codes of a given length without factoring $x^n - 1$ at all!

We extend the theory a little further. Again we make the restriction $q = 2$. First observe that from the proof of Theorem 6.4.1 it follows that if $c(x)$ is the idempotent of the code C, with generator $g(x)$ and check polynomial $h(x)$, then $1 + c(x)$ is the idempotent of the code with generator $h(x)$. Therefore $1 + x^n c(x^{-1})$ is the idempotent of the dual code.

(6.4.2) Definition. The idempotent of an irreducible cyclic code M_i^- is called a *primitive idempotent* and denoted by $\theta_i(x)$. For example in (6.1.5) the polynomial $(x^2 + 1)g(x) = x^6 + x^5 + x^3 + 1$ is a primitive idempotent.

Let α be a primitive nth root of unity in an extension field of $\mathbb{F}_2$. If the polynomial $c(x)$ is idempotent, then $c(\alpha^i) = 0$ or 1 for all values of i and the converse is clearly also true. If $c(x)$ is a primitive idempotent, then there is an irreducible factor $f(x)$ of $x^n - 1$ such that $c(\alpha^i) = 1$ iff $f(\alpha^i) = 0$, i.e. $c(\alpha^i) = 1$ iff i belongs to one of the cyclotomic cosets $\{a, 2a, \ldots\}$. Such a primitive idempotent is often denoted by θ_a, i.e. in (6.4.2) the index i is chosen from the representatives of different cyclotomic cosets. For example, consider $n = 15$ and let α be a zero of $x^4 + x + 1$. Then the primitive idempotent belonging to the minimal cyclic code with check polynomial $x^4 + x + 1$ is denoted by θ_1 and in this case θ_{-1} corresponds to nonzeros $\alpha^{-1}, \alpha^{-2}, \alpha^{-4}, \alpha^{-8}$, i.e. to the check polynomial $x^4 + x^3 + 1$. In the following, if no such α has been fixed, we simply number the irreducible cyclic codes $M_1^-, M_2^-, \ldots, M_t^-$.

(6.4.3) Theorem. *If C_1 and C_2 are cyclic codes with idempotents $c_1(x)$ and $c_2(x)$, then:*

(i) $C_1 \cap C_2$ *has idempotent* $c_1(x)c_2(x)$;
(ii) $C_1 + C_2$, *i.e. the set of all words* $\mathbf{a} + \mathbf{b}$ *with* $\mathbf{a} \in C_1$ *and* $\mathbf{b} \in C_2$, *has idempotent* $c_1(x) + c_2(x) + c_1(x)c_2(x)$.

PROOF.

(i) is a trivial consequence of Theorem 6.4.1;
(ii) follows in the same way since $c_1(x) + c_2(x) + c_1(x)c_2(x)$ is clearly in $C_1 + C_2$ and is again easily seen to be an identity element for this code because all codewords have the form $a(x)c_1(x) + b(x)c_2(x)$.   □

(6.4.4) Theorem. *For the primitive idempotents we have:*

(i) $\theta_i(x)\theta_j(x) = 0$ *if* $i \neq j$;
(ii) $\sum_{i=1}^{t} \theta_i(x) = 1$;
(iii) $1 + \theta_{i_1}(x) + \theta_{i_2}(x) + \cdots + \theta_{i_r}(x)$ *is the idempotent of the code with generator* $f_{i_1}(x)f_{i_2}(x)\ldots f_{i_r}(x)$.

PROOF.

(i) follows from Theorem 6.4.3(i) since $M_i^- \cap M_j^- = \{0\}$;
(ii) follows from Theorem 6.4.3(ii) and Theorem 6.4.4(i) because $M_1^- + M_2^- + \cdots + M_t^-$ is the set of all words of length n; and finally
(iii) is proved by observing that the check polynomial of $M_{i_1}^- + \cdots + M_{i_r}^-$ is $f_{i_1}(x) \ldots f_{i_r}(x)$. $\square$

It is not too difficult to find the primitive idempotents, using these theorems. One then has an easy way of finding the idempotent of a code if the generator is given in the form $f_{i_1}(x) \ldots f_{i_r}(x)$.

In several more advanced topics in coding theory, one finds proof techniques involving idempotents. In this book we shall not reach that stage but nevertheless we wish to show a little more about idempotents. The reader who wishes to study the literature will find the following remarks useful.

Consider a cyclic code C of length n with generator $g(x)$. Let $x^n - 1 = g(x)h(x)$. We consider the formal derivatives of both sides (cf. Section 1.1). We find

$$x^{n-1} = g'(x)h(x) + g(x)h'(x).$$

Here the degree of $g(x)h'(x)$ is $n - 1$ iff the degree of $h(x)$ is odd. Multiply both sides by x and reduce mod $x^n - 1$. We find

$$1 = xg'(x)h(x) + xg(x)h'(x) + (x^n - 1),$$

where the final term cancels the term x^n which occurs in one of the other two polynomials. We see that the idempotent of C is $xg(x)h'(x) + \delta(x^n - 1)$, where $\delta = 1$ if the degree of $h(x)$ is odd, 0 otherwise. As an example consider the minimal code of length 15 with check polynomial $x^4 + x + 1$. The idempotent θ_1 is $xg(x) = x(x^{15} - 1)/(x^4 + x + 1)$.

The following correspondence between idempotents is another useful exercise. The example above can serve as an illustration. Let $f(x)$ be a primitive divisor of $x^n - 1$, where $n = 2^k - 1$. Let α be a primitive element of $\mathbb{F}_{2^k}$ for which $f(\alpha) = 0$. The primitive idempotents θ_1, resp. θ_{-1} correspond to the cyclotomic cosets $\{1, 2, \ldots, 2^{k-1}\}$, resp. $\{-1, -2, \ldots, -2^{k-1}\}$. We claim that

$$\theta_{-1}(x) = \sum_{i=0}^{n-1} \mathrm{Tr}(\alpha^i)x^i,$$

where Tr is the trace function (cf. (1.1.29)). In order to show this, we must calculate $\theta_{-1}(\alpha^l)$ for $l = 0, 1, \ldots, n - 1$. We have

$$\theta_{-1}(\alpha^l) = \sum_{i=0}^{n-1} (\alpha^l)^i \sum_{j=0}^{k-1} (\alpha^i)^{2^j} = \sum_{j=0}^{k-1} \sum_{i=0}^{n-1} (\alpha^{l+2^j})^i.$$

The inner sum is 0 unless $\alpha^{l+2^j} = 1$. Hence $\theta_{-1}(\alpha^l) = 1$ if $l = -2^j$ for some value of j and $\theta_{-1}(\alpha^l) = 0$ otherwise. This proves the assertion.

Idempotents are used in many places, e.g. to calculate weight enumerators. We do not go into this subject but refer the reader to [42] and [46]. The theory treated in this section, especially Theorem 6.4.4, is a special case of the general theory of idempotents for semi-simple algebras. We refer the reader to [16].

§6.5. Other Representations of Cyclic Codes

There are several other ways of representing cyclic codes than the standard way which was treated in Section 6.1. Sometimes a proof is easier when one of these other representations is used. The first one that we discuss makes use of the trace function (cf. (1.1.29)).

(6.5.1) Theorem. *Let k be the multiplicative order of p mod n, $q = p^k$, and let β be a primitive nth root of unity in $\mathbb{F}_q$. Then the set*

$$V := \{\mathbf{c}(\xi) := (\mathrm{Tr}(\xi), \mathrm{Tr}(\xi\beta), \ldots, \mathrm{Tr}(\xi\beta^{n-1}))|\xi \in \mathbb{F}_q\}$$

is an $[n, k]$ irreducible cyclic code over $\mathbb{F}_p$.

PROOF. By Theorem 1.1.30, V is a linear code. Next, observe that $\mathbf{c}(\xi\beta^{-1})$ is a cyclic shift of $\mathbf{c}(\xi)$. Hence V is a cyclic code. Since β is in no subfield of $\mathbb{F}_q$ we know that β is a zero of an irreducible polynomial $h(x) = h_0 + h_1 x + \cdots + h_k x^k$ of degree k. If $\mathbf{c}(\xi) = (c_0, c_1, \ldots, c_{n-1})$ then

$$\sum_{i=0}^{k} c_i h_i = \mathrm{Tr}(\xi h(\beta)) = \mathrm{Tr}(0) = 0,$$

i.e. we have a parity check equation for the code V.

Since $h(x)$ is irreducible, we see that $x^k h(x^{-1})$ is the check polynomial for V and V is therefore an irreducible cyclic $[n, k]$ code. $\quad\square$

We shall now introduce a discrete analog of the Fourier transform, which in coding theory is always referred to as the *Mattson-Solomon polynomial*. Let β be a primitive nth root of unity in the extension field $\mathscr{F}$ of $\mathbb{F}_q$. Let T be the set of polynomials over $\mathscr{F}$ of degree at most $n - 1$. We define $\Phi: T \to T$ as follows. Let $a(x) \in T$. Then $A(X) = (\Phi a)(X)$ is defined by

$$(6.5.2) \qquad\qquad A(X) := \sum_{j=1}^{n} a(\beta^j) X^{n-j}.$$

If $\mathbf{a} = (a_0, a_1, \ldots, a_{n-1})$, then the polynomial $A(X)$ obtained from $a_0 + a_1 x + \cdots + a_{n-1} x^{n-1}$ is called the Mattson-Solomon polynomial of the vector $\mathbf{a}$.

(6.5.3) Lemma. *The inverse of Φ is given by*

$$a(x) = n^{-1}(\Phi A)(x^{-1}) \qquad (\mathrm{mod}\ x^n - 1).$$

PROOF.

$$A(\beta^k) = \sum_{j=1}^{n} \sum_{i=0}^{n-1} a_i \beta^{ij} \beta^{-kj} = \sum_{i=0}^{n-1} a_i \sum_{j=1}^{n} \beta^{(i-k)j} = na_k. \qquad\square$$

Let $\circ$ denote multiplication of polynomials $\mathrm{mod}(x^n - 1)$ and let $*$ be defined by

$$\left(\sum a_i x^i\right) * \left(\sum b_i x^i\right) := \sum a_i b_i x^i.$$

Then it is easily seen that Φ is an isomorphism of the ring $(T, +, \circ)$ onto the ring $(T, +, *)$.

Now let us use these polynomials to study cyclic codes.

(6.5.4) Lemma. *Let V be a cyclic code over $\mathbb{F}_q$ generated by*

$$g(x) = \prod_{k \in K} (x - \beta^k).$$

Suppose $\{1, 2, \ldots, d - 1\} \subset K$ and $\mathbf{a} \in V$. Then the degree of the Mattson-Solomon polynomial A of $\mathbf{a}$ is at most $n - d$.

PROOF. $a(\beta^j) = 0$ for $1 \le j \le d - 1$ since $a(x)$ is divisible by $g(x)$. The result follows from (6.5.2).   □

(6.5.5) Theorem. *If there are r n-th roots of unity which are zeros of the Mattson-Solomon polynomial A of a word $\mathbf{a}$, then $w(\mathbf{a}) = n - r$.*

PROOF. This is an immediate consequence of Lemma 6.5.3.   □

We can also make a link between cyclic codes and the theory of *linear recurring sequences* for which there exists extensive literature (cf. e.g. [61]). A linear recurring sequence with elements in $\mathbb{F}_q$ is defined by an initial sequence $a_0, a_1, \ldots, a_{k-1}$ and a recursion

$$(6.5.6) \qquad\qquad a_l + \sum_{i=1}^{k} b_i a_{l-i} = 0, \qquad (l \ge k).$$

The standard technique for finding a solution is to try $a_l = \beta^l$. This is a solution of (6.5.6) if β is a zero of $h(x)$, where $h(x) := x^k + \sum_{i=1}^{k} b_i x^{k-i}$. Let us assume that the equation $h(x) = 0$ has k distinct roots $\beta_1, \beta_2, \ldots, \beta_k$ in some extension field of $\mathbb{F}_q$. Then, if $c_1, c_2, \ldots, c_k$ are arbitrary, the sequence $a_l = \sum_{i=1}^{k} c_i \beta_i^l$ is a solution of (6.5.6). We must choose the c_i in such a way that $a_0, a_1, \ldots, a_{k-1}$ have the prescribed values. This amounts to solving a system of k linear equations for which the determinant of coefficients is the Vandermonde determinant

$$(6.5.7) \qquad \begin{bmatrix} 1 & 1 & \cdots & 1 \\ \beta_1 & \beta_2 & \cdots & \beta_k \\ \beta_1^2 & \beta_2^2 & \cdots & \beta_k^2 \\ \cdots\cdots\cdots\cdots\cdots\cdots\cdots \\ \beta_1^{k-1} & \beta_2^{k-1} & \cdots & \beta_k^{k-1} \end{bmatrix} = \prod_{i>j} (\beta_i - \beta_j) \ne 0.$$

So we can indeed find the required sequence.

Suppose $h(x)$ is a divisor of $x^n - 1$ (again $(n, q) = 1$). Then the linear recurring sequence is periodic with period a divisor of n. Now consider all partial sequences $(a_0, a_1, \ldots, a_{n-1})$ where $(a_0, a_1, \ldots, a_{k-1})$ runs through $\mathbb{F}_q^k$. We then have an $[n, k]$ cyclic code with $x^k h(x^{-1})$ as check polynomial. So

$$ C = \left\{ (a_0, \ldots, a_{n-1}) \,\middle|\, a_l = \sum_{i=1}^{k} c_i \beta_i^l (0 \le l < n), (c_1, c_2, \ldots, c_k) \in \mathbb{F}_q^k \right\} $$

is another representation of a cyclic code.

§6.6. BCH Codes

An important class of cyclic codes, still used a lot in practice, was discovered by R. C. Bose and D. K. Ray-Chaudhuri (1960) and independently by A. Hocquenghem (1959). The codes are known as BCH codes.

(6.6.1) Definition. A cyclic code of length n over $\mathbb{F}_q$ is called a *BCH code of designed distance* δ if its generator $g(x)$ is the least common multiple of the minimal polynomials of $\beta^l, \beta^{l+1}, \ldots, \beta^{l+\delta-2}$ for some l, where β is a primitive nth root of unity. Usually we shall take $l = 1$ (sometimes called a *narrow-sense* BCH code). If $n = q^m - 1$, i.e. β is a primitive element of $\mathbb{F}_{q^m}$, then the BCH code is called *primitive*.

The terminology "designed distance" is explained by the following theorem.

(6.6.2) Theorem. *The minimum distance of a* BCH *code with designed distance d is at least d.*

FIRST PROOF. In the same way as in Section 6.3 we form the $m(d-1)$ by n matrix H:

$$ H := \begin{bmatrix} 1 & \beta^l & \beta^{2l} & \cdots & \beta^{(n-1)l} \\ 1 & \beta^{l+1} & \beta^{2(l+1)} & \cdots & \beta^{(n-1)(l+1)} \\ \multicolumn{5}{c}{\dotfill} \\ 1 & \beta^{l+d-2} & \beta^{2(l+d-2)} & \cdots & \beta^{(n-1)(l+d-2)} \end{bmatrix} $$

where each entry is interpreted as a column vector of length m over $\mathbb{F}_q$. A word $\mathbf{c}$ is in the BCH code iff $\mathbf{c}H^T = \mathbf{0}$. The $m(d-1)$ rows of H are not necessarily independent. Consider any $d-1$ columns of H and let $\beta^{i_1 l}, \ldots, \beta^{i_{d-1} l}$ be the top elements in these columns. The determinant of the submatrix of H obtained in this way is again a Vandermonde determinant (cf. (6.5.7)) with value $\beta^{(i_1 + \cdots + i_{d-1})l} \prod_{r>s} (\beta^{i_r} - \beta^{i_s}) \ne 0$, since β is a primitive nth root of unity. Therefore any $d-1$ columns of H are linearly independent and hence a codeword $\mathbf{c} \ne \mathbf{0}$ has weight $\ge d$.

SECOND PROOF. W.l.o.g. we take $l = 1$. By Lemma 6.5.4 the degree of the Mattson-Solomon polynomial of a codeword $\mathbf{c}$ is at most $n - d$. Therefore in Theorem 6.5.5 we have $r \leq n - d$, i.e. $w(\mathbf{c}) \geq d$. $\qquad\qquad\qquad\qquad\qquad\square$

REMARK. Theorem 6.6.2 is usually called the *BCH bound*. From now on we usually consider narrow sense BCH codes. If we start with $l = 0$ instead of $l = 1$ we find the even weight subcode of the narrow sense code.

EXAMPLE. Let $n = 31, m = 5, q = 2$ and $d = 8$. Let α be a primitive element of $\mathbb{F}_{32}$. The minimal polynomial of α is

$$(x - \alpha)(x - \alpha^2)(x - \alpha^4)(x - \alpha^8)(x - \alpha^{16}).$$

In the same way we find the polynomial $m_3(x)$. But

$$m_5(x) = (x - \alpha^5)(x - \alpha^{10})(x - \alpha^{20})(x - \alpha^9)(x - {}^{18}) = m_9(x).$$

It turns out that $g(x)$ is the least common multiple of $m_1(x), m_3(x), m_5(x), m_7(x)$ and $m_9(x)$. Therefore the minimum distance of the primitive BCH code with designed distance 8 (which was obviously at least 9) is in fact at least 11.

Several generalizations of the BCH bound have been proved. We now describe a method of estimating the minimum distance of a cyclic code. The method is due to J. H. van Lint and R. M. Wilson [76]. Earlier improvements of Theorem 6.6.2 are consequences of the method.

If $A = \{\alpha^{i_1}, \ldots, \alpha^{i_l}\}$ is a set of n-th roots of unity such that for a cyclic code C of length n

$$c(x) \in C \Leftrightarrow \forall_{\xi \in A}[c(\xi) = 0],$$

then we shall say that A is a *defining set* for C. If A is the maximal defining set for C, then we shall call A *complete*.

(6.6.3) Definition. We denote by $M(A)$ or $M(\alpha^{i_1}, \ldots, \alpha^{i_l})$ the matrix of size l by n that has $1, \alpha^{i_k}, \alpha^{2i_k}, \ldots, \alpha^{(n-1)i_k}$ as its kth row; that is

$$M(\alpha^{i_1}, \ldots, \alpha^{i_k}) = \begin{bmatrix} 1 & \alpha^{i_1} & \alpha^{2i_1} & \ldots & \alpha^{(n-1)i_1} \\ 1 & \alpha^{i_2} & \alpha^{2i_2} & \ldots & \alpha^{(n-1)i_2} \\ . & . & . & \ldots & . \\ 1 & \alpha^{i_l} & \alpha^{2i_l} & \ldots & \alpha^{(n-1)i_l} \end{bmatrix}.$$

We refer to $M(A)$ as the parity check matrix corresponding to A. This is the same notation as in Theorem 6.6.2. (Note that over $\mathbb{F}_q$ the matrix $M(A)$ has rows that are not necessarily independent.)

(6.6.4) Definition. A set $A = \{\alpha^{i_1}, \ldots, \alpha^{i_l}\}$ will be called a *consecutive set* of length l if there exists a primitive nth root of unity β and an exponent i such that $A = \{\beta^i, \beta^{i+1}, \ldots, \beta^{i+l-1}\}$.

So, Theorem 6.6.2 states that if a defining set A for a cyclic code contains a consecutive set of length $d - 1$, then the minimum distance is at least d. A consequence of our proof of Theorem 6.6.2 is the following lemma.

(6.6.5) Lemma. *If A is a consecutive set of length l, then the submatrix of $M(A)$ obtained by taking any l columns has rank l.*

We shall frequently use the following corollary of this lemma.

(6.6.6) Corollary. *If β is a primitive n-th root of unity and*

$$i_1 < i_2 < \cdots < i_k = i_1 + t - 1,$$

then if we take any t columns of $M(\beta^{i_1}, \beta^{i_2}, \ldots, \beta^{i_k})$, the resulting matrix has rank k.

We now introduce the notation

$$AB := \{\xi\eta \,|\, \xi \in A, \eta \in B\}.$$

Subsequently, we consider a product operation for matrices that will be applied in the special situation where the matrices are parity check matrices of the form $M(A)$ defined in (6.6.3).

(6.6.7) Definition. The matrix $A * B$ is the matrix that has as its rows all products **ab**, where **a** runs through the rows of A and **b** runs through the rows of B.

The following (nearly trivial) lemma is the basis of the method to be described. We consider matrices A and B with n columns.

(6.6.8) Lemma. *If a linear combination of all the columns of $A * B$ with nonzero coefficients is $\mathbf{0}$, then*

$$rank(A) + rank(B) \leq n.$$

PROOF. If the coefficients in the linear combination are λ_j ($j = 1, \ldots, n$) then multiply column j of B by λ_j ($j = 1, \ldots, n$). This yields a matrix B' with the same rank as B. The condition of the lemma states that every row of A has inner product 0 with every row of B'. Since this implies that $rank(A) + rank(B') \leq n$, we are done. $\square$

Now we are in a position to state the theorem that will enable us to find the minimum distance of a large number of cyclic codes. If **c** is a codeword in a cyclic code, then the *support* I of **c** is the set of coordinate positions i such that $c_i \neq 0$. If A is a matrix, then A_I denotes the submatrix obtained by deleting the positions not in I.

(6.6.9) Theorem. *Let A and B be matrices with entries from a field* $\mathbb{F}$. *Let* $A * B$ *be a parity check matrix for the code C over* $\mathbb{F}$. *If I is the support of a codeword in C, then*

$$rank(A_I) + rank(B_I) \leq |I|.$$

PROOF. This is an immediate corollary of Lemma 6.6.8.   □

We shall apply this theorem in the following way. Lemma 6.6.5 allows us to say something about the rank of suitable matrices of type A_I, respectively B_I. If the sum of these ranks is $> |I|$ for every subset I of $\{1, 2, \ldots, n\}$ of size $< \delta$, then the code has minimum distance at least δ.

(6.6.10) EXAMPLE. We illustrate the method by proving the so-called *Roos bound*. This bound states that if A is a defining set for a cyclic code with minimum distance d_A and if B is a set of nth roots of unity such that the shortest consecutive set that contains B has length $\leq |B| + d_A - 2$, then the code with defining set AB has minimum distance $d \geq |B| + d_A - 1$.

To prove this, we first observe that we have

$$rank(M(A)_I) = \begin{cases} |I|, & \text{for } |I| < d_A \\ \geq d_A - 1, & \text{for } |I| \geq d_A. \end{cases}$$

Then Corollary 6.6.6 provides us with information on the rank of submatrices of $M(B)$, namely

$$rank(M(B)_I) \geq \begin{cases} 1, & \text{for } |I| < d_A \\ |I| - d_A + 2, & \text{for } d_A \leq |I| \leq |B| + d_A - 2. \end{cases}$$

We now apply Theorem 6.6.9. We find from the above that

$$rank(M(A)_I) + rank(M(B)_I) > |I| \text{ for } |I| \leq |B| + d_A - 2,$$

and hence for these values of $|I|$, the set I cannot be the support of a codeword of a code with defining set AB. (Here we use the fact that the rows of $M(A) * M(B)$ are the same as the rows of $M(AB)$.)

Remark. This bound is due to C. Roos [80]. The special case where B is a consecutive set was proved by C. R. P. Hartmann and K. K. Tzeng in 1972; cf. [33].

EXAMPLE. Consider the cyclic code C of length 35 with generator

$$g(x) = m_1(x)m_5(x)m_7(x).$$

If α is a primitive 35th root of unity, then the defining set of C contains the set $\{\alpha^i | i = 7, 8, 9, 10, 11, 20, 21, 22, 23\}$. This set can be written as AB, where $A = \{\alpha^i | i = 7, 8, 9, 10\}$ and $B = \{\beta^j | j = 0, 3, 4\}$ with $\beta = \alpha^{12}$ (also a primitive 35th root of unity). The set A is the defining set for a cyclic code with minimum distance $d_A = 5$. The set B is contained in a consecutive set of length

5. The condition on $|B|$ of Example 6.6.10 is satisfied. It follows that C has minimum distance at least $3 + 5 - 1 = 7$. This is in fact the minimum distance of this code. Note that the BCH bound only shows that the minimum distance is at least 6.

Before giving one of the nicest examples of our method, we prove a special case of a theorem due to R. J. McEliece.

(6.6.11) Lemma. *Let C be a binary cyclic code of length n with complete defining set R. Suppose that no two nth roots of unity that are not in R have product 1. Then the weight of every codeword in C is divisible by 4.*

PROOF. Clearly $1 \in R$ and for every nth root of unity γ, we have $\gamma \in R$ or $\gamma^{-1} \in R$. Let $c(x) = x^{i_1} + x^{i_2} + \cdots + x^{i_k}$ be a codeword. Since $1 \in R$, k must be even. Since $c(x)c(x^{-1})$ is zero for every nth root of unity, it is the zero polynomial. If $x^{i-j} = x^{l-m}$, then $x^{j-i} = x^{m-l}$, i.e. in the product $c(x)c(x^{-1})$ the terms cancel four at a time. There are k terms equal to 1 and hence $k(k-1) \equiv 0 \pmod 4$, so $4|k$. $\qquad\square$

A consequence of Lemma 6.6.11 is that the dual C of the primitive BCH code of length 127 and designed distance 11, has minimum distance divisible by 4. By the BCH bound, C has minimum distance at least 16. By the Roos bound the distance is at least 22, so in fact at least 24 from Lemma 6.6.11. Since the code contains the shortened second order Reed-Muller code $\mathscr{R}(2, 7)$, its minimum distance is at most 32. We shall now show that the method treated above shows that $d \geq 30$, thus showing that in fact $d = 32$.

EXAMPLE. Let R be the defining set of C. Note that R contains the sets $\{\alpha^i | 81 \leq i \leq 95\}, \{\alpha^i | 98 \leq i \leq 111\}, \{\alpha^i | 113 \leq i \leq 127\}$, where α is a primitive 127th root of unity. Let

$$A = \{\alpha^i | 83 \leq i \leq 95\} \cup \{\alpha^i | 98 \leq i \leq 111\}$$
$$B = \{\beta^j | j = -7, 0, 1\}, \qquad \beta = \alpha^{16}.$$

Then $R \supseteq AB$. The set A contains 14 consecutive powers of α, and furthermore, it is a subset of a set of 29 consecutive powers of α, with the powers α^{96} and α^{97} missing. So, from Lemma 6.6.5 and Corollary 6.6.6 we have

$$\text{rank}(M(A)_I) \geq \begin{cases} |I|, & \text{for } 1 \leq |I| \leq 14 \\ 14, & \text{for } 14 \leq |I| \leq 16 \\ |I| - 2, & \text{for } 17 \leq |I| \leq 29. \end{cases}$$

In the same way we find

$$\text{rank}(M(B)_I) \geq \begin{cases} |I|, & \text{for } 1 \leq |I| \leq 2 \\ 2, & \text{for } 2 \leq |I| \leq 8 \\ 3, & \text{for } |I| \geq 9. \end{cases}$$

By Theorem 6.6.9 a set I with $|I| < 30$ cannot be the support of a codeword in C.

It was shown by Van Lint and Wilson [76] that the method described above gives the exact minimum distance for all binary cyclic codes of length < 63 with only two exceptions.

Finding the actual minimum distance of a BCH code is in general a hard problem. However, something can be said. To illustrate this we shall restrict ourselves to binary primitive BCH codes. We first must prove a lemma. Consider $\mathbb{F}_{2^k}$ as the space $\mathbb{F}_2^k$ and let U be a subspace of dimension l. We define $\sum_i(U) := \sum_{x \in U} x^i$.

(6.6.12) Lemma. *If i has less than l ones in its binary expansion then $\sum_i(U) = 0$.*

PROOF. We use induction. The case $l = 1$ is trivial. Let the assertion be true for some l and let V have dimension $l + 1$ and $V = U \cup (U + b)$, where U has dimension l. Then

$$\sum_i(V) = \sum_i(U) + \sum_{x \in U} (x + b)^i = \sum_{v=0}^{i-1} \binom{i}{v} b^{i-v} \sum_v(U).$$

If the binary expansion of i has at most l ones, then by Theorem 4.5.1 the binomial coefficient $\binom{i}{v}$, where $v < i$, is 0 unless the binary expansion of v has less than l ones, in which case $\sum_v(U)$ is 0 by the induction hypothesis. $\qquad\square$

(6.6.13) Theorem. *The primitive binary BCH code C of length $n = 2^m - 1$ and designed distance $\delta = 2^l - 1$ has minimum distance δ.*

PROOF. Let U be an l-dimensional subspace of $\mathbb{F}_{2^m}$. Consider a vector c which has its ones exactly in the positions corresponding to nonzero elements of U, i.e.

$$c(x) = \sum_{j : \alpha^j \in U \setminus \{0\}} x^j.$$

Let $1 \le i < 2^l - 1$. Then the binary expansion of i has less than l ones. Furthermore $c(\alpha^i) = \sum_i(U)$ and hence by Lemma 6.6.12 we have $c(\alpha^i) = 0$ for $1 \le i < 2^l - 1$, i.e. $c(x)$ is a codeword in C. $\qquad\square$

(6.6.14) Corollary. *A primitive BCH code of designed distance δ has distance $d \le 2\delta - 1$.*

PROOF. In Theorem 6.6.13 take l such that $2^{l-1} \le \delta \le 2^l - 1$. The code of Theorem 6.6.13 is a subcode of the code with designed distance δ. $\qquad\square$

Although it is not extremely difficult, it would take us too long to also give reasonable estimates for the actual dimension of a BCH code. In the binary case we have the estimate $2^m - 1 - mt$ if $\delta = 2t + 1$, which is clearly poor for large t although it is accurate for small t (compared to m). We refer the interested reader to [46]. Combining the estimates one can easily show that long primitive BCH codes are bad in the sense of Chapter 5, i.e. if C_v is a primitive $[n_v, k_v, d_v]$ BCH code for $v = 1, 2, \ldots$, and $n_v \to \infty$, then either $k_v/n_v \to 0$ or $d_v/n_v \to 0$.

In Section 6.1 we have already pointed out that the automorphism group of a cyclic code of length n over $\mathbb{F}_q$ not only contains the cyclic permutations but also π_q. For BCH codes we can prove much more. Consider a primitive BCH code C of length $n = q^m - 1$ over $\mathbb{F}_q$ with designed distance d (i.e. α, α^2, $\ldots, \alpha^{d-1}$ are the prescribed zeros of the codewords, where α is a primitive element of $\mathbb{F}_{q^m}$).

We denote the *positions* of the symbols in the codewords by X_i ($i = 0, 1, \ldots, n - 1$), where $X_i = \alpha^i$. We extend the code to $\bar{C}$ by adding an overall parity check. We denote the additional position by ∞ and we make the obvious conventions concerning arithmetic with the symbol ∞. We represent the codeword $(c_0, c_1, \ldots, c_\infty)$ by $c_0 + c_1 x + \cdots + c_{n-1} x^{n-1} + c_\infty x^\infty$ and make the further conventions $1^\infty := 1$, $(\alpha^i)^\infty := 0$ for $i \not\equiv 0 \pmod{n}$.

We shall now show that $\bar{C}$ is invariant under the permutations of the *affine permutation group* $AGL(1, q^m)$ acting on the positions (cf. Section 1.1). This group consists of the permutations

$$P_{u,v}(X) := uX + v, \qquad (u \in \mathbb{F}_{q^m}, v \in \mathbb{F}_{q^m}, u \neq 0).$$

The group is 2-transitive. First observe that $P_{\alpha,0}$ is the cyclic shift on the positions of C and that it leaves ∞ invariant. Let $(c_0, c_1, \ldots, c_{n-1}, c_\infty) \in \bar{C}$ and let $P_{u,v}$ yield the permuted word $(c_0', c_1', \ldots, c_\infty')$. Then for $0 \leq k \leq d - 1$ we have

$$\sum_i c_i' \alpha^{ik} = \sum_i c_i (u\alpha^i + v)^k = \sum_i c_i \sum_{l=0}^{k} \binom{k}{l} u^l \alpha^{il} v^{k-l}$$

$$= \sum_{l=0}^{k} \binom{k}{l} u^l v^{k-l} \sum_i c_i (\alpha^l)^i = 0 .$$

because the inner sum is 0 for $0 \leq l \leq d - 1$ since $\mathbf{c} \in \bar{C}$. So we have the following theorem.

(6.6.15) Theorem. *Every extended primitive BCH code of length $n + 1 = q^m$ over $\mathbb{F}_q$ has $AGL(1, q^m)$ as a group of automorphisms.*

(6.6.16) Corollary. *The minimum weight of a primitive binary BCH code is odd.*

PROOF. Let C be such a code. We have shown that $Aut(\bar{C})$ is transitive on the positions. The same is true if we consider only the words of minimum weight in $\bar{C}$. So $\bar{C}$ has words of minimum weight with a 1 in the final check position.

□

§6.7. Decoding BCH Codes

Once again consider a BCH code of length n over $\mathbb{F}_q$ with designed distance $\delta = 2t + 1$ and let β be a primitive nth root of unity in $\mathbb{F}_{q^m}$. We consider a codeword $C(x)$ and assume that the received word is

$$R(x) = R_0 + R_1 x + \cdots + R_{n-1} x^{n-1}.$$

Let $E(x) := R(x) - C(x) = E_0 + E_1 x + \cdots + E_{n-1} x^{n-1}$ be the error vector. We define:

$$M := \{i \mid E_i \neq 0\}, \qquad \text{the positions where an error occurs,}$$

$$e := |M|, \qquad \text{the number of errors,}$$

$$\sigma(z) := \prod_{i \in M} (1 - \beta^i z), \qquad \text{which we call the } \textit{error-locator polynomial,}$$

$$\omega(z) := \sum_{i \in M} E_i \beta^i z \prod_{j \in M \setminus \{i\}} (1 - \beta^j z).$$

It is clear that if we can find $\sigma(z)$ and $\omega(z)$, then the errors can be corrected. In fact an error occurs in position i iff $\sigma(\beta^{-i}) = 0$ and in that case the error is $E_i = -\omega(\beta^{-i})\beta^i/\sigma'(\beta^{-i})$. From now on we assume that $e \leq t$ (if $e > t$ we do not expect to be able to correct the errors). Observe that

$$\frac{\omega(z)}{\sigma(z)} = \sum_{i \in M} \frac{E_i \beta^i z}{1 - \beta^i z} = \sum_{i \in M} E_i \sum_{l=1}^{\infty} (\beta^i z)^l$$

$$= \sum_{l=1}^{\infty} z^l \sum_{i \in M} E_i \beta^{li} = \sum_{l=1}^{\infty} z^l E(\beta^l),$$

where all calculations are with formal power series over $\mathbb{F}_{q^m}$. For $1 \leq l \leq 2t$ we have $E(\beta^l) = R(\beta^l)$, i.e. the receiver knows the first $2t$ coefficients on the right-hand side. Therefore $\omega(z)/\sigma(z)$ is known mod z^{2t+1}. We claim that the receiver must determine polynomials $\sigma(z)$ and $\omega(z)$ such that degree $\omega(z) \leq$ degree $\sigma(z)$ and degree $\sigma(z)$ is as small as possible under the condition

$$(6.7.1) \qquad \frac{\omega(z)}{\sigma(z)} \equiv \sum_{l=1}^{2t} z^l R(\beta^l) \qquad (\bmod\ z^{2t+1}).$$

Let $S_l := R(\beta^l)$ for $l = 1, \ldots, 2l$ and let $\sigma(z) = \sum_{i=0}^{e} \sigma_i z^i$. Then

$$\omega(z) \equiv \left(\sum_{l=1}^{2t} S_l z^l \right) \left(\sum_{i=0}^{e} \sigma_i z^i \right) = \sum_{k} z^k \left(\sum_{i+l=k} S_l \sigma_i \right) \qquad (\bmod\ z^{2t+1}).$$

Because $\omega(z)$ has degree $\leq e$ we have

$$\sum_{i+l=k} S_l \sigma_i = 0, \qquad \text{for } e + 1 \leq k \leq 2t.$$

This is a system of $2t - e$ linear equations for the unknowns $\sigma_1, \ldots, \sigma_e$ (we know that $\sigma_0 = 1$). Let $\tilde{\sigma}(z) = \sum_{i=0}^{e} \tilde{\sigma}_i z^i$ (where $\tilde{\sigma}_0 = 1$) be the polynomial of lowest degree found by solving these equations (we know there is at least the solution $\sigma(z)$). For $e + 1 \leq k \leq 2t$ we have

$$0 = \sum_l S_{k-l}\tilde{\sigma}_l = \sum_{i \in M} \sum_l E_i \beta^{(k-l)i}\tilde{\sigma}_l = \sum_{i \in M} E_i \beta^{ik}\tilde{\sigma}(\beta^{-i}).$$

We can interpret the right-hand side as a system of linear equations for $E_i\tilde{\sigma}(\beta^{-i})$ with coefficients β^{ik}. So the determinant of coefficients is again Vandermonde, hence $\neq 0$. So $E_i\tilde{\sigma}(\beta^{-i}) = 0$ for $i \in M$. Since $E_i \neq 0$ for $i \in M$ we see that $\sigma(z)$ divides $\tilde{\sigma}(z)$, i.e. $\tilde{\sigma}(z) = \sigma(z)$. So indeed, the solution $\tilde{\sigma}(z)$ of lowest degree solves our problem and we have seen that finding it amounts to solving a system of linear equations. The advantage of this approach is that the decoder has an algorithm that does not depend on e. Of course, in practice it is even more important to find a fast algorithm that actually does what we have only considered from a theoretical point of view. Such an algorithm (with implementation) was designed by E. R. Berlekamp (cf. [2], [24]) and is often referred to as the *Berlekamp-decoder*.

If we call the (known) polynomial on the right hand side of (6.7.1) $S(z)$ and define $G(z) := z^{2t+1}$, then (6.7.1) reads

$$(6.7.1) \qquad S(z)\sigma(z) \equiv \omega(z) \pmod{G(z)}.$$

We need to find a solution of this congruence with σ of degree $\leq t$ and ω of degree smaller than the degree of σ. The (unique) solution makes the error correction possible. In §8.5 we encounter the same congruence.

§6.8. Reed-Solomon Codes and Algebraic Geometry Codes

One of the simplest examples of BCH codes, namely the case $n = q - 1$, turns out to have many important applications.

(6.8.1) Definition. A *Reed-Solomon code* (RS code) is a primitive BCH code of length $n = q - 1$ over $\mathbb{F}_q$. The generator of such a code has the form $g(x) = \prod_{i=1}^{d-1}(x - \alpha^i)$ where α is primitive in $\mathbb{F}_q$.

By the BCH bound (6.6.2) the minimum distance of an RS code with this generator $g(x)$ is at least d. By Section 6.2 this code has dimension $k = n - d + 1$. Therefore Corollary 5.2.2 implies that the minimum distance is d and the RS code is a maximum distance separable code.

Suppose we need a code for a channel that does not have random errors (like the B.S.C.) but instead has errors occurring in *bursts* (i.e. several errors close together). This happens quite often in practice (telecommunication, magnetic tapes). For such a channel RS codes are often used. We illustrate this briefly. Suppose binary information is taken in strings of m symbols which are interpreted as elements of $\mathbb{F}_{2^m}$. If these are encoded using an RS code then a burst of several errors (in the 0s and 1s) will influence only a few consecutive symbols in a codeword of the RS code. Of course this idea can be used for any code but since the RS codes are MDS they are particularly useful. A more important application will occur in Section 9.2. In connection with this application we mention the original approach of Reed and Solomon. Let $n = q - 1$, α a primitive element of $\mathbb{F}_q$. As usual identify $\mathbf{a} = (a_0, a_1, \ldots, a_{k-1}) \in \mathbb{F}_q^k$ with $a_0 + a_1 x + \cdots + a_{k-1} x^{k-1} = a(x)$. Then

$$C = \{(c_0, c_1, \ldots, c_{n-1}) | c_i = a(\alpha^i), 0 \le i < n, \mathbf{a} \in \mathbb{F}_q^k\}$$

is the RS code with $d = n - k + 1$. To see this first observe that C is obviously cyclic. The definition of C and Lemma 6.5.3 imply that a codeword $\mathbf{c}$ has $na(x)$ as its Mattson-Solomon polynomial. Since the degree of $a(x)$ is $\le k - 1$ this means that $c(\alpha^i) = 0$ for $i = 1, 2, \ldots, n - k$. Hence C is an RS code. This representation gives a very efficient encoding procedure for RS codes even though it is not systematic.

If we extend the words of C by adjoining a symbol $c_n = a(0)$, then $\sum_{i=0}^{n} c_i = a_0 q = 0$. So, we indeed obtain $\bar{C}$. If $c_n = 0$, i.e. $c(1) = 0$, then the word has weight $\ge n - k + 2$ and clearly this is also true if $c_n \ne 0$. So, the code $\bar{C}$ is also an MDS code.

Our second description of RS codes allows us to give a rough idea of the codes that are defined using algebraic geometry. In (1.3.4) we saw that the projective line of order q can be described by giving the points coordinates (x, y), where (x, y) and (cx, cy) are the same point ($c \in \mathbb{F}_q$). If $a(x, y)$ and $b(x, y)$ are homogeneous polynomials of the same degree, then it makes sense to study the rational function $a(x, y)/b(x, y)$ on the projective line (since a change of coordinates does not change the value of the fraction). We pick the point $Q := (1, 0)$ as a special point on the line. The remaining points have as coordinates $(0, 1)$ and $(\alpha^i, 1)$, $(0 \le i < q - 1)$, where α again denotes a primitive element of $\mathbb{F}_q$. We now consider those rational functions $a(x, y)/y^l$ for which $l < k$ (and of course $a(x, y)$ is homogeneous of degree l). This is a vector space (say K) of dimension k and one immediately sees that the description of RS codes given above amounts to numbering the points of the line in some fixed order (say $P_0, P_1, \ldots, P_{q-1}$), and taking as codewords $(f(P_0), \ldots, f(P_{q-1})$, where f runs through the space K. The functions have been chosen in such a way that we can indeed calculate their values in all the points P_i; this is not so for Q. In terms of analysis, the point Q is a *pole* of order at most $k - 1$ for the functions in K.

The simplest examples of algebraic geometry codes generalize this construction by replacing the projective line by a projective curve in some projective space. We shall give one example of this idea.

As alphabet we take $\mathbb{F}_q$, where $q = r^2$ (r a power of a prime p). We consider the so-called *hermitean curve* X in PG(2, q) given by

$$x^{r+1} + y^{r+1} + z^{r+1} = 0.$$

We count how many points there are on X (with coordinates in $\mathbb{F}_q$). If one of the coordinates is 0, then we may take another to be 1, and then we have $r + 1$ solutions for the third coordinate, since $x^{r+1} = 1$ has $r + 1$ solutions in $\mathbb{F}_q$. So, there are $3(r + 1)$ points with $xyz = 0$. If $xyz \neq 0$, then we may take $z = 1$ and we can choose the value of y^{r+1} to be any element in $\mathbb{F}_r \backslash \{0, 1\}$. This again leaves us with $r + 1$ choices for x. In this way we find $(r - 2)(r + 1)^2$ solutions. The total number of points on X therefore is $1 + q\sqrt{q}$.

Again we pick a "special" point, say $Q := (0, 1, 1)$. We pick a number m (where for reasons connected to the theorems from algebraic geometry that we do not mention, we must require $q - \sqrt{q} < m < q\sqrt{q}$). We number the points of X not equal to Q in some way $P_1, P_2, \ldots, P_n$, where $n = q\sqrt{q}$. Again we define a vector space $K := \mathscr{L}(mQ)$, namely the space of all rational functions defined on X that have *no pole* except possibly in Q and in that case a pole of order at most m. Corresponding to each function $f \in K$, we define a codeword $\mathbf{c}_f$, where $\mathbf{c}_f := (f(P_1), f(P_1), \ldots, f(P_n))$. The definition is easy enough. What we need is the dimension of the code, its minimum distance and preferably a basis. The last question is not difficult. The first two require deep theorems from algebraic geometry. In our example, the code has dimension $k := m - g + 1$ and minimum distance $d \geq n - m$, where $g := \frac{1}{2}(q - \sqrt{q})$.

The following example of the previous construction was used successfully a few years ago by the author to convince engineers, who believed firmly in RS codes as the only useful codes for them, that it was worth their while to have a closer look at the codes from algebraic geometry.

We consider as alphabet $\mathbb{F}_{16}$. We assume that we are using a very poor channel with error probability $p_e = 0.04$. We shall compare two codes over this alphabet. One is the extended RS code of length 16 with rate $\frac{1}{2}$ and the other is the code corresponding to the hermitean curve with equation $x^5 + y^5 + z^5 = 0$, where m is chosen in such a way that the rate is also $\frac{1}{2}$. As we saw above, the second code has word length 64. We have $g = \frac{1}{2}(16 - 4) = 6$ and hence $m = 37$ (from $32 = k = m - 6 + 1$). The second code therefore has minimum distance $n - m = 27$. (Note that this is also better than a corresponding BCH code.) The word error probability is $8 \cdot 10^{-4}$ for the RS code, whereas it is about $2 \cdot 10^{-7}$ for the hermitean code!

We remarked above that it is not difficult to find a basis for these codes. We demonstrate this for the example. Consider the functions

$$f(x, y, z) := \frac{x^i y^j}{(y + z)^l}, \qquad 0 \leq i \leq 4, j \geq 0, i + j = l.$$

On the curve X, the denominator $(y + z)^l$ is equal to $(y^4 + y^3 z + y^2 z^2 + yz^3 + z^4)^l x^{-5l}$. This shows that f has Q as only pole and in fact it is a pole of order $5l - i$. There are exactly 32 triples (i, j, l) that yield a pole of order at most 37, i.e. we have the required basis for our space and by substitution a basis for the code.

§6.9. Quadratic Residue Codes

In this section we shall consider codes for which the word length n is an odd prime. The alphabet $\mathbb{F}_q$ must satisfy the condition: q is a quadratic residue (mod n), i.e. $q^{(n-1)/2} \equiv 1$ (mod n). As usual α will denote a primitive nth root of unity in an extension field of $\mathbb{F}_q$. Later it will turn out that we shall require that α satisfies one more condition. We define

$$R_0 := \{i^2 \ (\text{mod } n) | i \in \mathbb{F}_n, i \neq 0\}, \qquad \text{the quadratic residues in } \mathbb{F}_n,$$

$$R_1 := \mathbb{F}_n^* \backslash R_0, \qquad \text{i.e. the set of nonsquares in } \mathbb{F}_n,$$

$$g_0(x) := \prod_{r \in R_0} (x - \alpha^r), \qquad g_1(x) := \prod_{r \in R_1} (x - \alpha^r).$$

Since we have required that q (mod n) is in R_0, the polynomials $g_0(x)$ and $g_1(x)$ both have coefficients in $\mathbb{F}_q$ (cf. Theorem 1.1.22). Furthermore

$$x^n - 1 = (x - 1)g_0(x)g_1(x).$$

(6.9.1) Definition. The cyclic codes of length n over $\mathbb{F}_q$ with generators $g_0(x)$ resp. $(x - 1)g_0(x)$ are both called *quadratic residue codes* (QR codes).

We shall only consider extended QR codes in the binary case, where the definition is as in (3.2.7). Such a code is obtained by adding an overall parity check to the code with generator $g_0(x)$.

For other fields the definition of extended code is usually modified in such a way that the extended code is self-dual if $n \equiv -1$ (mod 4), resp. dual to the extension of the code with generator $g_1(x)$ if $n \equiv 1$ (mod 4) (cf. [46]). In the binary case the code with generator $(x - 1)g_0(x)$ is the even-weight subcode of the other QR code. If G is a generator matrix for the first of these codes then we obtain a generator matrix for the latter code by adding a row of 1s to G. If we do the same thing after adding a column of 0s to G we obtain a generator matrix for the extended code.

In the binary case the condition that q is a quadratic residue mod n simply means that $n \equiv \pm 1$ (mod 8) (cf. Section 1.1). The permutation $\pi_j : i \mapsto ij$ (mod n) acting on the positions of the codewords maps the code with generator $g_0(x)$ into itself if $j \in R_0$ resp. into the code with generator $g_1(x)$ if $j \in R_1$. So the codes with generators $g_0(x)$ resp. $g_1(x)$ are equivalent. If $n \equiv -1$ (mod 4) then $-1 \in R_1$ and in that case the transformation $x \to x^{-1}$ maps a codeword of the code with generator $g_0(x)$ into a codeword of the code with generator $g_1(x)$.

(6.9.2) Theorem. *If* $\mathbf{c} = c(x)$ *is a codeword in the* QR *code with generator* $g_0(x)$ *and if* $c(1) \neq 0$ *and* $w(\mathbf{c}) = d$, *then*

(i) $d^2 \geq n$,
(ii) *if* $n \equiv -1$ (mod 4) *then* $d^2 - d + 1 \geq n$,
(iii) *if* $n \equiv -1$ (mod 8) *and* $q = 2$ *then* $d \equiv 3$ (mod 4).

PROOF.

(i) Since $c(1) \neq 0$ the polynomial $c(x)$ is not divisible by $(x - 1)$. By a suitable permutation π_j we can transform $c(x)$ into a polynomial $\hat{c}(x)$ which is divisible by $g_1(x)$ and of course again not divisible by $(x - 1)$. This implies that $c(x)\hat{c}(x)$ is a multiple of $1 + x + x^2 + \cdots + x^{n-1}$. Since the polynomial $c(x)\hat{c}(x)$ has at most d^2 nonzero coefficients we have proved the first assertion.

(ii) In the proof above we may take $j = -1$. In that case it is clear that $c(x)\hat{c}(x)$ has at most $d^2 - d + 1$ nonzero coefficients.

(iii) Let $c(x) = \sum_{i=1}^{d} x^{l_i}$, $\hat{c}(x) = \sum_{i=1}^{d} x^{-l_i}$. If $l_i - l_j = l_k - l_l$ then $l_j - l_i = l_l - l_k$. Hence, if terms in the product $c(x)\hat{c}(x)$ cancel then they cancel four at a time. Therefore $n = d^2 - d + 1 - 4a$ for some $a \geq 0$. □

The idempotent of a cyclic code, introduced in Section 6.4, will prove to be a powerful tool in the analysis of QR codes.

(6.9.3) Theorem. *For a suitable choice of the primitive n-th root of unity α, the polynomial*

$$\theta(x) := \sum_{r \in R_0} x^r$$

is the idempotent of the binary QR code with generator $(x - 1)g_0(x)$ if $n \equiv 1$ (mod 8) resp. the QR code with generator $g_0(x)$ if $n \equiv -1$ (mod 8).

PROOF. $\theta(x)$ is obviously an idempotent polynomial. Therefore $\{\theta(\alpha)\}^2 = \theta(\alpha)$, i.e. $\theta(\alpha) = 0$ or 1. By the same argument $\theta(\alpha^i) = \theta(\alpha)$ if $i \in R_0$ and

$$\theta(\alpha^i) + \theta(\alpha) = 1$$

if $i \in R_1$. The "suitable choice" of α is such that $\theta(\alpha) = 0$. (The reader should convince himself that it is impossible that all primitive elements of $\mathbb{F}_q$ satisfy $\theta(\alpha) = 1$.) Our choice implies that $\theta(\alpha^i) = 0$ if $i \in R_0$ and $\theta(\alpha^i) = 1$ if $i \in R_1$. Finally we have $\theta(\alpha^0) = (n - 1)/2$. This proves the assertion. □

With the aid of $\mathbf{\theta}$ we now make a $(0, 1)$-matrix C (called a circulant) by taking the word $\mathbf{\theta}$ as the first row and all cyclic shifts as the other rows. Let $\mathbf{c} := (00\ldots0)$ if $n \equiv 1$ (mod 8) and $\mathbf{c} := (11\ldots1)$ if $n \equiv -1$ (mod 8). We have

$$G := \begin{bmatrix} 1 & 1 & \cdots & 1 \\ \mathbf{c}^T & & C & \end{bmatrix}.$$

It follows from Theorem 6.9.3 that the rows of G (which are clearly not independent) generate the extended binary QR code of length $n + 1$. We now number the coordinate places of codewords in this code with the points of the projective line of order n, i.e. $\infty, 0, 1, \ldots, n - 1$. The overall parity check is in front and it has number ∞. We make the usual conventions about arithmetic operations involving ∞. The group $\mathrm{PSL}(2, n)$ consists of all transformations

$x \to (ax + b)/(cx + d)$ with a, b, c, d in $\mathbb{F}_n$ and $ad - bc = 1$. It is not difficult to check that this group is generated by the transformations $S: x \to x + 1$ and $T: x \to -x^{-1}$. Clearly S is a cyclic shift on the positions different from ∞ and it leaves ∞ invariant. By the definition of a QR code, S leaves the extended code invariant. To check the effect of T on the extended QR code it is sufficient to analyse what T does to the rows of G. It is a simple (maybe somewhat tedious) exercise to show that T maps a row of G into a linear combination of at most three rows of G (the reader who does not succeed is referred to [42]). Therefore both S and T leave the extended QR code invariant, proving the following theorem.

(6.9.4) Theorem. *The automorphism group of the extended binary* QR *code of length* $n + 1$ *contains* PSL$(2, n)$.

The modified definition of extended code which we mentioned earlier ensures that Theorem 6.9.4 is also true for the nonbinary case (cf. [46]).

(6.9.5) Corollary. *A word of minimum weight in a binary* QR *code satisfies the conditions of Theorem 6.9.2.*

PROOF. The proof is the same as for Corollary 6.6.16. In this case we use the fact that PSL$(2, n)$ is transitive. Therefore the minimum weight is odd.   □

EXAMPLES. (a) Let $q = 2, n = 7$. We find

$$x^7 - 1 = (x - 1)(x^3 + x + 1)(x^3 + x^2 + 1).$$

We take $g_0(x)$ as generator. The choice of α specified in Theorem 6.9.3 implies that $x + x^2 + x^4$ is also a generator. Hence $g_0(x) = 1 + x + x^3$. Of course this code is the (perfect) [7, 4] Hamming code (see Section 3.3 and Theorem 6.31). The corresponding even weight subcode was treated in (6.1.5).
   (b) Let $q = 2, n = 23$. We have

$$x^{23} - 1 = (x - 1)(x^{11} + x^9 + x^7 + x^6 + x^5 + x + 1)$$
$$\times (x^{11} + x^{10} + x^6 + x^5 + x^4 + x^2 + 1).$$

Again we take $g_0(x)$ to be the multiple of $\theta(x)$, which is

$$x^{11} + x^9 + x^7 + x^6 + x^5 + x + 1.$$

By Corollary 6.9.5 the corresponding QR code C has minimum distance $d \geq 7$.

Since $\sum_{i=0}^{3} \binom{23}{i} = 2^{11}$ and $|C| = 2^{12}$ it follows that d is equal to 7 and by (3.1.6) C is a perfect code. Since the binary Golay code of Section 4.2 is unique we have now shown that it is in fact a QR code.

We leave several other examples as exercises (Section 6.12).

§6.10. Binary cyclic codes of length $2n$ (n odd)

Let n be odd and $x^n - 1 = f_1(x)f_2(x)\ldots f_t(x)$ the factorization of $x^n - 1$ into irreducible factors in $\mathbb{F}_2[x]$.

We define $g_1(x) := f_1(x)\ldots f_k(x)$, $g_2(x) := f_{k+1}(x)\ldots f_l(x)$, where $k < l < t$. Let $r_1 := \deg g_1$, $r_2 := \deg g_1g_2$.

Let C_1 be the cyclic code of length n and dimension $n - r_1$ with generator $g_1(x)$, and let C_2 be the cyclic code of length n and dimension $n - r_2$ with generator $g_1(x)g_2(x)$, and let d_i be the minimum distance of C_i ($i = 1, 2$). Clearly $d_2 \geq d_1$.

We shall study the cyclic code C of length $2n$ and dimension $2n - r_1 - r_2$ with generator $g(x) := g_1^2(x)g_2(x)$. We claim that this code has the following structure:

Let $\mathbf{a} = (a_0, a_1, \ldots, a_{n-1}) \in C_1$ and $\mathbf{c} = (c_0, c_1, \ldots, c_{n-1}) \in C_2$. Define $b :=$ $\mathbf{a} + \mathbf{c}$. Since n is odd, we can define words that belong to C by

$$\mathbf{w} := (a_0, b_1, a_2, \ldots, b_{n-2}, a_{n-1}, b_0, a_1, \ldots, a_{n-2}, b_{n-1})$$

and in this way we find *all* words of C; (the final assertion follows from dimension arguments). To demonstrate this, we proceed as follows. Write

$$a(x) = a_0 + a_1 x + \cdots + a_{n-1} x^{n-1}$$
$$= (a_0 + a_2 x^2 + \cdots + a_{n-1} x^{n-1}) + x(a_1 + \cdots + a_{n-2} x^{n-3})$$
$$= a_e(x^2) + xa_o(x^2),$$

and analogously for $c(x)$ and $b(x)$. We then have the following two (equal) representations for the polynomial $w(x)$ corresponding to the codeword $\mathbf{w}$:

$$(6.10.1) \qquad w(x) = \{a_e(x^2) + x^{n+1} a_o(x^2)\} + \{xb_o(x^2) + x^n b_e(x^2)\}$$

and

$$(6.10.2) \quad w(x) = \{a(x) + x(x^n + 1)a_o(x^2)\} + \{b(x) + (x^n + 1)b_e(x^2)\}.$$

Both terms in (6.10.2) are divisible by $g_1(x)$. From (6.10.1) we see that the first term only contains even powers of x, the second one only odd powers of x. Since $g_1(x)$ has no multiple factors, this implies that both terms are actually divisible by $g_1^2(x)$.

From (6.10.2) we find

$$w(x) = (x^n + 1)a(x) + c(x) + (x^n + 1)c_e(x^2)$$

in which every term is divisible by $g_2(x)$.

Since $\mathbf{b} = \mathbf{a} + \mathbf{c}$, the word $\mathbf{w}$ is a permutation of the word $|\mathbf{a}|\mathbf{a} + \mathbf{c}|$, (cf. 4.4.1). We have proved the following theorem.

(6.10.3) Theorem. *Let C_1 be a binary cyclic code of length n (odd) with generator $g_1(x)$, and let C_2 be a binary cyclic code of length n with generator $g_1(x)g_2(x)$. Then the binary cyclic code C of length $2n$ with generator $g_1^2(x)g_2(x)$*

is equivalent to the $|\mathbf{u}|\mathbf{u} + \mathbf{v}|$ sum of C_1 and C_2. Therefore C has minimum distance $\min\{2d_1, d_2\}$.

There are not many good binary cyclic codes of even length. However, the following theorem shows the existence of a class of optimal examples.

(6.10.4) Theorem. *The even weight subcode of a shortened binary Hamming code is cyclic (for a suitable ordering of the symbols).*

PROOF. It is not difficult to see that it makes no difference on which position the code is shortened (all resulting codes are equivalent). Let $n = 2^s - 1$. Let $m_1(x)$ denote the minimal polynomial of a primitive element α of $\mathbb{F}_{2^s}$. Then $m_1(x)$ is the generator polynomial of the $[n, n - s]$ binary Hamming code and $(x + 1)m_1(x)$ is the generator polynomial of the corresponding even weight subcode. In Theorem 6.10.3 we take $g_1(x) = (x + 1)$ and $g_2(x) = m_1(x)$. We then find a cyclic code C of length $2n$, dimension $2n - s - 2$, with minimum distance 4. It follows from the $|\mathbf{u}|\mathbf{u} + \mathbf{v}|$ construction that all weights in C are even. Therefore C has a parity check matrix with a top row of 1's and all columns distinct. Hence C is equivalent to the even weight subcode of a shortened Hamming code.   □

We observe that there is a different way of proving the previous theorem. We shall use the Hasse derivative (see Chapter 1). The generator of C has 1 as a zero with multiplicity 2 and α as a zero with multiplicity 1. This means that if $c(x) = \sum c_i x^i$ is a codeword, then

$$\sum c_i = 0, \qquad \sum i c_i = 0, \qquad \sum c_i \alpha^i = 0,$$

i.e.

$$H_1 := \begin{pmatrix} 1 & 1 & 1 & \cdots & 1 & 1 & 1 & \cdots & 1 & 1 \\ 0 & 1 & 0 & \cdots & 0 & 1 & 0 & \cdots & 0 & 1 \\ 1 & \alpha & \alpha^2 & \cdots & \alpha^{n-1} & \alpha^n & \alpha^{n+1} & \cdots & \alpha^{2n-2} & \alpha^{2n-1} \end{pmatrix}$$

is a parity check matrix for C; here the second row is obtained by using the property of the Hasse derivative and multiple zeros. Note that $\alpha^n = 1$. Hence the matrix H_1 consists of all possible columns with a 1 at the top, except for $(1000\ldots0)^{\mathsf{T}}$ and $(1100\ldots0)^{\mathsf{T}}$, i.e. the code is indeed equivalent to the even weight subcode of a shortened Hamming code.

§6.11. Comments

The reader who is interested in seeing the trace function and idempotents used heavily in proofs should read [46, Chapter 15].

A generalization of BCH codes will be treated in Chapter 8. There is extensive literature on weights, dimension, covering radius, etc. of BCH codes. We mention the Carlitz-Uchiyama bound which depends on a deep theorem in number theory by A. Weil. For the bound we refer to [42]. For a generalization of QR codes to word length n a prime power, in which case the theory is similar to Section 6.9 we refer to a paper by J. H. van Lint and F. J. MacWilliams (1978; [45]).

§6.12. Problems

6.12.1. Show that the [4, 2] ternary Hamming code is a negacyclic code.

6.12.2. Determine the idempotent of the [15, 11] binary Hamming code.

6.12.3. Show that the rth order binary Reed-Muller code of Definition 4.5.6 is equivalent to an extended cyclic code.

6.12.4. Construct a ternary BCH code with length 26 and designed distance 5.

6.12.5. Let α be a primitive element of $\mathbb{F}_{2^5}$ satisfying $\alpha^5 = \alpha^2 + 1$. A narrow-sense BCH code of length 31 with designed distance 5 is being used. We receive

$$(1001 \quad 0110 \quad 1111 \quad 0000 \quad 1101 \quad 0101 \quad 0111 \quad 111).$$

Decode this message using the method of Section 6.7.

6.12.6. Let m be odd. Let β be a primitive element of $\mathbb{F}_{2^m}$. Consider a binary cyclic code C of length $n = 2^m - 1$ with generator $g(x)$ such that $g(\beta) = g(\beta^{-1}) = 0$. Show that the minimum distance d of C is at least 5.

6.12.7. Let C be a $[q + 1, 2, d]$ code over $\mathbb{F}_q(q \text{ odd})$. Show that $d < q$ (i.e. C is not an MDS code, cf. (5.2.2)).

6.12.8. Show that the [11, 6] ternary QR code is perfect. (This code is equivalent to the code of Section 4.3.)

6.12.9. Determine the minimum distance of the binary QR code with length 47.

6.12.10. Determine all perfect single error-correcting QR codes.

6.12.11. Generalize the ideas of Section 6.9 in the following sense. Let $e > 2$, n a prime such that $e|(n - 1)$ and q a prime power such that $q^{(n-1)/e} \equiv 1 \pmod{n}$. Instead of using the squares in $\mathbb{F}_n$ use the eth powers. Show that Theorem 6.9.2(i) can be generalized to $d^e > n$. Determine the minimum distance of the binary cubic residue code of length 31.

6.12.12. Let m be odd, $n = 2^m - 1$, α a primitive element of $\mathbb{F}_{2^m}$. Let $g(x)$ be a divisor of $x^n - 1$ such that $g(\alpha) = g(\alpha^5) = 0$. Prove that the binary cyclic code with generator $g(x)$ has minimum distance $d \geq 4$ in two ways:

(a) by applying a theorem of this chapter,
(b) by showing that $1 + \xi + \eta = 0$ and $1 + \xi^5 + \eta^5 = 0$ with ξ and η in $\mathbb{F}_{2^m}$ is impossible.
(c) Using the idea of (b), show that in fact $d \geq 5$.

6.12.13. Show that the ternary Golay code has a negacyclic representation.

6.12.14. By Theorem 6.9.2 the [31, 16] QR code has $d \geq 7$, whereas the BCH bound only yields $d \geq 5$. Show that the AB-method of §6.6 also yields $d \geq 7$.

CHAPTER 7

Perfect Codes and Uniformly Packed Codes

§7.1. Lloyd's Theorem

In this chapter we shall restrict ourselves to *binary* codes. To obtain insight into the methods and theorems of this part of coding theory this suffices. Nearly everything can be done (with a little more work) for arbitrary fields $\mathbb{F}_q$. In the course of time many ways of studying perfect codes and related problems have been developed. The algebraic approach which will be discussed in the next section is perhaps the most elegant one. We start with a completely different method. We shall give an extremely elementary proof of a strong necessary condition for the existence of a binary perfect e-error-correcting code. The theorem was first proved by S. P. Lloyd (1957) (indeed for $q = 2$) using analytic methods. Since then it has been generalized by many authors (cf. [44]) but it is still referred to as Lloyd's theorem. The proof in this section is due to D. M. Cvetković and J. H. van Lint (1977; cf. [17]).

(7.1.1) Definition. The square matrix A_k of size 2^k is defined as follows. Number the rows and columns in binary from 0 to $2^k - 1$. The entry $A_k(i, j)$ is 1 if the representations of i and j have Hamming distance 1, otherwise $A_k(i, j) = 0$.

From (7.1.1) we immediately see

$$(7.1.2) \qquad\qquad A_{k+1} = \begin{pmatrix} A_k & I \\ I & A_k \end{pmatrix}.$$

(7.1.3) Lemma. *The eigenvalues of A_k are $-k + 2j$ $(0 \le j \le k)$ with multiplicities $\binom{k}{j}$.*

PROOF. The proof is by induction. For $k = 1$ it is easily checked. Let the column vector $\mathbf{x}$ be eigenvector of A_k belonging to the eigenvalue λ. Then by (7.1.2) we have

$$A_{k+1}\begin{pmatrix}\mathbf{x}\\\mathbf{x}\end{pmatrix} = (\lambda + 1)\begin{pmatrix}\mathbf{x}\\\mathbf{x}\end{pmatrix},$$

$$A_{k+1}\begin{pmatrix}\mathbf{x}\\-\mathbf{x}\end{pmatrix} = (\lambda - 1)\begin{pmatrix}\mathbf{x}\\-\mathbf{x}\end{pmatrix}.$$

The proof now follows from well-known properties of binomial coefficients. $\square$

The technically most difficult part of this section is determining the eigenvalues of certain tridiagonal matrices which occur in the proof of the theorem. To keep the notation compact we use the following definition.

(7.1.4) Definition. The matrix $Q_e = Q_e(a, b)$ is the tridiagonal matrix with

$$(Q_e)_{i,i} := a, \qquad 0 \le i \le e,$$
$$(Q_e)_{i,i+1} := b - i, \qquad 0 \le i \le e - 1,$$
$$(Q_e)_{i,i-1} := i, \qquad 1 \le i \le e.$$

Furthermore, we define

$$P_e := P_e(a, b) := \begin{bmatrix} & & & & 1 \\ & & & & 1 \\ & Q_{e-1}(a, b) & & & \vdots \\ & & & & 1 \\ \hline 0\,0 & \cdots & 0 & e & 1 \end{bmatrix}.$$

The determinants of these matrices are denoted by $\bar{Q}_e$ resp. $\bar{P}_e$.

(7.1.5) Lemma. *Let $\Psi_e(x)$ be the Krawtchouk polynomial $K_e(x - 1; n - 1, 2)$ defined in (1.2.1) and (1.2.15). Then*

$$\bar{P}_e(2y - n, n) = (-1)^e e!\,\Psi_e(y).$$

PROOF. By adding all columns to the last one and then developing by the last row we find

$$\bar{Q}_e = (a + e)\bar{Q}_{e-1} - e(a + b)\bar{P}_{e-1}.$$

Developing $\bar{P}_e$ by the last row yields

$$\bar{P}_e = \bar{Q}_{e-1} - e\bar{P}_{e-1}.$$

Combining these relations yields the following recurrence relation for $\bar{P}_e$:

$$(7.1.6) \qquad \bar{P}_{e+1} = (a - 1)\bar{P}_e - e(b - e)\bar{P}_{e-1}.$$

It is easy to check that the assertion of the lemma is true for $e = 1$ and $e = 2$. From (1.2.9) and (7.1.6) it follows that the two polynomials in the assertion satisfy the same recurrence relation. This proves the lemma.   □

We need one more easy lemma on eigenvalues.

(7.1.7) Lemma. *Let A be a matrix of size m by m which has the form*

$$A = \begin{bmatrix} A_{11} & A_{12} & \cdots & A_{1k} \\ A_{21} & A_{22} & \cdots & A_{2k} \\ \cdots\cdots\cdots\cdots\cdots\cdots \\ A_{k1} & A_{k2} & \cdots & A_{kk} \end{bmatrix},$$

where A_{ij} has size m_i by m_j ($i = 1, 2, \ldots, k$; $j = 1, 2, \ldots, k$). Suppose that for each i and j the matrix A_{ij} has constant row sums b_{ij}. Let B be the matrix with entries b_{ij}. Then each eigenvalue of B is also an eigenvalue of A.

PROOF. Let $B\mathbf{x} = \lambda\mathbf{x}$, where $\mathbf{x} = (x_1, x_2, \ldots, x_k)^T$. Define $\mathbf{y}$ by

$$\mathbf{y}^T := (x_1, x_1, \ldots, x_1, x_2, x_2, \ldots, x_2, \ldots, x_k, x_k, \ldots, x_k)$$

where each x_i is repeated m_i times. By definition of B it is obvious that $A\mathbf{y} = \lambda\mathbf{y}$.   □

We now come to the remarkable theorem which will have important consequences.

(7.1.8) Theorem. *If a binary perfect e-error-correcting code of length n exists, then $\Psi_e(x)$ has e distinct zeros among the integers $1, 2, \ldots, n$.*

PROOF. The fact that the zeros are distinct is a well-known property of Krawtchouk polynomials (cf. (1.2.13)). To show that they are integers, we assume that C is a code as in the theorem. Consider the matrix A_n (cf. (7.1.1)). Reorder the rows and column as follows. First take the rows and columns with a number corresponding to a codeword. Then successively those with numbers corresponding to words in $C_i := \{\mathbf{x} \in \mathbb{F}_2^n | d(\mathbf{x}, C) = i\}$, $1 \le i \le e$. Since C is perfect, this yields a partitioning of A_n into blocks such as in Lemma 7.1.7, where now

$$B = \begin{bmatrix} 0 & n & 0 & 0 & 0 & \cdots\cdots\cdots\cdots \\ 1 & 0 & n-1 & 0 & 0 & \cdots\cdots\cdots\cdots \\ 0 & 2 & 0 & n-2 & 0 & \cdots\cdots\cdots\cdots \\ \cdots\cdots\cdots\cdots\cdots\cdots\cdots\cdots\cdots \\ 0 & \cdots\cdots\cdots\cdots & 0 & e-1 & 0 & n-e+1 \\ 0 & \cdots\cdots\cdots\cdots & 0 & 0 & e & n-e \end{bmatrix}.$$

The substitution $x = n - 2y$ in $\det(B - xI_{e+1})$ yields

$$\det(B - xI_{e+1}) = 2y\bar{P}_e(2y - n, n).$$

The result now follows from Lemmas 7.1.3, 7.1.5 and 7.1.7.   □

The proof given in this section gives no insight into what is going on (e.g. Do the zeros of Ψ_e have a combinatorial meaning?) but it has the advantage of being completely elementary (except for the unavoidable knowledge of properties of Krawtchouk polynomials). In Section 7.5 we shall use Theorem 7.1.8 to find all binary perfect codes.

§7.2. The Characteristic Polynomial of a Code

We consider a binary code C of length n. In (3.5.1) we defined the weight distribution of a code and in (5.3.2) generalized this to distance distribution or inner distribution $(A_i)_{i=0}^n$. Corresponding to this sequence we have the *distance enumerator*

$$(7.2.1) \qquad A_C(z) := \sum_{i=0}^n A_i z^i = |C|^{-1} \sum_{\substack{u \in C \\ v \in C}} z^{d(u, v)}.$$

To get even more information on distances we now define the *outer distribution* to be a matrix B (rows indexed by elements of $\mathcal{R} = \mathbb{F}_2^n$, columns indexed $0, 1, \ldots, n$), where

$$(7.2.2) \qquad B(\mathbf{x}, i) := |\{\mathbf{c} \in C \mid d(\mathbf{x}, \mathbf{c}) = i\}|.$$

The row of B indexed by $\mathbf{x}$ is denoted by $B(\mathbf{x})$. Observe that

$$(7.2.3) \qquad (A_0, A_1, \ldots, A_n) = |C|^{-1} \sum_{\mathbf{x} \in C} B(\mathbf{x}),$$

and

$$(7.2.4) \qquad \mathbf{x} \in C \Leftrightarrow B(\mathbf{x}, 0) = 1.$$

(7.2.5) Definition. A code C is called a *regular* code if all rows of B with a 1 in position 0 are equal. The code is called *completely regular* if

$$\forall_{\mathbf{x} \in \mathcal{R}} \forall_{\mathbf{y} \in \mathcal{R}} [(\rho(\mathbf{x}, C) = \rho(\mathbf{y}, C)) \Rightarrow (B(\mathbf{x}) = B(\mathbf{y}))],$$

where $\rho(\mathbf{x}, C)$ is the distance from $\mathbf{x}$ to the code C.

Observe that if a code C is regular and $\mathbf{0} \in C$, then the weight enumerator of C is equal to $A_C(z)$.

In order to study the matrix B, we first introduce some algebra (cf. (1.1.11)).

(7.2.6) Definition. If G is an additive group and $\mathbb{F}$ a field, then the *group algebra* $\mathbb{F}G$ (or better $(\mathbb{F}G, \oplus, *)$) is the vector space over $\mathbb{F}$ with elements of

G as basis, with addition $\oplus$ and a multiplication $*$ defined by

$$\sum_{g \in G} \alpha(g)g * \sum_{h \in G} \beta(h)h := \sum_{k \in G} \left(\sum_{g+k=k} \alpha(g)\beta(h) \right) k.$$

Some authors prefer introducing an extra symbol z and using formal multiplication as follows

$$\sum_{g \in G} \alpha(g)z^g * \sum_{h \in G} \beta(h)z^h = \sum_{k \in G} \left(\sum_{g+h=k} \alpha(g)\beta(h) \right) z^k.$$

We shall take G to be $\mathscr{R} = \mathbb{F}_2^n$ and $\mathbb{F} = \mathbb{C}$. We denote this algebra by $\mathscr{A}$. In order not to confuse addition in G with the addition of elements of $\mathscr{A}$ we write the elements of the group algebra as $\sum_{x \in \mathscr{R}} \alpha(x)x$. If S is a subset of $\mathscr{R}$ we shall identify this subset with the element $\sum_{x \in S} x$ in $\mathscr{A}$ (i.e. we also denote this element by S). We introduce a notation for the sets of words of fixed weight resp. the spheres around $\mathbf{0}$:

(7.2.7) $Y_i := \{\mathbf{x} \in \mathscr{R} \mid w(\mathbf{x}) = i\},$

(7.2.8) $S_j := \{\mathbf{x} \in \mathscr{R} \mid w(\mathbf{x}) \le j\}.$

If C is a code with outer distribution B, then the conventions made above imply that

(7.2.9) $Y_i * C = \sum_{\mathbf{x} \in \mathscr{R}} B(\mathbf{x}, i)\mathbf{x}.$

If $D(\mathbf{x}, j)$ denotes the number of codewords with distance at most j to $\mathbf{x}$ (i.e. $D(\mathbf{x}, j) = \sum_{i \le j} B(\mathbf{x}, i)$), then we have

(7.2.10) $S_j * C = \sum_{\mathbf{x} \in \mathscr{R}} D(\mathbf{x}, j)\mathbf{x}.$

Let χ be the character of $\mathbb{F}_2$ with $\chi(1) = -1$. For every $\mathbf{u} \in \mathscr{R}$ we define a mapping $\chi_\mathbf{u}: \mathscr{R} \to \mathbb{C}$ by

(7.2.11) $\forall_{\mathbf{v} \in \mathscr{R}}[\chi_\mathbf{u}(\mathbf{v}) := \chi(\langle \mathbf{u}, \mathbf{v} \rangle) = (-1)^{\langle \mathbf{u}, \mathbf{v} \rangle},$

i.e. $\chi_\mathbf{u}(\mathbf{v}) = 1$ if $\mathbf{u} \perp \mathbf{v}$ and -1 otherwise.

We extend this mapping to a linear functional on the group algebra $\mathscr{A}$ by

(7.2.12) $\chi_\mathbf{u}(\sum \alpha(\mathbf{x})\mathbf{x}) := \sum \alpha(\mathbf{x})\chi_\mathbf{u}(\mathbf{x}).$

The following two assertions follow immediately from our definition. We leave the proofs as easy exercises for the reader.

(7.2.13) $\forall_{\mathbf{u} \in \mathscr{R}} \forall_{A \in \mathscr{A}} \forall_{B \in \mathscr{A}} [\chi_\mathbf{u}(A * B) = \chi_\mathbf{u}(A)\chi_\mathbf{u}(B)],$

(7.2.14) $(\chi_\mathbf{0}(S) = 2^n$ and $\forall_{\mathbf{u} \ne \mathbf{0}}[\chi_\mathbf{u}(S) = 0]) \Leftrightarrow S = S_n.$

The result of Lemma 5.3.1 (where we now have $q = 2$) can be written as

(7.2.15) $\chi_\mathbf{u}(Y_k) = K_k(w(\mathbf{u})).$

From this it follows that if $w(\mathbf{u}) = x$

$$(7.2.16) \qquad \chi_{\mathbf{u}}(S_j) = \sum_{k=0}^{j} K_k(x) = \Psi_j(x).$$

(Cf. (1.2.15).)

Let C be a code. We consider the numbers

$$C_j := |C|^{-1} \sum_{\mathbf{u} \in Y_j} \chi_{\mathbf{u}}(C).$$

We have seen these numbers before. If C is a linear code, then the proof of Theorem 3.5.3 shows us that C_j is the number of words of weight j in $C^{\perp}$. If C is not linear, we can still consider the numbers C_j and continue the proof of Theorem 3.5.3 to find that $2^{-n}|C|\sum_{j=0}^{n} C_j(1-z)^j(1+z)^{n-j}$ is the weight enumerator of C. This relation between the weight enumerator and the numbers C_j, defined with the aid of χ, is a nonlinear form of the MacWilliams relation.

We now define a second sequence of numbers, again using the character χ.

(7.2.17) Definition. The *characteristic numbers* B_j ($0 \le j \le n$) of the code C are defined by

$$B_j := |C|^{-2} \sum_{\mathbf{u} \in Y_j} |\chi_{\mathbf{u}}(C)|^2.$$

As before we see that B_j is the number of words of weight j in the code $C^{\perp}$ if C is a linear code. Let $N(C) := \{ j \,|\, 1 \le j \le n, B_j \ne 0 \}$. We define the *characteristic polynomial* F_C of the code C by

$$(7.2.18) \qquad F_C(x) := 2^n |C|^{-1} \prod_{j \in N(C)} \left(1 - \frac{x}{j} \right).$$

(7.2.19) Theorem. *Let* $\alpha_0, \alpha_1, \ldots, \alpha_n$ *be the coefficients in the Krawtchouk expansion of* F_C. *Then in* $\mathscr{A}$ *we have*

$$\sum \alpha_i Y_i * C = S_n.$$

PROOF. Let $\mathbf{u} \in \mathscr{R}$, $w(\mathbf{u}) = j$. By (7.2.13) and (7.2.15) we have

$$\chi_{\mathbf{u}}(\sum \alpha_i Y_i * C) = \chi_{\mathbf{u}}(\sum \alpha_i Y_i)\chi_{\mathbf{u}}(C) = \chi_{\mathbf{u}}(C) \sum \alpha_i K_i(j) = \chi_{\mathbf{u}}(C)F_C(j).$$

If $\mathbf{u} \ne \mathbf{0}$ the right-hand side is 0 by definition of F_C. If $\mathbf{u} = \mathbf{0}$ then the right-hand side is 2^n. The assertion now follows from (7.2.14). $\qquad \square$

(7.2.20) Corollary. *If* $\alpha_0, \alpha_1, \ldots, \alpha_n$ *are the coefficients in the Krawtchouk expansion of* F_C *and* $\mathbf{u} \in \mathscr{R}$ *then*

$$\sum_{i=0}^{n} \alpha_i B(\mathbf{u}, i) = 1.$$

PROOF. Apply (7.2.9). $\qquad \square$

(7.2.21) Definition. The number $s := |N(C)|$ is called the *external distance* of C.

Note that if C is linear, then s is the number of nonzero weights occurring in $C^\perp$. The somewhat strange name is slightly justified by Corollary 7.2.20 which shows that the covering radius $\rho(C)$ of a code (see (3.14)) is at most equal to s.

§7.3. Uniformly Packed Codes

In this section we consider codes which are generalizations of perfect codes (cf. (5.1.5)). Note that if C is a perfect e-error-correcting code, then in $\mathscr{A}$ we have $S_e * C = S_n$. We now consider codes C with $d \geq 2e + 1$ and $\rho(C) = e + 1$. (If $d = 2e + 3$ then this means that C is perfect.) The spheres with radius $e - 1$ around codewords are disjoint and each word not in one of these spheres has distance e or $e + 1$ to at least one codeword.

(7.3.1) Definition. A code C with $\rho(C) = e + 1$ and $d \geq 2e + 1$ is called *uniformly packed* with parameter r if each word $\mathbf{u}$ with $\rho(\mathbf{u}, C) \geq e$ has distance e or $e + 1$ to exactly r codewords.

Note that if $r = 1$, then C is a perfect $(e + 1)$-error-correcting code. Of course a word $\mathbf{u}$ with $\rho(\mathbf{u}, C) = e$ has distance e to exactly one codeword. Let $\rho(\mathbf{u}, C) = e + 1$ and w.l.o.g. take $\mathbf{u} = \mathbf{0}$. Then the codewords with distance $e + 1$ to $\mathbf{u}$ have weight $e + 1$. Since they must have mutual distances $\geq 2e + 1$, it follows that

$$(7.3.2) \qquad\qquad r \leq \frac{n}{e + 1}.$$

We now assume that $e + 1$ does not divide $n + 1$. A code for which $r = \lfloor n/(e + 1) \rfloor$ is called *nearly perfect*. It is easy to check that this means that C satisfies the Johnson bound (5.2.16) with equality. In a paper by J.-M. Goethals and H. C. A. van Tilborg [25], (7.3.1) is generalized by replacing r by two numbers depending on whether $\rho(\mathbf{u}, C) = e$ or $e + 1$.

(7.3.3) Theorem. *A code C with $\rho(C) = e + 1$ and $d \geq 2e + 1$ is uniformly packed with parameter r iff in $\mathscr{A}$ we have*

$$\left\{ Y_0 \oplus Y_1 \oplus \cdots \oplus Y_{e-1} \oplus \frac{1}{r}(Y_e \oplus Y_{e+1}) \right\} * C = S_n.$$

PROOF. This follows from (7.2.2), (7.2.9) and (7.3.1).   □

(7.3.4) Theorem. *A code C with $\rho(C) = e + 1$ and $d \geq 2e + 1$ is uniformly packed with parameter r iff the characteristic polynomial has degree $s = e + 1$*

and Krawtchouk coefficients

$$\alpha_0 = \alpha_1 = \cdots = \alpha_{e-1} = 1, \qquad \alpha_e = \alpha_{e+1} = \frac{1}{r}.$$

PROOF.

(i) The if part follows from Theorem 7.2.19 and Theorem 7.3.3.

(ii) Let C be uniformly packed. We know that F_C has degree $s \geq e + 1$. Let $F(x) := \sum_{i=0}^{e+1} \alpha_i K_i(x)$ with $\alpha_0 = \alpha_1 = \cdots = \alpha_{e-1} = 1$, $\alpha_e = \alpha_{e+1} = 1/r$. If $\mathbf{u} \in \mathcal{R}$, $w(\mathbf{u}) = j \neq 0$ and $\chi_{\mathbf{u}}(C) \neq 0$, then $F(j) = 0$ by (7.2.13), (7.2.14), (7.2.15) and Theorem 7.3.3. Then by (7.2.18) it follows that $F_C(x)$ divides $F(x)$. Hence $s = e + 1$ and $F(x) = aF_C(x)$ for some a. Substituting $x = 0$ we find $a = 1$ (again using Theorem 7.3.3). $\qquad\qquad\qquad\square$

The following is a different formulation of Theorem 7.3.4.

(7.3.5) Theorem. *If a uniformly packed code C with $\rho(C) = e + 1$ and $d \geq 2e + 1$ exists, then the polynomial*

$$F(x) := \sum_{i=0}^{e-1} K_i(x) + \frac{1}{r}[K_e(x) + K_{e+1}(x)]$$

has $e + 1$ distinct integral zeros in $[1, n]$ and $F(0) = 2^n|C|^{-1}$.

First observe that if C is a perfect code, i.e. $d = 2e + 3$, then $r = 1$ and $F(x) = \Psi_{e+1}(x)$ by (1.2.15) and Theorem 7.3.5 is Lloyd's theorem (7.1.8).

Next we remark that the requirement about $F(0)$ can be written as

(7.3.6)
$$|C| \left\{ \sum_{i=0}^{e-1} \binom{n}{i} + \frac{1}{r}\binom{n+1}{e+1} \right\} = 2^n,$$

which is (3.1.6) if $r = 1$, resp. (5.2.16) if $r = \lfloor n/(e+1) \rfloor$.

In fact (7.3.6) is true in general if we interpret r as the average number of codewords with distance e or $e + 1$ to a word $\mathbf{u}$ for which $\rho(\mathbf{u}, C) \geq e$.

In general it is not easy to check if a given code is uniformly packed using the definition.

We shall now consider a special case, namely a linear code C with $e = 1$. In order for C to be uniformly packed, the characteristic polynomial must have degree 2 (by Theorem 7.3.4). We have already remarked that this means that in $C^\perp$ only two nonzero weights w_1 and w_2 occur. Now suppose that $C^\perp$ is such a *two-weight code* with weight enumerator

$$A_{C^\perp}(z) = 1 + N_1 z^{w_1} + N_2 z^{w_2}.$$

Consider the MacWilliams relation (cf. Section 7.2) and substitute

$$\sum_{k=0}^{\infty} K_k(x) z^k$$

for $(1 + z)^{n-x}(1 - z)^x$ (cf. (1.2.3)). Since we have assumed that C has minimum distance $d \geq 3$, we find three equations from the coefficients of z^0, z^1, z^2, namely

$$1 + N_1 + N_2 = 2^n |C|^{-1},$$

$$K_k(0) + N_1 K_k(w_1) + N_2 K_k(w_2) = 0, \qquad (k = 1, 2).$$

By definition we have $F_C(w_1) = F_C(w_2) = 0$ and $F_C(0) = 2^n |C|^{-1}$. For the coefficients α_0, α_1, α_2 in the Krawtchouk expansion of $F_C(x)$ we then find, using (1.2.7)

$$\alpha_0 + \alpha_1 n + \alpha_2 \binom{n}{2} = 2^n |C|^{-1},$$

$$\alpha_0 + \alpha_1(n - 2w_i) + \alpha_2 \left\{ 2w_i^2 - 2nw_i + \binom{n}{2} \right\} = 0, \qquad (i = 1, 2).$$

We compare these equations with the equations for N_1 and N_2. This shows that $\alpha_0 = 1$. We define

$$r := 2(n + 1)w_1 - 2w_1^2 - \tfrac{1}{2}n(n + 1).$$

It then follows that $\alpha_1 = \alpha_2 = 1/r$ if $w_1 + w_2 = n + 1$. We have thus proved the following characterization of 1-error-correcting uniformly packed codes.

(7.3.7) Theorem. *A linear code C with $\rho(C) = 2$ and $d \geq 3$ is uniformly packed iff $C^\perp$ is a two-weight code with weights w_1, w_2 satisfying $w_1 + w_2 = n + 1$.*

In [25] it is shown that if we adopt the more general definition of uniformly packed codes, we can drop the restriction $w_1 + w_2 = n + 1$. The theorem is also true for $e > 1$ with $e + 1$ weights in $C^\perp$ instead of two.

§7.4. Examples of Uniformly Packed Codes

(7.4.1) *A Hadamard code* (cf. Section 4.1)

Consider the (12, 24, 6) Hadamard code. Puncture the code to obtain the (11, 24, 5) code C. It is obvious that any word $\mathbf{z}$ can have distance 2 or 3 to at most four codewords and if this happens we have the following situation (after changing back to $\pm$ notation and suitable multiplications of columns by -1):

$$\mathbf{z} = -\, -\quad +\, +\, +\quad +\, +\, +\quad +\, +\, +,$$

$$\mathbf{x}_1 = +\, +\quad +\, +\, +\quad +\, +\, +\quad +\, +\, +,$$

$$\mathbf{x}_2 = -\, -\quad -\, -\, -\quad +\, +\, +\quad +\, +\, +,$$

$$\mathbf{x}_3 = -\, -\quad +\, +\, +\quad -\, -\, -\quad +\, +\, +,$$

$$\mathbf{x}_4 = -\, -\quad +\, +\, +\quad +\, +\, +\quad -\, -\, -,$$

This would mean that the original Hadamard matrix of order 12 had the four rows $(+, \mathbf{x}_1), (-, \mathbf{x}_2), (-, \mathbf{x}_3), (-, \mathbf{x}_4)$. The row vector $(-4, -4, -4, 0, 0, \ldots, 0)$ is a linear combination of these four rows and must therefore be orthogonal to the remaining rows of the Hadamard matrix, which is clearly impossible. It follows that a word $\mathbf{z}$ has distance 2 or 3 to at most three codewords. From (7.3.6) it follows that the average number of codewords with distance 2 or 3 to a word $\mathbf{z}$ with $\rho(\mathbf{z}, C) > 1$ is three. Hence this number is always three. So C is uniformly packed with $r = 3$. In this example C is nonlinear.

(7.4.2) *A Punctured* RM *Code*

Let V be the six-dimensional vector space over $\mathbb{F}_2$. Let W be the set of 35 points $\mathbf{x}$ in $V \backslash \{\mathbf{0}\}$ on the quadric with equation $x_1 x_2 + x_3 x_4 + x_5 x_6 = 0$. We take these vectors as columns of a 6 by 35 matrix G. As in Section 4.5 we see that the ith row of G is the characteristic function of the intersection of W and the hyperplane with equation $x_i = 1$ ($1 \leq i \leq 6$). Hence the weight of a linear combination $\mathbf{a}^T G$ ($\mathbf{a} \in V$) is the number of solutions of

$$x_1 x_2 + x_3 x_4 + x_5 x_6 = 0 \quad \text{and} \quad \sum_{i=1}^6 a_i x_i = 1.$$

W.l.o.g. we may take $a_1 = 1$ (unless $\mathbf{a} = \mathbf{0}$). By substitution and the affine transformation

$$y_2 = x_2, \qquad y_3 = x_3 + a_4 x_2, \qquad y_4 = x_4 + a_3 x_2,$$

$$y_5 = x_5 + a_6 x_2, \qquad y_6 = x_6 + a_5 x_2$$

(which is invertible) we see that we must count the number of solutions of the equation

$$(1 + a_2 + a_3 a_4 + a_5 a_6) y_2 + y_3 y_4 + y_5 y_6 = 0.$$

If the coefficient of y_2 is 1 this number is 16, if it is 0 the number of solutions is 20. Therefore the code C which has G as parity check matrix has a dual $C^\perp$ which is a two-weight code with weights 16 and 20. The code C has $d \geq 3$ since it is projective. By the remark following (7.2.21) we have $\rho(C) = 2$. So by Theorem 7.3.7, C is uniformly packed with $r = 10$ (by (7.3.6)). The same method works in higher dimensions.

(7.4.3) *Preparata-codes*

In 1968, F. P. Preparata [57] introduced a class of nonlinear double-error-correcting codes which turned out to have many interesting properties. His definition was based on a combination of Hamming codes and 2-error-correcting BCH codes. The analysis of the codes involves tedious calculation (cf. [11]). The following description of the Preparata codes is due to R. D. Baker, R. M. Wilson and the author (cf. [72]).

In the following m is odd ($m \geq 3$), $n = 2^m - 1$. We shall define a code $\bar{\mathcal{P}}$ of length $2n + 2 = 2^{m+1}$. The words will be described by pairs (X, Y), where $X \subset \mathbb{F}_{2^m}$ and $Y \subset \mathbb{F}_{2^m}$. As usual, we interpret the pair (X, Y) as the corresponding characteristic function, which is a $(0, 1)$-vector of length 2^{m+1}.

(7.4.4) Definition. The extended *Preparata code* $\bar{\mathcal{P}}$ of length 2^{m+1} consists of the codewords described by all pairs (X, Y) satisfying

(i) $|X|$ is even, $|Y|$ is even,

(ii) $\sum_{x \in X} x = \sum_{y \in Y} y$,

(iii) $\sum_{x \in X} x^3 + (\sum_{x \in X} x)^3 = \sum_{y \in Y} y^3$.

The code $\mathcal{P}$ is obtained by leaving out the coordinate corresponding to the zero position in the first half.

We first show that $\mathcal{P}$ has 2^{2n-2m} words. We can choose X, satisfying (i) in 2^n ways. Next, we observe that since m is odd the minimal polynomial $m_3(x)$ for $\mathbb{F}_{2^m}$ has degree m. Therefore the BCH code of length n and designed distance 5 has dimension $n - 2m$. This in turn implies that for a given X the equations (ii) and (iii) have 2^{n-2m} solutions $Y \subset \mathbb{F}_{2^m}^*$. We can add the zero element to this Y if necessary to satisfy (i). This proves our assertion.

The next claim is that $\bar{\mathcal{P}}$ has minimum distance 6. From (7.4.4)(i) we see that the minimum distance is even and also that if (X, Y) satisfies the conditions, then so does (Y, X). Suppose we have two words (X, Y_1) and (X, Y_2) and let $Y := Y_1 \triangle Y_2$. Then from (7.4.4)(ii) and (iii) we find that

$$\sum_{y \in Y} y = \sum_{y \in Y} y^3 = 0,$$

i.e. $|Y| \geq 5$ by the BCH bound. So in this case the two words have distance ≥ 6. It remains to consider the possibility $(X_1, Y_1), (X_2, Y_2)$ with

$$|X_1 \triangle X_2| = |Y_1 \triangle Y_2| = 2.$$

Let $X_1 \triangle X_2 = \{\alpha, \beta\}$, $Y_1 \triangle Y_2 = \{\gamma, \delta\}$ and let $s + \alpha$ be the sum of the elements in X_1. Then (7.4.4)(ii) and (iii) imply

$$\alpha + \beta = \gamma + \delta,$$

$$s^2(\alpha + \beta) + s(\alpha + \beta)^2 = \gamma^3 + \delta^3.$$

From these we find $(s + \gamma)^3 + (s + \delta)^3 = 0$, i.e. $\gamma = \delta$, a contradiction. This proves our claim. We have proved the following theorem.

(7.4.5) Theorem. *The Preparata code $\mathcal{P}$ of length $2^{m+1} - 1$ (m odd, $m \geq 3$) has $|\mathcal{P}| = 2^k$, where $k = 2^{m+1} - 2m - 2$, and minimum distance 5.*

From (7.3.6) we find that the average value of r for the code $\mathcal{P}$ is $(2^{m+1} - 1)/3$ and then (7.3.2) implies that r is constant and equal to $(2^{m+1} - 1)/3$, i.e. $\mathcal{P}$ is nearly perfect.

If we take $m = 3$ in (7.4.4) then we find the Nordstrom-Robinson code which was introduced in Section 4.4.

Remark. The exponents 3 in (7.4.4)(iii) are not essential. We can replace 3 by $s := 2^t + 1$, where we require that $x \to x^s$ and $x \to x^{s-2}$ are 1-1 mappings of $\mathbb{F}_m$ to itself. The first part of the argument concerning minimum distance is then replaced by one involving Theorem 6.6.3. We leave this as an easy exercise for the reader.

Observe that the code satisfying only (i) and (ii) in (7.4.4) is the extended Hamming code of length 2^{m+1}. From this and a counting argument it follows that if we take $\mathscr{P}$ and adjoin to it all words at distance 3 to $\mathscr{P}$, we obtain the Hamming code of length $2^{m+1} - 1$.

§7.5. Nonexistence Theorems

It was shown by A. Tietäväinen [68] and J. H. van Lint [41] that the Golay codes are the only nontrivial e-error-correcting perfect codes with $e > 1$ over any alphabet Q for which $|Q|$ is a prime power. For $e > 2$ the restriction on Q can be dropped as was shown by M. R. Best [7] and Y. Hong [74] but that is much more difficult to prove. For $e = 1$ we have seen the Hamming codes. There are also examples of nonlinear perfect codes with $e = 1$ (cf. (7.7.4)).

In 1975 van Tilborg [69] showed that e-error-correcting uniformly packed codes with $e > 3$ do not exist and those with $e \leq 3$ are all known. In this section we wish to give some idea of the methods which were used to establish these results. It suffices to consider the binary case.

(7.5.1) Theorem. *If C is a perfect e-error-correcting binary code with $e > 1$, then C is a repetition code or the binary Golay code.*

PROOF. By Lloyd's theorem (7.1.8) the polynomial Ψ_e has zeros $x_1 < x_2 < \cdots < x_e$ which are integers in $[1, n]$. By the definition of Ψ_e and (1.2.8), the elementary symmetric functions of degree 1 and 2 of the zeros are known:

$$(7.5.2) \qquad \sum_{i=1}^{e} x_i = \frac{1}{2} e(n + 1),$$

$$(7.5.3) \qquad \sum_{i<j} x_i x_j = \frac{1}{24} e(e - 1)\{3n^2 + 3n + 2e + 2\}.$$

Observe that (7.5.2) also follows from (1.2.2) which also shows that

$$(7.5.4) \qquad x_{e-i+1} = n + 1 - x_i.$$

From (7.5.2) and (7.5.3) we find

$$(7.5.5) \qquad \sum_{i=1}^{e} \sum_{j=1}^{e} (x_i - x_j)^2 = \frac{1}{2} e^2(e - 1)\left\{n - \frac{2e - 1}{3}\right\}.$$

To find the product of the zeros, we calculate $\Psi_e(0)$. From (1.2.1) we find $\Psi_e(0) = \sum_{j=0}^{e} \binom{n}{j}$. Combining this with (3.1.6) and (1.2.8), we find

(7.5.6) $\prod_{i=1}^{e} x_i = e! 2^l,$ (for some integer l).

In a similar way we calculate $\Psi_e(1)$ and $\Psi_e(2)$, which leads to

(7.5.7) $\prod_{i=1}^{e} (x_i - 1) = 2^{-e}(n-1)(n-2)...(n-e),$

(7.5.8) $\prod_{i=1}^{e} (x_i - 2) = 2^{-e}(n-1-2e)(n-2)(n-3)...(n-e).$

We now draw conclusions about $x_1, x_2, \ldots, x_e$ from these relations. Let $A(x)$ denote the largest odd divisor of x. Then (7.5.6) shows that

$$\prod_{i=1}^{e} A(x_i) = A(e!) < e!.$$

This implies that there must be two zeros x_i and x_j such that $A(x_i) = A(x_j)$ $(i < j)$. Hence $2x_i \leq x_j$ and therefore $2x_1 \leq x_e$ and then (7.5.4) implies

(7.5.9) $x_e - x_1 \geq \frac{1}{3}(n+1).$

If we fix x_1 and x_e, then the left-hand side of (7.5.5) is minimal if $x_2 = x_3 = \cdots = x_{e-1} = \frac{1}{2}(x_1 + x_e)$.
Substitution of these values in (7.5.5) leads to

(7.5.10) $(x_e - x_1)^2 \leq \frac{1}{2}e(e-1)\left(n - \frac{2e-1}{3}\right),$

which we combine with (7.5.9). The result is

(7.5.11) $n + 1 \leq \frac{9}{2}e(e-1).$

Now consider (7.5.7) and (7.5.8). Since $(x-1)(x-2)$ is always even if $x \in \mathbb{N}$, we find

(7.5.12) $(n-1-2e)(n-1)(n-2)^2(n-3)^2 \cdots (n-e)^2 \equiv 0$ (mod 2^{3e}).

This is a triviality if $e = \frac{1}{2}(n-1)$, i.e. C is the repetition code. Suppose $e < \frac{1}{2}(n-1)$. Let 2^α be the highest power of 2 in any factor $n - j$ on the left-hand side of (7.5.12), including $n - 1 - 2e$. Then the highest power of 2 that divides the left-hand side of (7.5.12) is at most $2^{3\alpha+2e-3}$, which implies that $\alpha \geq \frac{1}{3}e + 1$.
Hence

(7.5.13) $n > 2^{1+(1/3)e}.$

If e is large then (7.5.13) contradicts (7.5.11). Small values of e which by

(7.5.11) imply small values of n are easily checked. In fact, if we are a little more accurate in estimating n, there are only very few cases left to analyze. It turns out that $e = 3$ is the only possibility. Actually $e = 3$ can be treated completely without even using Lloyd's theorem. This was shown in Problem 3.7.1.   □

The reasoning used to show that all uniformly packed codes are known (i.e. those satisfying (7.3.1)) follows the same lines but a few extra tricks are necessary because of the occurrence of the parameter r.

(7.5.14) Theorem. *Table 7.5.18 lists all uniformly packed codes.*

PROOF. We start from the generalization of Lloyd's theorem, i.e. Theorem 7.3.5. In exactly the same way as we proved (7.5.10) resp. (7.5.13), we find

$$(7.5.15) \qquad\qquad x_{e+1} - x_1 \le (e + 1)\left(\frac{n + 1}{2}\right)^{1/2},$$

$$(7.5.16) \qquad\qquad n > 2^{e/7}.$$

The argument which led to (7.5.9) has to be modified. We number the zeros in a different way as $y_1, \ldots, y_{e+1}$, where $y_j = A(y_j)2^{\alpha_j}$ and $\alpha_1 \le \alpha_2 \le \cdots \le \alpha_{e+1}$. On the one hand we have (writing (a, b) for the g.c.d. of a and b):

$$\prod_{i=1}^{e} \frac{|y_i - y_{i+1}|}{y_i} \ge \prod_{i=1}^{e} \frac{(y_i, y_{i+1})}{y_i} = \prod_{i} \frac{(A(y_i), A(y_{i+1}))2^{\alpha_i}}{y_i}$$

$$\ge \prod_{i=1}^{e} \frac{1}{A(y_i)} \ge \frac{1}{A(y_1 \ldots y_{e+1})} = \frac{A(|C|)}{A(r)A((e + 1)!)}$$

$$\ge \frac{1}{rA((e + 1)!)}.$$

Here, the last equality follows from (7.3.6). On the other hand, we have

$$\prod_{i=1}^{e} \frac{|y_i - y_{i+1}|}{y_i} \le \frac{(x_{e+1} - x_1)^e}{y_1 \ldots y_e} \le \frac{n(x_{e+1} - x_1)^e}{x_1 x_2 \ldots x_{e+1}}$$

$$= \frac{n(x_{e+1} - x_1)^e}{r(e + 1)!} \cdot \frac{2^{e+1}|C|}{2^n}.$$

Combining these two inequalities we find

$$(x_{e+1} - x_1)^e \ge \frac{(e + 1)!}{A((e + 1)!)} \cdot \frac{1}{2^{e+1}} \cdot \frac{2^n}{n|C|}$$

$$\ge \frac{(e + 1)!}{A((e + 1)!)} \cdot \frac{1}{2^{e+1}} \cdot \frac{1}{n} \sum_{i=0}^{e} \binom{n}{i} \ge \frac{(e + 1)!}{A((e + 1)!)} \cdot \frac{1}{2^{e+1}} \cdot \frac{1}{n} \binom{n}{e},$$

and hence

$$(7.5.17) \quad (x_{e+1} - x_1)^e \geq \frac{(e+1)}{A((e+1)!)} \frac{1}{2^{e+1}} (n-1)(n-2)\ldots(n-e+1).$$

We now compare (7.5.15), (7.5.16) and (7.5.17). If $e \geq 3$ only a finite number of pairs (e, n) satisfy all three inequalities. The cases $e = 1$ and $e = 2$ can easily be treated directly with Theorem 7.3.5. As a result finitely many cases have to be analyzed separately. We omit the details (cf. [69]). As a result we find the codes listed in the table below.   □

(7.5.18) Table of all Perfect, Nearly Perfect, and Uniformly Packed Binary codes

e	n	$\lvert C \rvert$	Type	Description
0	n	2^n	perfect	$\{0, 1\}^n$
1	$2^m - 1$	2^{n-m}	perfect	Hamming code (and others)
1	$2^m - 2$	2^{n-m}	nearly perfect	shortened Hamming code (cf. (7.7.1))
1	$2^{2m-1} \pm 2^{m-1} - 1$	2^{n-2m}	uniformly packed	cf. (7.4.2)
2	$2^{2m} - 1$	2^{n+1-4m}	nearly perfect	Preparata code
2	$2^{2m+1} - 1$	2^{n-4m-2}	uniformly packed	BCH code (cf. (7.7.2))
2	11	24	uniformly packed	cf. (7.4.1)
3	23	2^{12}	perfect	Golay code
e	$2e + 1$	2	perfect	repetition code
e	e	1	perfect	$\{\mathbf{0}\}$

(Here the entries "Hamming code" and "Preparata code" are to be interpreted as all codes with the same parameters as these codes.)

§7.6. Comments

Perfect codes have been generalized in several directions (e.g. other metrics than Hamming distance, mixed alphabets). For a survey (including many references) the reader should consult [44].

A modification of Tietäväinen's nonexistence proof can be found in [46], also many references.

The most complete information on uniformly packed codes can be found in [69]. For connections to design theory we refer to [11] and [46].

The problem of the possible existence of unknown 2-error-correcting codes over alphabets Q with $\lvert Q \rvert$ not a prime power seems to be very hard but probably not impossible. The case $e = 1$ looks hopeless.

Many of the ideas and methods which were used in this chapter (e.g. Section 7.2) were introduced by P. Delsarte (cf. [18]).

§7.7. Problems

7.7.1. Show that the $[2^m - 2, 2^m - m - 2]$ shortened binary Hamming code is nearly perfect.

7.7.2. Let C be the binary BCH code of length $n = 2^{2m+1} - 1$ with designed distance 5. Show that C is uniformly packed with parameter $r = \frac{1}{6}(n - 1)$ by explicitly calculating the number of codewords with distance 3 to a word $\mathbf{u}$ with $\rho(\mathbf{u}, C) \geq 2$.

7.7.3. Show that there is a nearly perfect code C for which $\overline{C}$ is the Nordstrom-Robinson code.

7.7.4. Let H be the $[7, 4]$ binary Hamming code. Define f on H by $f(\mathbf{0}) = 0$, $f(\mathbf{c}) = 1$ if $\mathbf{c} \neq \mathbf{0}$. Let C be the code of length 15 with codewords

$$\left(\mathbf{x}, \mathbf{x} + \mathbf{c}, \sum_{i=1}^{7} x_i + f(\mathbf{c}) \right), \qquad \text{where } \mathbf{c} \in H, \mathbf{x} \in \mathbb{F}_2^7.$$

Show that C is perfect and C is not equivalent to a linear code.

7.7.5. Show that a perfect binary 2-error-correcting code is trivial.

7.7.6. Let C be a uniformly packed code of length n with $e = 1$ and $r = 6$. Show that $n = 27$ and give a construction of C.

CHAPTER 8

Goppa Codes

§8.1. Motivation

Consider once again the parity check matrix of a (narrow sense) BCH code as given in the proof of Theorem 6.6.2, i.e.

$$
H = \begin{bmatrix}
1 & \beta & \beta^2 & \cdots & \beta^{n-1} \\
1 & \beta^2 & \beta^4 & \cdots & \beta^{2(n-1)} \\
\vdots & \vdots & \vdots & & \vdots \\
1 & \beta^{d-1} & \beta^{2(d-1)} & \cdots & \beta^{(d-1)(n-1)}
\end{bmatrix},
$$

where β is a primitive nth root of unity in $\mathbb{F}_{q^m}$ and each entry is interpreted as a column vector of length m over $\mathbb{F}_q$; existence of β implies that $n \mid (q^m - 1)$.

In Theorem 6.6.2 we proved that the minimum distance is at least d by using the fact that any submatrix of H formed by taking $d - 1$ columns is a Vandermonde matrix and therefore has determinant $\neq 0$. Many authors have noticed that the same argument works if we replace H by

$$
\hat{H} = \begin{bmatrix}
h_0 \beta_0 & h_1 \beta_1 & \cdots & h_{n-1} \beta_{n-1} \\
\vdots & \vdots & & \vdots \\
h_0 \beta_0^{d-1} & h_1 \beta_1^{d-1} & \cdots & h_{n-1} \beta_{n-1}^{d-1}
\end{bmatrix},
$$

where $h_j \in \mathbb{F}_{q^m}^*$ and the β_i are different elements of $\mathbb{F}_{q^m}^*$. If $h_j \in \mathbb{F}_q$ ($0 \leq j \leq n - 1$) then the factors h_j have no essential effect; the code is replaced by an equivalent code. However, if the h_j are elements of $\mathbb{F}_{q^m}$, then the terms $h_j \beta_j^i$ considered as column vectors over $\mathbb{F}_q$ can be very different from the original entries.

We shall consider two ways of generalizing BCH codes in this manner. That we really get something more interesting will follow from the fact that the new classes of codes contain sequences meeting the Gilbert bound whereas long BCH codes are known to be bad.

§8.2. Goppa Codes

Let $(c_0, c_1, \ldots, c_{n-1})$ be a codeword in a BCH code with designed distance d (word length n, β a primitive nth root of unity). Then, by definition $\sum_{i=0}^{n-1} c_i(\beta^j)^i = 0$ for $1 \leq j < d$. We wish to write this condition in another way. Observe that

(8.2.1)
$$\frac{z^n - 1}{z - \beta^{-i}} = \sum_{k=0}^{n-1} z^k (\beta^{-i})^{n-1-k} = \sum_{k=0}^{n-1} \beta^{i(k+1)} z^k.$$

It follows that

(8.2.2)
$$\sum_{i=0}^{n-1} \frac{c_i}{z - \beta^{-i}} = \frac{z^{d-1} p(z)}{z^n - 1}$$

for some polynomial $p(z)$.

If $g(z)$ is any polynomial and $g(\gamma) \neq 0$, we define $1/(z - \gamma)$ to be the unique polynomial mod $g(z)$ such that $(z - \gamma) \cdot 1/(z - \gamma) \equiv 1 \pmod{g(z)}$, i.e.

(8.2.3)
$$\frac{1}{z - \gamma} = \frac{-1}{g(\gamma)} \cdot \left(\frac{g(z) - g(\gamma)}{z - \gamma} \right).$$

These observations serve as preparation for the following definition.

(8.2.4) Definition. Let $g(z)$ be a (monic) polynomial of degree t over $\mathbb{F}_{q^m}$. Let $L = \{\gamma_0, \gamma_1, \ldots, \gamma_{n-1}\} \subset \mathbb{F}_{q^m}$, such that $|L| = n$ and $g(\gamma_i) \neq 0$ for $0 \leq i \leq n - 1$. We define the *Goppa code* $\Gamma(L, g)$ with *Goppa polynomial* $g(z)$ to be the set of codewords $\mathbf{c} = (c_0, c_1, \ldots, c_{n-1})$ over the alphabet $\mathbb{F}_q$ for which

(8.2.5)
$$\sum_{i=0}^{n-1} \frac{c_i}{z - \gamma_i} \equiv 0 \pmod{g(z)}.$$

Observe that Goppa codes are linear.

(8.2.6) EXAMPLE. From the introductory remarks we see that if we take the Goppa polynomial $g(z) = z^{d-1}$ and $L := \{\beta^{-i} | 0 \leq i \leq n - 1\}$, where β is a primitive nth root of unity in $\mathbb{F}_{q^m}$, the resulting Goppa code $\Gamma(L, g)$ is the narrow sense BCH code of designed distance d (cf. Problem 8.8.2).

In order to establish the connection with Section 8.1, we try to find a suitable parity check matrix for $\Gamma(L, g)$. From (8.2.5) and (8.2.3) we see that

$$\left(\frac{1}{g(\gamma_0)} \cdot \frac{g(z) - g(\gamma_0)}{(z - \gamma_0)}, \ldots, \frac{1}{g(\gamma_{n-1})} \cdot \frac{g(z) - g(\gamma_{n-1})}{(z - \gamma_{n-1})} \right),$$

with each entry interpreted as a column vector, is, in a sense, a parity check matrix. Let $h_j := g(\gamma_j)^{-1}$ and hence $h_j \neq 0$. If $g(z) = \sum_{i=0}^t g_i z^i$, then in the same way as (8.2.1) we have

$$\frac{g(z) - g(x)}{z - x} = \sum_{i+j \leq t-1} g_{i+j+1} x^j z^i.$$

Leaving out the factors z^i, we find as parity check matrix for $\Gamma(L, g)$

$$
\begin{bmatrix}
h_0 g_t & \cdots & h_{n-1} g_t \\
h_0(g_{t-1} + g_t \gamma_0) & \cdots & h_{n-1}(g_{t-1} + g_t \gamma_{n-1}) \\
\vdots & \cdots & \vdots \\
h_0(g_1 + g_2 \gamma_0 + \cdots + g_t \gamma_0^{t-1}) & \cdots & h_{n-1}(g_1 + g_2 \gamma_{n-1} + \cdots + g_t \gamma_{n-1}^{t-1})
\end{bmatrix}
$$

By a linear transformation we find the matrix we want, namely

$$
H = \begin{bmatrix}
h_0 & \cdots & h_{n-1} \\
h_0 \gamma_0 & \cdots & h_{n-1} \gamma_{n-1} \\
\vdots & & \vdots \\
h_0 \gamma_0^{t-1} & \cdots & h_{n-1} \gamma_{n-1}^{t-1}
\end{bmatrix}
$$

(here we have used the fact that $g_t \neq 0$).

This does not have the full generality of the matrix $\hat{H}$ of Section 8.1, where the h_j were arbitrary, since we now have $h_j = g(\gamma_j)^{-1}$.

(8.2.7) Theorem. *The Goppa code $\Gamma(L, g)$ defined in (8.2.4) has dimension $\geq n - mt$ and minimum distance $\geq t + 1$.*

PROOF. This follows from the parity check matrix H in exactly the same way as for BCH codes. ☐

The example given in (8.2.6) shows that the BCH bound (for narrow-sense BCH codes) is a special case of Theorem 8.2.7.

§8.3. The Minimum Distance of Goppa Codes

If we change our point of view a little, it is possible to obtain (8.2.7) in another way and also some improvements. As before, let $\mathcal{R}$ denote $(\mathbb{F}_q)^n$ with Hamming distance. Let L be as in (8.2.4). We define

$$
\mathcal{R}^* := \left\{ \xi(z) = \sum_{i=0}^{n-1} \frac{b_i}{z - \gamma_i} \,\middle|\, (b_0, b_1, \ldots, b_{n-1}) \in \mathcal{R} \right\}
$$

and we define the distance of two rational functions $\xi(z)$, $\eta(z)$ by

$$
d(\xi(z), \eta(z)) := \|\xi(z) - \eta(z)\|,
$$

where $\|\xi(z)\|$ denotes the degree of the denominator when $\xi(z)$ is written as $n(z)/d(z)$ with $(n(z), d(z)) = 1$. This is easily seen to be a distance function and in fact the mapping $(b_0, \ldots, b_{n-1}) \to \sum_{i=0}^{n-1} b_i/(z - \gamma_i)$ is an isometry from $\mathcal{R}$ onto $\mathcal{R}^*$. We shall use this terminology to study Goppa codes by considering the left-hand side of (8.2.5) as an element of $\mathcal{R}^*$ (i.e. we do not apply (8.2.3)). If $\xi(z) = n(z)/d(z)$ corresponds to a nonzero codeword, then degree $d(z) \geq \deg$

$n(z) + 1$. The requirement $\xi(z) \equiv 0 \pmod{g(z)}$ implies that $g(z)$ divides $n(z)$, i.e. degree $d(z) \geq t + 1$. So we have $\|\xi(z)\| \geq t + 1$, which is the result of Theorem 8.2.7.

This proof shows that we can improve our estimate for the minimum distance if the degrees of $n(z)$ and $d(z)$ differ by more than 1. The coefficient of z^{n-1} in $n(z)$ is $\sum_{i=0}^{n-1} b_i$. It follows that if we add an extra parity check equation $\sum_{i=0}^{n-1} b_i = 0$, the estimate for the minimum distance will increase by 1 and the dimension of the code will decrease by at most 1. We can use the same idea for other coefficients. The coefficient of z^{n-s-1} in the numerator $n(z)$ is $(-1)^s \sum_{i=0}^{n-1} b_i \sum'_{j_1, j_2, \ldots, j_s} \gamma_{j_1} \gamma_{j_2} \cdots \gamma_{j_s}$ (where $\sum'$ indicates that $j_v \neq i$ for $v = 1$, 2, ..., s). This coefficient is a linear combination of the sums $\sum_{i=0}^{n-1} b_i \gamma_i^r$ ($0 \leq r \leq s$). It follows that if we add $s + 1$ parity check equations, namely $\sum_{i=0}^{n-1} b_i \gamma_i^r = 0$ ($0 \leq r \leq s$), we find a code with dimension at least $n - tm - (1 + sm)$ and minimum distance at least $t + s + 2$. How does this compare to simply replacing $g(z)$ by another Goppa polynomial with degree $t + s$? The first method has the advantage that $\sum_{i=0}^{n-1} b_i \gamma_i = 0$ implies that $\sum_{i=0}^{n-1} b_i \gamma_i^q = 0$. Hence, once in q times we are sure that the dimension does not decrease.

We remark that the procedure sketched above is more or less the same thing as taking the intersection of the Goppa code with a BCH code.

The method which we have described turns out to be particularly useful in the case of binary codes as shown by the following theorem.

(8.3.1) Theorem. *Let $q = 2$ and let $g(z)$ have no multiple zeros. Then $\Gamma(L, g)$ has minimum distance at least $2t + 1$ (where $t = \text{degree } g(z)$).*

PROOF. Let $(c_0, c_1, \ldots, c_{n-1})$ be a codeword. Define $f(z) = \prod_{i=0}^{n-1} (z - \gamma_i)^{c_i}$. Then $\xi(z) = \sum_{i=0}^{n-1} c_i/(z - \gamma_i) = f'(z)/f(z)$, where $f'(z)$ is the formal derivative. In $f'(z)$ only even powers of z occur, i.e. $f'(z)$ is a perfect square. Since we require that $g(z)$ divides $f'(z)$ we must actually have $g^2(z)$ dividing $f'(z)$. So our previous argument yields $d \geq 2t + 1$. $\qquad\square$

Of course one can combine Theorem 8.3.1 with the idea of intersecting with a BCH code.

§8.4. Asymptotic Behaviour of Goppa Codes

In Section 6.6 we pointed out that long primitive BCH codes are bad. This fact is connected with Theorem 6.6.7. It was shown by T. Kasami (1969; [39]) that a family of cyclic codes for which the extended codes are invariant under the affine group is bad in the same sense: a subsequence of codes C_i with length n_i, dimension k_i and distance d_i must have $\lim \inf(k_i/n_i) = 0$ or $\lim \inf(d_i/n_i) = 0$. We shall now show that the class of Goppa is considerably larger.

(8.4.1) Theorem. *There exists a sequence of Goppa codes over $\mathbb{F}_q$ which meets the Gilbert bound.*

PROOF. We first pick parameters $n = q^m$, t and d, choose $L = \mathbb{F}_{q^m}$, and we try to find an irreducible polynomial $g(z)$ of degree t over $\mathbb{F}_{q^m}$ such that $\Gamma(L, g)$ has minimum distance at least d. Let $\mathbf{c} = (c_0, c_1, \ldots, c_{n-1})$ be any word of weight $j < d$, i.e. a word we do not want in $\Gamma(L, g)$. Since $\sum_{i=0}^{n-1} c_i/(z - \gamma_i)$ has numerator of degree at most $j - 1$, there are at most $\lfloor (j - 1)/t \rfloor$ polynomials $g(z)$ for which $\Gamma(L, g)$ does contain $\mathbf{c}$. This means that to ensure distance d, we have to exclude at most $\sum_{j=1}^{d-1} \lfloor (j - 1)/t \rfloor (q - 1)^j \binom{n}{j}$ irreducible polynomials of degree t. This number is less than $(d/t)V_q(n, d - 1)$ (cf. (5.1.4)). By (1.1.19) the number of irreducible polynomials of degree t over $\mathbb{F}_{q^m}$ exceeds $(1/r)q^{mt}(1 - q^{-(1/2)mt+m})$. So a sufficient condition for the existence of the code $\Gamma(L, g)$ that we are looking for is

$$(8.4.2) \qquad \frac{d}{t} V_q(n, d - 1) < \frac{1}{t} q^{mt}(1 - q^{-(1/2)mt+m}).$$

By Theorem 8.2.7 the code has at least q^{n-mt} words. On both sides of (8.4.2) we take logarithms to base q and divide by n. Suppose n is variable, $n \to \infty$, and $d/n \to \delta$. Using Lemma 5.1.6 we find

$$H_q(\delta) + o(1) < \frac{mt}{n} + o(1).$$

The information rate of the code $\Gamma(L, g)$ is $\geq 1 - mt/n$. It follows that we can find a sequence of polynomials $g(z)$ such that the corresponding Goppa codes have information rate tending to $1 - H_q(\delta)$. This is the Gilbert bound (5.1.9).
$\square$

§8.5. Decoding Goppa Codes

The Berlekamp decoder for BCH codes which was mentioned at the end of Section 6.7 can also be used to decode Goppa codes. In order to show this, we shall proceed in the same way as in Section 6.7.

Let $(C_0, C_1, \ldots, C_{n-1})$ be a codeword in $\Gamma(L, g)$ as defined in (8.2.4) and suppose we receive $(R_0, R_1, \ldots, R_{n-1})$. We denote the error vector by $(E_0, E_1, \ldots, E_{n-1}) = \mathbf{R} - \mathbf{C}$. Let $M := \{i | E_i \neq 0\}$. We denote the degree of $g(x)$ by t and assume that $|M| = e < \frac{1}{2}t$. Again using the convention (8.2.3) we define a polynomial $S(x)$, called the *syndrome*, by

$$(8.5.1) \qquad S(x) \equiv \sum_{i=0}^{n-1} \frac{E_i}{x - \gamma_i} \qquad (\mathrm{mod}\ g(x)).$$

Observe that $S(x)$ can be calculated by the receiver using $\mathbf{R}$ and (8.2.5). We now define the *error-locator polynomial* $\sigma(z)$ and a companion polynomial $\omega(z)$ in a manner similar to Section 6.7 (but this time using the locations themselves instead of inverses).

(8.5.2)
$$\sigma(z) := \prod_{i \in M} (z - \gamma_i),$$

(8.5.3)
$$\omega(z) := \sum_{i \in M} E_i \prod_{j \in M \setminus \{i\}} (z - \gamma_i).$$

From the definitions it follows that $\sigma(z)$ and $\omega(z)$ have no common factors, $\sigma(z)$ has degree e, and $\omega(z)$ has degree $< e$. The computation of $\omega(z)/\sigma(z)$ of Section 6.7 is replaced by the following argument.

(8.5.4)
$$S(z)\sigma(z) \equiv \sum_{i=0}^{n-1} \frac{E_i}{z - \gamma_i} \prod_{i \in M} (z - \gamma_i)$$

$$\equiv \omega(z) \qquad (\mathrm{mod}\ g(z)).$$

Now suppose we have an algorithm which finds the monic polynomial $\sigma_1(z)$ of lowest degree $(\sigma_1(z) \neq 0)$ and a polynomial $\omega_1(z)$ of lower degree, such that

(8.5.5)
$$S(z)\sigma_1(z) \equiv \omega_1(z) \qquad (\mathrm{mod}\ g(z)).$$

It follows that

$$\omega_1(z)\sigma(z) - \omega(z)\sigma_1(z) \equiv 0 \qquad (\mathrm{mod}\ g(z)).$$

Since the degree of the left-hand side is less than the degree of $g(z)$, we find that the left-hand side is 0. Then $(\sigma(z), \omega(z)) = 1$ implies that $\sigma(z)$ divides $\sigma_1(z)$ and therefore we must have $\sigma_1(z) = \sigma(z)$. Once we have found $\sigma(z)$ and $\omega(z)$, it is clear that we know **E**. The Berlekamp-algorithm is an efficient way of computing $\sigma_1(z)$. There are other methods, based on Euclid's algorithm for finding the g.c.d. of two polynomials (cf. [51]).

§8.6. Generalized BCH Codes

Let us take another look at Goppa codes. We consider $L = \{1, \beta, \beta^2, \ldots, \beta^{n-1}\}$ where β is a primitive nth root of unity in $\mathbb{F}_{2^m}$, $g(z)$ a suitable polynomial. Let $(a_0, a_1, \ldots, a_{n-1}) \in \Gamma(L, g)$. As in (6.5.2) we denote by $A(X)$ the Mattson-Solomon polynomial of $a_0 + a_1 x + \cdots + a_{n-1} x^{n-1}$.

Consider the polynomial

$$(X^n - 1) \sum_{i=0}^{n-1} \frac{A(\beta^i)}{X - \beta^i} = (X^n - 1)n \sum_{i=0}^{n-1} \frac{a_i}{X - \beta^i}.$$

(by Lemma 6.5.3). The left-hand side is a polynomial of degree $\leq n - 1$ which takes on the value $n\beta^{-i}A(\beta^i)$ for $X = \beta^i$ $(0 \leq i \leq n - 1)$. We can replace n by 1 since we are working over $\mathbb{F}_2$. Therefore the left-hand side is the polynomial $X^{n-1} \circ A(X)$ (using the notation of Section 6.5) because this also has degree

$\leq n - 1$ and takes on the same values in the nth roots of unity. Hence we have proved the following theorem.

(8.6.1) Theorem. *If $L = \{1, \beta, \ldots, \beta^{n-1}\}$ where β is a primitive nth root of unity in $\mathbb{F}_{2^m}$ and $(g(z), z^n - 1) = 1$, then the binary Goppa code $\Gamma(L, g)$ consists of the words $(a_0, a_1, \ldots, a_{n-1})$ such that the Mattson-Solomon polynomial $A(X)$ of $a(x)$ satisfies*

$$X^{n-1} \circ A(X) \equiv 0 \qquad (\bmod\ g(X)).$$

In Theorem 6.6.2 we proved the BCH bound by applying Theorem 6.5.5 and by using the fact that the Mattson-Solomon polynomial of a codeword has sufficiently small degree. For Goppa codes a similar argument works. The polynomial $g(X)$ has degree t and $(g(X), X^n - 1) = 1$. It then follows from Theorem 8.6.1 that at most $n - 1 - t$ nth roots of unity are zeros of $A(X)$. This means that **a** has weight at least $t + 1$, yielding a second proof of Theorem 8.2.7.

The argument above shows how to generalize these codes. The trick is to ensure that the Mattson-Solomon polynomial of a codeword has few nth roots of unity as zeros. This idea was used by R. T. Chien and D. M. Choy (1975; [13]) in the following way.

(8.6.2) Definition. Let $(T, +, \circ)$ be as in Section 6.5 with $\mathscr{F} = \mathbb{F}_{q^m}$ and $S = \mathbb{F}_q[x] \bmod(x^n - 1)$. Let $P(X)$ and $G(X)$ be two polynomials in T such that $(P(X), X^n - 1) = (G(X), X^n - 1) = 1$. The *generalized BCH code* (= GBCH code) of length n over $\mathbb{F}_q$ with polynomial pair $(P(X), G(X))$ is defined as

$$\{a(x) \in S \mid P(X) \circ (\Phi a)(X) \equiv 0 \qquad (\bmod\ G(X))\}.$$

A GBCH code is obviously linear.

(8.6.3) Theorem. *The minimum distance of the GBCH code of (8.6.2) is at least $1 + \text{degree } G(X)$.*

PROOF. We apply Theorem 6.5.5. A common factor $f(X)$ of Φa and $X^n - 1$ is also a factor of $P(X) \circ (\Phi a)(X)$. But $(G(X), f(X)) = 1$. So the degree of $f(X)$ must be at most $n - 1 - \text{degree } G(X)$. $\qquad\square$

Notice that the special Goppa codes of Theorem 8.6.1 are examples of GBCH codes. If we take $P(X) = X^{n-1}$ and $G(X) = X^{d-1}$ we obtain a BCH code.

The GBCH codes have a parity check matrix like $\hat{H}$ of Section 8.1. In order to show this, we consider the polynomials $p(x) = (\Phi^{-1} P)(x) = \sum_{i=0}^{n-1} p_i x^i$ and $g(x) = (\Phi^{-1} G)(x) = \sum_{i=0}^{n-1} g_i x^i$. By Lemma 6.5.3 all the coefficients of $p(x)$ and $g(x)$ are nonzero since nth roots of unity are not zeros of $P(X)$ or $G(X)$. Let $a(x)$ be a codeword and $A(X) = (\Phi a)(X)$. By (8.6.2) there is a polynomial $B(X)$ of degree at most $n - 1 - \text{degree } G(X)$ such that

$$P(X) \circ A(X) = B(X)G(X) = B(X) \circ G(X).$$

Define $b(x) := (\Phi^{-1}B)(x) = \sum_{i=0}^{n-1} b_i x^i$. Then we have

$$p(x) * a(x) = b(x) * g(x),$$

i.e.

$$\sum_{i=0}^{n-1} p_i a_i x^i = \sum_{i=0}^{n-1} b_i g_i x^i.$$

So we have found that $b_i = p_i g_i^{-1} a_i$ ($0 \le i \le n - 1$). Let $h_i := p_i g_i^{-1}$ and define

$$H := \begin{bmatrix} h_0 & h_1\beta & \cdots & h_{n-1}\beta^{n-1} \\ h_0 & h_1\beta^2 & \cdots & h_{n-1}\beta^{2(n-1)} \\ \vdots & \vdots & & \vdots \\ h_0 & h_1\beta^t & \cdots & h_{n-1}\beta^{t(n-1)} \end{bmatrix}$$

Let $1 \le j \le t = $ degree $G(X)$. Then $B_{n-j} = 0$. By (6.5.2)

$$B_{n-j} = b(\beta^j) = \sum_{i=0}^{n-1} b_i\beta^{ij} = \sum_{i=0}^{n-1} h_i a_i \beta^{ij}.$$

So $\mathbf{a}H^T = \mathbf{0}$. Conversely, if $\mathbf{a}H^T = \mathbf{0}$ we find that the degree of $B(X)$ is at most $n - 1 - t$. Hence $B(X)G(X) = B(X) \circ G(X) = P(X) \circ A(X)$, i.e. $\mathbf{a}$ is in the GBCH code.

§8.7. Comments

The codes described in Section 8.1 are called *alternant codes*. The codes treated in this chapter are special cases depending on the choice of h_i and β_i. The first interesting subclass seems to be the class of *Srivastava codes* introduced by J. N. Srivastava in 1967 (unpublished). E. R. Berlekamp [2] recognized their possibilities and recommended further study of this area. The alternant codes were introduced by H. J. Helgert (1974; [35]). The most interesting turned out to be the Goppa codes introduced by V. D. Goppa [27] in 1970 (cf. [4]).

BCH codes are the only cyclic Goppa codes (cf. Problem 8.8.2) but E. R. Berlekamp and O. Moreno [5] showed that extended 2-error-correcting binary Goppa codes are cyclic. Later K. K. Tzeng and K. P. Zimmerman [71] proved a similar result for other Goppa codes and the same authors have generalized the idea of Goppa codes.

§8.8. Problems

8.8.1. Let L consist of the primitive 15th roots of unity in $\mathbb{F}_{2^4}$ (take $\alpha^4 + \alpha + 1 = 0$). Let $g(z) := z^2 + 1$. Analyze the binary Goppa code $\Gamma(L, g)$.

8.8.2. Let α be a primitive nth root of unity in $\mathbb{F}_{2^m}$ and let $L := \{1, \alpha, \alpha^2, \ldots, \alpha^{n-1}\}$. Let the binary Goppa code $C = \Gamma(L, g)$ be a cyclic code. Show that $g(z) = z^t$ for some t, i.e. C is a BCH code.

8.8.3. Let $n = q^m - 1$, $L = \mathbb{F}_{q^m} \backslash \{0\}$. Let C_1 be the BCH code of length n over $\mathbb{F}_q$ obtained by taking $l = 0$ and $\delta = d_1$ in (6.6.1). Let C_2 be a Goppa code $\Gamma(L, g)$. Show that $C_1 \cap C_2$ has minimum distance $d \geq d_1 + d_2 - 1$, where $d_2 := 1 + \deg g$.

8.8.4. Consider the GBCH code with polynomial pair $(P(X), G(X))$ where $G(X)$ has degree t. Show that there is a polynomial $\hat{P}(X)$ such that the pair $(\hat{P}(X), X^t)$ defines the same code.

8.8.5. Let C be the binary cyclic code of length 15 with generator $x^2 + x + 1$. Show that C is a BCH code but not a Goppa code.

CHAPTER 9

Asymptotically Good Algebraic Codes

§9.1. A Simple Nonconstructive Example

In the previous chapters we have described several constructions of codes. If we considered these codes from the point of view of Chapter 5, we would be in for a disappointment. The Hadamard codes of Section 4.1 have $\delta = \frac{1}{2}$ and if $n \to \infty$ their rate R tends to 0. For Hamming codes R tends to 1 but δ tends to 0. For BCH codes we also find $\delta \to 0$ if we fix the rate. For all examples of codes which we have treated, an explicitly defined sequence of these codes, either has $\delta \to 0$ or $R \to 0$.

As an introduction to the next section we shall now show that one can give a simple algebraic definition which yields good codes. However, the definition is not constructive and we are left at the point we reached with Theorem 2.2.3. We shall describe binary codes with $R = \frac{1}{2}$. Fix m and choose an element $\alpha_m \in \mathbb{F}_{2^m}$. How this element is to be chosen will be explained below. We interpret vectors $\mathbf{a} \in \mathbb{F}_2^m$ as elements of $\mathbb{F}_{2^m}$ and define

$$C_\alpha := \{(\mathbf{a}, \alpha\mathbf{a}) | \mathbf{a} \in \mathbb{F}_2^m\}.$$

Let $\lambda = \lambda_m$ be given. If C_α contains a nonzero word $(\mathbf{a}, \alpha\mathbf{a})$ of weight $< 2m\lambda$, then this word uniquely determines α as the quotient (in $\mathbb{F}_{2^m}$) of $\alpha\mathbf{a}$ and $\mathbf{a}$. It follows that at most $\sum_{i<2m\lambda} \binom{2m}{i}$ choices of α will lead to a code C_α which has minimum distance $< 2m\lambda$. Now we take $\lambda := H^{\leftarrow}(\frac{1}{2} - (1/\log m))$. By Theorem 1.4.5 the number of "bad" choices for α is $o(2^m)$ $(m \to \infty)$. Therefore for almost all choices of α we have

$$d \geq 2mH^{\leftarrow}\left(\frac{1}{2} - \frac{1}{\log m}\right),$$

where d denotes the minimum distance of C_α. Letting $m \to \infty$ and taking suitable choices for α_m we thus have a sequence of codes with rate $\frac{1}{2}$ such that the corresponding δ satisfies

$$\delta = H^-(\tfrac{1}{2}) + o(1), \qquad (m \to \infty).$$

So this sequence meets the Gilbert bound (5.1.9). If we could give an explicit way of choosing α_m, that would be a sensational result. For a long time there was serious doubt whether it is at all possible to give an explicit algebraic construction of a sequence of codes such that both the rate and d/n are bounded away from zero. In 1972, J. Justesen [37] succeeded in doing this. The essential idea is a variation of the construction described above. Instead of one (difficult to choose) value of α, all possible multipliers α occur within one codeword. The average effect is nearly as good as one smart choice of α.

§9.2. Justesen Codes

The codes we shall describe are a generalization of *concatenated codes* which were introduced by G. D. Forney [22] in 1966. The idea is to construct a code in two steps by starting with a code C_1 and interpreting words of C_1 as symbols of a new alphabet with which C_2 is constructed. We discuss this in more detail. Let C_2 be a code over $\mathbb{F}_{2^m}$. The symbols c_i of a codeword $(c_0, c_1, \ldots, c_{n-1})$ can be written as m-tuples over $\mathbb{F}_2$, i.e. $c_i = (c_{i1}, c_{i2}, \ldots, c_{im})$ ($i = 0, 1, \ldots, n-1$), where $c_{ij} \in \mathbb{F}_2$. Such an m-tuple is the sequence of information symbols for a word in the so-called *inner code* C_1. Let us consider the simplest case where the rate is $\frac{1}{2}$. Corresponding to $c_i = (c_{i1}, c_{i2}, \ldots, c_{im})$ we have a word of length $2m$ in the inner code.

The rate of the concatenated code is half of the rate of C_2. Justesen's idea was to vary the inner code C_1, i.e. to let the choice of C_1 depend on i. As in the previous section, the inner codes are chosen in such a way that a word of length $2m$ starts with the symbols of c_i. For the *outer code* C_2 we take a Reed-Solomon code.

The details of the construction are as follows. Since we intend to let m tend to infinity, we must have a simple construction for $\mathbb{F}_{2^m}$. We use Theorem 1.1.28. So take $m = 2 \cdot 3^{l-1}$ and $\mathbb{F}_{2^m}$ in the representation as $\mathbb{F}_2[x]$ (mod $g(x)$), where $g(x) = x^m + x^{m/2} + 1$. The Reed-Solomon code C_2 which is our outer code is represented as follows (cf. Section 6.8). An m-tuple of information symbols $(i_0, i_1, \ldots, i_{m-1})$ is interpreted as the element $i_0 + i_1 x + \cdots + i_{m-1} x^{m-1} \in \mathbb{F}_{2^m}$. Take K successive m-tuples $a_0, a_1, \ldots, a_{K-1}$ and form the polynomial $a(Z) := a_0 + a_1 Z + \cdots + a_{K-1} Z^{K-1} \in \mathbb{F}_{2^m}[Z]$. For $j = 1, 2, \ldots, 2^m - 1 =: N$, define $j(x)$ by $j(x) = \sum_{i=0}^{m-1} \varepsilon_i x^i$ if $\sum_{i=0}^{m-1} \varepsilon_i 2^i$ is the binary representation of j. Then $j(x)$ runs through the nonzero elements of $\mathbb{F}_{2^m}$. We substitute these in $a(Z)$ and thus obtain a sequence of N elements of $\mathbb{F}_{2^m}$. This is a codeword in the linear code C_2, which has rate K/N. Since $a(Z)$ has degree $\leq K - 1$, it has at most $K - 1$ zeros, i.e. C_2 has minimum weight $D \geq N - K + 1$ (cf. Section 6.8). This is a completely constructive way of producing a sequence of Reed-Solomon codes. We proceed in a similar way to form the inner codes. If c_j is the jth symbol in a codeword of the outer code (still in the representation as polynomial over $\mathbb{F}_2$) we replace it by $(c_j, j(x)c_j)$, where multiplication is again to be taken mod $g(x)$. Finally, we interpret this as a $2m$-tuple of elements of $\mathbb{F}_2$.

(9.2.1) Definition. Let $m = 2 \cdot 3^{l-1}$, $N = 2^m - 1$. K will be chosen in a suitable way below; $D = N + 1 - K$. The binary code with word length $n := n_m := 2mN$ defined above will be denoted by $\mathscr{C}_m$. It is called a *Justesen code*. The dimension of $\mathscr{C}_m$ is $k := mK$ and the rate is $\frac{1}{2}K/N$.

In our analysis of $\mathscr{C}_m$ we use the same idea as in Section 9.1., namely the fact that a nonzero $2m$-tuple $(c_j, j(x)c_j)$ occurring in a codeword of $\mathscr{C}_m$ determines the value of j.

(9.2.2) Lemma. *Let $\gamma \in (0, 1)$, $\delta \in (0, 1)$. Let $(M_L)_{L \in \mathbb{N}}$ be a sequence of natural numbers with the property $M_L \cdot 2^{-L\delta} = \gamma + o(1)$ $(L \to \infty)$. Let W be the sum of the weights of M_L distinct words in $\mathbb{F}_2^L$. Then*

$$W \geq \gamma L 2^{L\delta}\{H^{\leftarrow}(\delta) + o(1)\}, \qquad (L \to \infty).$$

PROOF. For L sufficiently large we define

$$\lambda := H^{\leftarrow}\left(\delta - \frac{1}{\log L}\right).$$

By Theorem 1.4.5 we have

$$\sum_{0 \leq i \leq \lambda L} \binom{L}{i} \leq 2^{L(\delta - (1/\log L))}.$$

Hence

$$W \geq \left\{M_L - \sum_{0 \leq i \leq \lambda L} \binom{L}{i}\right\} \lambda L \geq \lambda L\{M_L - 2^{L(\delta - (1/\log L))}\}$$

$$= \lambda L 2^{L\delta}\{\gamma + o(1)\} = \gamma L 2^{L\delta}\{H^{\leftarrow}(\delta) + o(1)\}, \qquad (L \to \infty). \qquad \square$$

We choose a rate R, $0 < R < \frac{1}{2}$. The number K in (9.2.1) is taken to be the minimal value for which $R_m := \frac{1}{2}K/N \geq R$. This ensures that the sequence of codes $\mathscr{C}_m$ obtained by taking $l = 1, 2, \ldots$ in (9.2.1) has rate $R_m \to R$ $(l \to \infty)$ What about the minimum distance of $\mathscr{C}_m$? A nonzero word in the outer code has weight at least $N - K + 1 = D$.

Furthermore

(9.2.3) $\quad N - K + 1 > N - K = N(1 - 2R_m)$

$$= (2^m - 1)\{1 - 2R + o(1)\}, \qquad (m \to \infty).$$

Every nonzero symbol in a codeword of the outer code yields a $2m$-tuple $(c_j, j(x)c_j)$ in the corresponding codeword $\mathbf{c}$ of $\mathscr{C}_m$ and these must all be different (by the remark following (9.2.1)). Apply Lemma 9.2.2 to estimate the weight of $\mathbf{c}$. We take $L = 2m$, $\delta = \frac{1}{2}$, $\gamma = 1 - 2R$ and $M_L = D$. By (9.2.3) the conditions of the lemma are satisfied. Hence

$$w(\mathbf{c}) \geq (1 - 2R) \cdot 2m \cdot 2^m \{H^{\leftarrow}(\tfrac{1}{2}) + o(1)\}, \qquad (m \to \infty).$$

Therefore

$$d_m/n \geq (1 - 2R)\{H^{\leftarrow}(\tfrac{1}{2}) + o(1)\}, \qquad (m \to \infty),$$

We have proved the following theorem.

(9.2.4) Theorem. *Let* $0 < R < \frac{1}{2}$. *The Justesen codes* $\mathscr{C}_m$ *defined above have word length* $n = 2m(2^m - 1)$, *rate* R_m *and minimum distance* d_m, *where*

(i) $R_m \to R$, $(m \to \infty)$,
(ii) $\liminf_{m \to \infty} d_m/n \geq (1 - 2R)H^{\leftarrow}(\tfrac{1}{2})$.

Using the notation of Chapter 5, we now have $\delta \geq (1 - 2R)H^{\leftarrow}(\tfrac{1}{2})$ for values of R less than $\frac{1}{2}$. For the first time δ does not tend to 0 for $n \to \infty$.

A slight modification of the previous construction is necessary to achieve rates larger than $\frac{1}{2}$. Let $0 \leq s < m$ (we shall choose s later). Consider $\mathscr{C}_m$. For every $2m$-tuple $(c_j, j(x)c_j)$ in a codeword $\mathbf{c}$ we delete the last s symbols. The resulting code is denoted by $\mathscr{C}_{m,s}$. Let R be fixed, $0 < R < 1$. Given m and s, we choose for K the minimal integer such that $R_{m,s} := [m/(2m - s)](K/N) \geq R$ (this is possible if $m(2m - s) \geq R$). In the proof of Theorem 9.2.4 we used the fact that a codeword $\mathbf{c}$ contained at least D distinct nonzero $2m$-tuples $(c_j, j(x)c_j)$. By truncating we have obtained $(2m - s)$-tuples which are no longer necessarily distinct but each possible value will occur at most 2^s times. So there are at least

$$M_s := 2^{-s}(N - K) = 2^{-s}N\left(1 - \frac{2m - s}{m}R_{m,s}\right)$$

distinct $(2m - s)$-tuples in a codeword $\mathbf{c}$ of $\mathscr{C}_{m,s}$.

Again we apply Lemma 9.2.2, this time with

$$L = 2m - s, \qquad \delta = \frac{m - s}{L}, \qquad \gamma = 1 - \frac{2m - S}{m}R, \qquad M_L = M_s.$$

Let $d_{m,s}$ be the minimum distance of $\mathscr{C}_{m,s}$. We find

$$d_{m,s} \geq \left(1 - \frac{2m - s}{m}R\right)(2m - s)2^{m-s}\left\{H^{\leftarrow}\left(\frac{m - s}{2m - s}\right) + o(1)\right\}2^s, \qquad (m \to \infty).$$

Therefore

$$(9.2.5) \quad \frac{d_{m,s}}{n} \geq \left(1 - \frac{2m-s}{m}\, R\right)\left\{H^{-}\left(\frac{m-s}{2m-s}\right) + o(1)\right\}, \qquad (m \to \infty).$$

We must now find a choice of s which produces the best result. Let r be fixed, $r \in (\frac{1}{2}, 1)$. Take $s := \lfloor m(2r-1)/r \rfloor + 1$. If $r \geq R$ then we also have $m/(2m-s) \geq R$. From (9.2.5) we find

$$(9.2.6) \qquad \frac{d_{m,s}}{n} \geq \left(1 - \frac{R}{r}\right)\{H^{-}(1-r) + o(1)\}, \qquad (m \to \infty).$$

The right-hand side of (9.2.6) is maximal if r satisfies

$$(9.2.7) \qquad\qquad R = \frac{r^2}{1 + \log\{1 - H^{-}(1-r)\}}.$$

If the solution of (9.2.7) is less than $\frac{1}{2}$, we take $r = \frac{1}{2}$ instead. The following theorem summarizes this construction.

(9.2.8) Theorem. *Let $0 < R < 1$ and let r be the maximum of $\frac{1}{2}$ and the solution of (9.2.7). Let $s = \lfloor m(2r-1)/r \rfloor + 1$.*
The Justesen codes $\mathscr{C}_{m,s}$ have word length n, rate $R_{m,s}$, and minimum distance $d_{m,s}$, where

$$\liminf \frac{d_{m,s}}{n} \geq \left(1 - \frac{R}{r}\right)H^{-}(1-r).$$

In Figure 3 we compare the Justesen codes with the Gilbert bound. For $r > \frac{1}{2}$ the curve is the envelope of the lines given by (9.2.6).

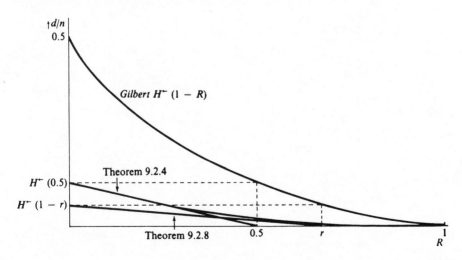

Figure 3

§9.3. Comments

The extremely simple idea of Section 9.1 has received very little attention up to now. A more serious attempt may lead to the discovery of explicit choices of α which yield relatively good codes (but see Problem 9.4.1). The discovery of the Justesen codes was one of the major developments in coding theory in the 1970s.

§9.4. Problems

9.4.1. Let $\mathbb{F}_{2^6}$ be represented as in Section 9.2. Show that there is no value of α for the construction of Section 9.1 such that C_α has distance greater than 3. Compare with other known $[12, k]$ codes with rate $\geq \frac{1}{2}$.

9.4.2. Let $\alpha(x)$ be a polynomial of degree $< k$. A $[2k, k]$ binary *double circulant code* consists of all words of the form $(a(x), \alpha(x)a(x))$, where multiplication is $\mod(x^k - 1)$. In this case the code is invariant under a simultaneous cyclic shift of both halves of the words. Construct a $[12, 6]$ code of this type which has $d = 4$.

9.4.3. Use the truncation method of Section 9.2 to show that the idea of Section 9.1 leads to codes meeting the Gilbert bound for any rate R.

CHAPTER 10

Arithmetic Codes

§10.1. AN Codes

In this chapter we shall give a brief introduction to codes which are used to check and correct arithmetic operations performed by a computer. Operations are now ordinary arithmetic and as a result the theory is quite different from the preceding chapters. However, there is in several places a similarity to the theory of cyclic codes. In some cases we shall leave the details of proofs to the reader. For further information on this area see the references mentioned in Section 10.4.

The arithmetic operations in this chapter are carried out with numbers represented in the number system with base r ($r \in \mathbb{N}, r \geq 2$). For practical purposes the binary case ($r = 2$) and the decimal case ($r = 10$) are the most important. The first thing we have to do is to find a suitable distance function. In the previous chapters we have used Hamming distance but that is not a suitable distance function for the present purposes. One error in an addition can cause many incorrect digits in the answer because of carry. We need a distance function that corresponds to arithmetical errors in the same way as Hamming distance corresponds to misprints in words.

(10.1.1) Definition. The *arithmetic weight* $w(x)$ of an integer x is the minimal $t \geq 0$ such that there is a representation

$$x = \sum_{i=1}^{t} a_i r^{n(i)},$$

with integers a_i, $n(i)$ for which $|a_i| < r$, $n(i) \geq 0$ ($i = 1, 2, \ldots, t$). The *arithmetic distance* $d(x, y)$ of two integers is defined by

$$d(x, y) := w(x - y).$$

It is easily checked that this is indeed a metric on $\mathbb{Z}$. Arithmetic distance is translation invariant, i.e. $d(x, y) = d(x + z, y + z)$. This is not true for the Hamming distance of two integers (in r-ary representation). Arithmetic distance is at most equal to the Hamming distance.

We shall consider codes C of the form

$$C := \{AN \mid N \in \mathbb{Z}, 0 \leq N < B\},$$

where A and B are fixed positive integers. Such codes are called *AN codes*. These codes are used in the following way. Suppose we wish to add two integers N_1 and N_2 (both positive and small compared to B). These are encoded as AN_1 and AN_2 and then these two integers are added. Let S be the sum. If no errors have been made, then we find $N_1 + N_2$ by dividing by A. If S is not divisible by A, i.e. errors have been made, we look for the code word AN_3 such that $d(S, AN_3)$ is minimal. The most likely value of $N_1 + N_2$ is N_3. In order to be able to correct all possible patterns of at most e errors it is again necessary and sufficient that the code C has minimum distance $\geq 2e + 1$. As before, that is equivalent to requiring that C has minimum weight at least $2e + 1$. These properties of the code C are based on the resemblance of C to the subgroup $H := \{AN \mid N \in \mathbb{Z}\}$ of $\mathbb{Z}$. It would not be a good idea to take H as our code because H has minimum weight ≤ 2 (see Problem 10.5.1).

In order to avoid this difficulty we shall consider so-called *modular AN codes*. Define $m := AB$. Now we can consider C as a subgroup of $\mathbb{Z}/m\mathbb{Z}$. This makes it necessary to modify our distance function. Consider the elements of $\mathbb{Z}/m\mathbb{Z}$ as vertices of a graph Γ_m and let $x \pmod m$ and $x' \pmod m$ be joined by an edge iff

$$x - x' \equiv \pm c \cdot r^j \pmod m$$

for some integers c, j with $0 < c < r, j \geq 0$.

(10.1.2) Definition. The *modular distance* $d_m(x, y)$ of two integers x and y (considered as elements of $\mathbb{Z}/m\mathbb{Z}$) is the distance of x and y in the graph Γ_m. The *modular weight* $w_m(x)$ of x is $d_m(x, 0)$. Note that

$$w_m(x) = \min\{w(y) \mid y \in \mathbb{Z}, y \equiv x \pmod m\}.$$

Although we now have achieved a strong resemblance to linear codes there is another difficulty. Not every choice of m makes good sense. For example, if we take $r = 3$, $A = 5$, $B = 7$, i.e. $m = 35$, then by (10.1.2) we have $d_m(0, 4) = 1$ because $4 \equiv 3^{10} \pmod{35}$. But it is not very realistic to consider errors in the position corresponding to 3^{10} when adding integers less than 35. Restricting j in the definition of edges of Γ_m also has drawbacks. It turns out that we get an acceptable theory if we take $m = r^n - 1$ ($n \in \mathbb{Z}, n \geq 2$). In practice this is also a good choice because many computers do arithmetic operations mod $2^n - 1$.

Every integer x has a unique representation

$$x \equiv \sum_{i=0}^{n-1} c_i r^i \quad (\text{mod } r^n - 1),$$

with $c_i \in \{0, 1, \ldots, r - 1\}$ $(0 \le i < n)$, not all $c_i = 0$. Hence $\mathbb{Z}/(r^n - 1)$ can be interpreted as the set of nonzero words of length n over the alphabet $\{0, 1, \ldots, r - 1\}$. Of course it would not have been necessary to exclude $\mathbf{0}$ if we had taken $m = r^n$, which is again a practical choice because many computers work mod 2^n. However, we cannot expect good codes for $r = 2$, $m = 2^n$. We would have to take $A = 2^k$ for some k and then the code C would consist of the integers $\sum_{i=0}^{n-1} c_i 2^i$, $c_i \in \{0, 1\}$, for which $c_0 = c_1 = \cdots = c_{k-1} = 0$. An integer x (mod B) would be encoded by adding k 0s to its representation. This would serve no purpose. For arbitrary r there are similar objections. The reader should convince himself that in the case $AB = m = r^n - 1$ modular distance is a natural function for arithmetic in $\mathbb{Z}/m\mathbb{Z}$ and that C behaves as a linear code. In fact we have an even stronger analogy with earlier chapters.

(10.1.3) Definition. A *cyclic AN code* of length n and base r is a subgroup C of $\mathbb{Z}/(r^n - 1)$. Such a code is a principal ideal in this ring, i.e. there are integers A and B such that $AB = r^n - 1$ and

$$C = \{AN | N \in \mathbb{Z}, 0 \le N < B\}.$$

As in Section 6.1, we call A the *generator* of C. By now it will not be surprising to the reader that we are primarily interested in codes C with a large *rate* $(= (1/n) \log_r B)$ and a large minimum distance. The terminology of (10.1.3) is in accordance with (6.1.1). If $x \in C$ then rx (mod $r^n - 1$) is also a codeword because C is a group and rx (mod $r^n - 1$) is indeed a cyclic shift of x (both represented in base r). The integer B can be compared with the check polynomial of a cyclic code.

The idea of negacyclic codes can be generalized in the same way by taking $m = r^n + 1$ and then considering subgroups of $\mathbb{Z}/m\mathbb{Z}$.

(10.1.4) EXAMPLE. Let $r = 2$, $n = 11$. Then $m = r^n - 1 = 2047$. We take $A = 23$, $B = 89$. We obtain the cyclic AN code consisting of 89 multiples of 23 up to 2047. There are 22 ways to make one error, corresponding to the integers $\pm 2^j$ $(0 \le j < 11)$. These are exactly the integers mod 23 except 0. Therefore every integer in $[1,2047]$ has modular distance 0 or 1 to exactly one codeword. This cyclic AN code is therefore *perfect*. It is a generalization of the Hamming codes.

§10.2. The Arithmetic and Modular Weight

In order to be able to construct AN codes that correct more than one error we need an easy way to calculate the arithmetic or modular weight of an integer.

By Definition 10.1.1 every integer x can be written as

$$x = \sum_{i=1}^{w(x)} a_i r^{n(i)}$$

with integers a_i, $n(i)$, $|a_i| < r$, $n(i) \geq 0$ $(i = 1, \ldots, w(x))$. It is easy to find examples which show that this representation is not unique. We shall put some more restrictions on the coefficients which will make the representation unique.

(10.2.1) Definition. Let $b \in \mathbb{Z}$, $c \in \mathbb{Z}$, $|b| < r$, $|c| < r$. The pair (b, c) is called *admissible* if one of the following holds

(i) $bc = 0$,
(ii) $bc > 0$ and $|b + c| < r$,
(iii) $bc < 0$ and $|b| > |c|$.

Note that if $r = 2$ we must have possibility (i). Therefore a representation $x = \sum_{i=0}^{\infty} c_i 2^i$ in which all pairs (c_{i+1}, c_i) are admissible has no two adjacent nonzero digits. This led to the name *nonadjacent form* (*NAF*) which we now generalize.

(10.2.2) Definition. A representation

$$x = \sum_{i=0}^{\infty} c_i r^i,$$

with $c_i \in \mathbb{Z}$, $|c_i| < r$ for all i and $c_i = 0$ for all large i is called an *NAF* for x if for every $i \geq 0$ the pair (c_{i+1}, c_i) is admissible.

(10.2.3) Theorem. *Every integer x has exactly one* NAF. *If this is*

$$x = \sum_{i=0}^{\infty} c_i r^i,$$

then

$$w(x) = |\{i \mid i \geq 0, c_i \neq 0\}|.$$

PROOF.

(a) Suppose x is represented as $\sum_{i=0}^{\infty} b_i r^i$, $|b_i| < r$. Let i be the minimal value such that the pair (b_{i+1}, b_i) is not admissible. W.l.o.g. $b_i > 0$ (otherwise consider $-x$). Replace b_i by $b_i' := b_i - r$ and replace b_{i+1} by $b_{i+1}' := b_{i+1} + 1$ (if $b_{i+1} + 1 = r$ we carry forward). If $b_{i+1} > 0$ we either have $b_{i+1}' = 0$ or $b_i' b_{i+1}' < 0$ and $b_{i+1}' = b_{i+1} + 1 > r - b_i = |b_i'|$ since (b_{i+1}, b_i) was not admissible. If $b_{i+1} < 0$ then $b_{i+1}' = 0$ or $b_i' b_{i+1}' > 0$ and $|b_i' + b_{i+1}'| = r - b_i - b_{i+1} - 1 < r$ because $-b_{i+1} \leq b_i$ as (b_{i+1}, b_i) is not admissible. So (b_{i+1}', b_i') is admissible and one checks in the same way that (b_i', b_{i-1}) is admissible. In this way we can construct an NAF and in the process the weight of the representation does not increase.

(b) It remains to show that the NAF is unique. Suppose some x has two such representations $x = \sum_{i=0}^{\infty} c_i r^i = \sum_{i=0}^{\infty} c_i' r^i$. W.l.o.g. we may assume $c_0 \neq c_0'$, $c_0 > 0$. Therefore $c_0' = c_0 - r$. It follows that $c_1' \in \{c_1 + 1 - r, c_1 + 1, c_1 + 1 + r\}$. If $c_1' = c_1 + 1 - r$ then $c_1 \geq 0$ and hence $c_0 + c_1 \leq r - 1$. Since $c_0' c_1' > 0$ we must have $-c_0' - c_1' < r$, i.e. $r - c_0 + r - c_1 - 1 < r$, so $c_0 + c_1 > r - 1$, a contradiction. In the same way the assumptions $c_1' = c_1 + 1$ resp. $c_1' = c_1 + 1 + r$ lead to a contradiction. Therefore the NAF is unique. $\square$

A direct way to find the NAF of an integer x is provided in the next theorem.

(10.2.4) Theorem. *Let $x \in \mathbb{Z}$, $x \geq 0$. Let the r-ary representations of $(r + 1)x$ and x be*

$$(r + 1)x = \sum_{j=0}^{\infty} a_j r^j, \qquad x = \sum_{j=0}^{\infty} b_j r^j.$$

with $a_j, b_j \in \{0, 1, \ldots, r - 1\}$ for all j and $a_j = b_j = 0$ for j sufficiently large. Then the NAF for x is

$$x = \sum_{j=0}^{\infty} (a_{j+1} - b_{j+1}) r^j.$$

PROOF. We calculate the numbers a_j by adding $\sum_{j=0}^{\infty} b_j r^j$ and $\sum_{j=0}^{\infty} b_j r^{j+1}$. Let the carry sequence be $\varepsilon_0, \varepsilon_1, \ldots$, so $\varepsilon_0 = 0$ and $\varepsilon_i := \lfloor (\varepsilon_{i-1} + b_{i-1} + b_i)/r \rfloor$. We find that $a_i = \varepsilon_{i-1} + b_{i-1} + b_i - \varepsilon_i r$. If we denote $a_i - b_i$ by c_i then $c_i = \varepsilon_{i-1} + b_{i-1} - \varepsilon_i r$. We must now check whether (c_{i+1}, c_i) is an admissible pair. That $|c_{i+1} + c_i| < r$ is a trivial consequence of the definition of ε_i. Suppose $c_i > 0$, $c_{i+1} < 0$. Then $\varepsilon_i = 0$. We then have $c_i = \varepsilon_{i-1} + b_{i-1}$, $c_{i+1} = b_i - r$ and the condition $|c_{i+1}| > |c_i|$ is equivalent to $\varepsilon_{i-1} + b_{i-1} + b_i < r$, i.e. $\varepsilon_i = 0$. The final case is similar. $\square$

The NAF for x provides us with a simple estimate for x as shown by the next theorem.

(10.2.5) Theorem. *If we denote the maximal value of i for which $c_i \neq 0$ in an NAF for x by $i(x)$ and define $i(0) := -1$ then*

$$i(x) \leq k \Leftrightarrow |x| < \frac{r^{k+2}}{r + 1}.$$

We leave the completely elementary proof to the reader.

From Section 10.1 it will be clear that we must now generalize these ideas in some way to modular representations. We take $m = r^n - 1$, $n \geq 2$.

(10.2.6) Definition. A representation

$$x \equiv \sum_{i=0}^{n-1} c_i r^i \quad (\bmod\ m),$$

with $c_i \in \mathbb{Z}$, $|c_i| < r$ is called a *CNAF* (=*cyclic NAF*) for x if (c_{i+1}, c_i) is admissible for $i = 0, 1, \ldots, n - 1$; here $c_n := c_0$.

The next two theorems on CNAF's are straightforward generalizations of Theorem 10.2.3 and can be obtained from this theorem or by using Theorem 10.2.4. A little care is necessary because of the exception but the reader should have no difficulty proving the theorems.

(10.2.7) Theorem. *Every integer x has a CNAF mod m; this CNAF is unique except if*

$$(r + 1)x \equiv 0 \not\equiv x \quad (\bmod\ m)$$

in which case there are two CNAFs for x (mod m). If $x \equiv \sum_{i=0}^{n-1} c_i r^i \pmod{m}$ is a CNAF for x then

$$w_m(x) = |\{i | 0 \le i < n, c_i \ne 0\}|.$$

(10.2.8) Theorem. *If $(r + 1)x \equiv 0 \not\equiv x \pmod{m}$ then $w_m(x) = n$ except if $n \equiv 0 \pmod{2}$ and $x \equiv \pm[m/(r + 1)] \pmod{m}$, in which case $w_m(x) = \frac{1}{2}n$.*

If we have an NAF for x for which $c_{n-1} = 0$ then the additional requirement for this to be a CNAF is satisfied. Therefore Theorem 10.2.5 implies the following theorem.

(10.2.9) Theorem. *An integer x has a CNAF with $c_{n-1} = 0$ iff there is a $y \in \mathbb{Z}$ with $x \equiv y \pmod{m}$, $|y| \le m/(r + 1)$.*

This theorem leads to another way of finding the modular weight of an integer.

(10.2.10) Theorem. *For $x \in \mathbb{Z}$ we have $w_m(x) = |\{ j | 0 \le j < n$, there is a $y \in \mathbb{Z}$ with*

$$m/(r + 1) < y \le mr/(r + 1),\ y \equiv r^j x \ (\bmod\ m)\}|.$$

PROOF. Clearly a CNAF for rx is a cyclic shift of a CNAF for x, i.e. $w_m(rx) = w_m(x)$. Suppose $x \equiv \sum_{i=0}^{n-1} c_i r^i \pmod{m}$ is a CNAF and $c_{n-1-j} = 0$. Then $r^j x$ has a CNAF with 0 as coefficient of r^{n-1}. By Theorem 10.2.9 this is the case iff there is a y with $y \equiv r^j x \pmod{m}$ and $|y| \le m/(r + 1)$. Since the modular weight is the number of nonzero coefficients, the assertion now follows unless we are in one of the exceptional cases of Theorem 10.2.7 but then the result follows from Theorem 10.2.8. $\qquad \square$

§10.3. Mandelbaum–Barrows Codes

We now introduce a class of cyclic multiple-error-correcting AN codes which is a generalization of codes introduced by J. T. Barrows and D. Mandelbaum. We first need a theorem on modular weights in cyclic AN codes.

(10.3.1) Theorem. *Let $C \subset \mathbb{Z}/(r^n - 1)$ be a cyclic AN code with generator A and let*

$$B := (r^n - 1)/A = |C|.$$

Then

$$\sum_{x \in C} w_m(x) = n\left(\left\lfloor \frac{rB}{r+1} \right\rfloor - \left\lfloor \frac{B}{r+1} \right\rfloor \right).$$

PROOF. We assume that every $x \in C$ has a unique CNAF

$$x \equiv \sum_{i=0}^{n-1} c_{i,x} r^i \quad (\text{mod } r^n - 1).$$

The case where C has an element with two CNAFs is slightly more difficult. We leave it to the reader. We must determine the number of nonzero coefficients $c_{i,x}$, where $0 \le i \le n - 1$ and $x \in C$, which we consider as elements of a matrix. Since C is cyclic every column of this matrix has the same number of zeros. So the number to be determined is equal to $n|\{x \in C | c_{n-1,x} \neq 0\}|$. By Theorem 10.2.9 we have $c_{n-1,x} \neq 0$ iff there is a $y \in \mathbb{Z}$ with $y \equiv x \pmod{r^n - 1}$, $m/(r+1) < y \le mr/(r+1)$. Since x has the form AN $(\text{mod } r^n - 1)$ $(0 \le N < B)$, we must have $B/(r+1) < N \le Br/(r+1)$. $\square$

The expression in Theorem 10.3.1 is nearly equal to $n|C|[(r-1)/(r+1)]$ and hence the theorem resembles our earlier result

$$\sum_{x \in C} w(x) = n|C| \cdot \frac{q-1}{q}$$

for a linear code C (cf. (3.7.5)).

The next theorem introduces the generalized *Mandelbaum–Barrows codes* and shows that these codes are *equidistant*.

(10.3.2) Theorem. *Let B be a prime number that does not divide r with the property that $(\mathbb{Z}/B\mathbb{Z})$ is generated by the elements r and -1. Let n be a positive integer with $r^n \equiv 1 \pmod{B}$ and let $A := (r^n - 1)/B$. Then the code $C \subset \mathbb{Z}/(r^n - 1)$ generated by A is an equidistant code with distance*

$$\frac{n}{(B-1)}\left(\left\lfloor \frac{rB}{r+1} \right\rfloor - \left\lfloor \frac{B}{r+1} \right\rfloor \right).$$

PROOF. Let $x \in C$, $x \neq 0$. Then $x = AN \pmod{r^n - 1}$, with $N \not\equiv 0 \pmod{B}$. Our assumptions imply that there is a j such that $N \equiv \pm r^j \pmod{B}$. Therefore $w_m(x) = w_m(\pm r^j A) = w_m(A)$. This shows that C is equidistant and then the constant weight follows from Theorem 10.3.1. $\qquad \square$

The Mandelbaum–Barrows codes correspond to the minimal cyclic codes M_i^- of Section 6.2. Notice that these codes have word length at least $\frac{1}{2}(B - 1)$ which is large with respect to the number of codewords which is B. So, for practical purposes these codes do not seem to be important.

§10.4. Comments

The reader interested in more information about arithmetic codes is referred to W. W. Peterson and E. J. Weldon [53], J. L. Massey and O. N. Garcia [48], T. R. N. Rao [58]. Perfect single error-correcting cyclic AN codes have been studied extensively. We refer to M. Goto [28], M. Goto and T. Fukumara [29], and V. M. Gritsenko [31]. A perfect single error-correcting cyclic AN code with $r = 10$ or $r = 2^k$ $(k > 1)$ does not exist.

For more details about the NAF and CNAF we refer to W. E. Clark and J. J. Liang [14], [15]. References for binary Mandelbaum–Barrows codes can be found in [48]. There is a class of cyclic AN codes which has some resemblance to BCH codes. These can be found in C. L. Chen, R. T. Chien and C. K. Liu [12].

For more information about perfect arithmetic codes we refer to a contribution with that title by H. W. Lenstra in the Séminaire Delange–Pisot–Poitou (Théorie des Nombres, 1977/78).

§10.5. Problems

10.5.1. Prove that $\min\{w(AN) | N \in \mathbb{Z}, N \neq 0\} \leq 2$ for every $A \in \mathbb{Z}$ if w is as defined in (10.1.1).

10.5.2. Generalize (10.1.4). Find an example with $r = 3$.

10.5.3. Consider ternary representations mod $3^6 - 1$. Find a CNAF for 455 using the method of the proof of Theorem 10.2.3.

10.5.4. Determine the words of the Mandelbaum–Barrows code with $B = 11$, $r = 3$, $n = 5$.

CHAPTER 11

Convolutional Codes

§11.1. Introduction

The codes which we consider in this chapter are quite different from those in previous chapters. They are not block codes, i.e., the words do not have constant length. Although there are analogies and connections to block codes, there is one big difference, namely that the mathematical theory of convolutional codes is not well developed. This is one of the reasons that mathematicians find it difficult to become interested in these codes.

However, in our introduction we gave communication with satellites as one of the most impressive examples of the use of coding theory and at present one of the main tools used in this area is convolutional coding! Therefore a short introduction to the subject seems appropriate. For a comparison of block and convolutional codes we refer to [51, Section 11.4]. After the introductory sections we treat a few of the more mathematical aspects of the subject. The main area of research of investigators of these codes is the reduction of decoding complexity. We do not touch on these aspects and we must refer the interested reader to the literature.

In this chapter we assume that the alphabet is binary. The generalization to $\mathbb{F}_q$ is straightforward. Every introduction to convolutional coding seems to use the same example. Adding one more instance to the list might strengthen the belief of some students that no other examples exist, but nevertheless we shall use this canonical example.

In Figure 4 we demonstrate the encoding device for our code. The three squares are storage elements (flip-flops) which can be in one of two possible states which we denote by 0 and 1. The system is governed by an external clock which produces a signal every t_0 seconds (for the sake of simplicity we choose our unit of time such that $t_0 = 1$). The effect of this signal is that the

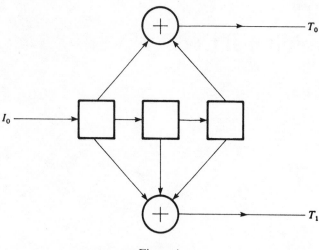

Figure 4

contents of the flip-flops move in the direction of the arrows to the next element of this so-called *shift register*. The elements ⊕ indicate mod 2 *adders*. For every pulse of the clock, we see that the contents of the first and third flip-flop are added and then leave the encoder via the stream T_0. The information to be processed enters on the left as stream I_0. Notice that the first flip-flop is actually superfluous since it only serves to divide the input stream into three directions. The second and third element of the shift register show the essential difference with block coding. They are *memory* elements which see to it that at time t the input signals for $t - 1$ and $t - 2$ are still available. The output depends on these three input symbols. In practice the output streams T_0 and T_1 are interlaced to produce one output stream. So, if we start with (0 0 0) in the register and have a message stream consisting of 1 followed by 0s, we see that the register first changes to (1 0 0) and yields the output (1 1); then it moves to (0 1 0) with output (0 1); subsequently (0 0 1) with output (1 1) and then back to the original state and a stream of 0s.

An efficient way of describing the action of this encoder is given by the *state diagram* of Figure 5. Here the contents of the second and third flip-flop are called the state of the register. We connect two states by a solid edge if the register goes from one to the other by an input 0. Similarly a dashed edge corresponds to an input 1. Along these edges we indicate in brackets the two outputs at T_0, T_1. An input stream I_0 corresponds to a walk through the graph of Figure 5.

A mathematical description of this encoding procedure can be given as follows. Describe the input stream $i_0, i_1, i_2, \ldots$ by the formal power series $I_0(x) := i_0 + i_1 x + i_2 x^2 + \cdots$ with coefficients in $\mathbb{F}_2$. Similarly describe the outputs at T_0 and T_1 by power series $T_0(x)$ resp. $T_1(x)$. We synchronize time in such a way that first input corresponds to first output. Then it is clear that

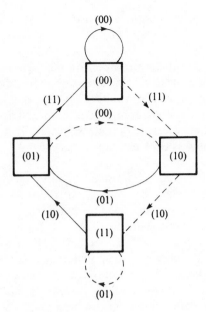

Figure 5

$$T_0(x) = (1 + x^2)I_0(x),$$
$$T_1(x) = (1 + x + x^2)I_0(x).$$

The interlacing of T_0 and T_1 then is described by

$$T(x) = T_0(x^2) + xT_1(x^2).$$

In our example we had input $I_0(x) = 1$ and the output sequence

$$11 \ 01 \ 11 \ 00 \ 00 \ \ldots$$

which is

$$G(x) := 1 + x + x^3 + x^4 + x^5 = (1 + (x^2)^2) + x(1 + (x^2) + (x^2)^2).$$

So if we define $I(x) := I_0(x^2)$, then

$$(11.1.1) \qquad\qquad T(x) = G(x)I(x).$$

For obvious reasons we say that the rate of this convolutional code is $\frac{1}{2}$. As usual, the code is the set of possible output sequences $T(x)$. The polynomial $G(x)$ is sometimes called the *generator polynomial* of this code.

In the description given above, the information symbol i_v entering the shift register influences six of the symbols of the transmitted sequence. This number is called the *constraint length* of the code. The constraint length equals $1 + $ degree $G(x)$. The reader is warned that there are at least two other definitions of constraint length used by other authors (one of these is: the length of the shift register, e.g. in Figure 4 this is 3). In our example we say that the *memory* associated with the convolutional code is 2 because the encoder must remember two previous inputs to generate output when i_v is presented.

We know that one of the most important numbers connected to a block code C is its minimum distance. For convolutional codes there is a similar concept which again plays a central rôle in the study of decoding. This number is called the *free distance* of the code and is defined to be the minimum weight of all nonzero output sequences. In the example treated above, this free distance is the weight of $G(x)$, i.e. 5.

In a completely analogous way, we now introduce rate $1/n$ convolutional codes. We have one sequence of information symbols given by the series $I_0(x)$. There are n sequences leaving the shift register: $T_0(x), T_1(x), \ldots, T_{n-1}(x)$, where each encoded sequence $T_i(x)$ is obtained by multiplying $I_0(x)$ by some polynomial $G_i(x)$. The transmitted sequence $T(x)$ is $\sum_{i=0}^{n-1} x^i T_i(x^n)$. As before, we define $I(x) := I_0(x^n)$ and $G(x) := \sum_{i=0}^{n-1} x^i G_i(x^n)$. Then $T(x) = G(x)I(x)$.

It is obvious that the choice of the polynomials $G_i(x)$ ($i = 0, 1, \ldots, n-1$) determines whether the code is good or bad, whatever we decide this to mean. Let us now describe a situation that is obviously bad. Suppose that the input stream $I_0(x)$ contains an infinite number of 1s but that the corresponding output stream $T(x)$ has only finitely many 1s. If the channel accidentally makes errors in the position of these 1s the resulting all-zero output stream will be interpreted by the receiver as coming from input $I_0(x) = 0$. Therefore a finite number of channel errors has then caused an infinite number of decoding errors! Such a code is called a *catastrophic code*. There is an easy way to avoid that the rate $1/n$ convolutional code is catastrophic, namely by requiring that

$$\text{g.c.d.}(G_0(x), G_1(x), \ldots, G_{n-1}(x)) = 1.$$

It is well known that this implies that there are polynomials $a_i(x)$ ($i = 0, \ldots, n-1$) such that $\sum_{i=0}^{n-1} a_i(x)G_i(x) = 1$. From this we find

$$\sum_{i=0}^{n-1} a_i(x^n) T_i(x^n) = \sum_{i=0}^{n-1} a_i(x^n) G_i(x^n) I_0(x^n) = I(x),$$

i.e. the input can be determined from the output and furthermore a finite number of errors in $T(x)$ cannot cause an infinite number of decoding errors.

There are two ways of describing the generalization to rate k/n codes. We now have k shift registers with input streams $I_0(x), \ldots, I_{k-1}(x)$. There are n output streams $T_i(x)$ ($i = 0, \ldots, n-1$), where $T_i(x)$ is formed using all the shift registers. We first use the method which was used above. Therefore we now need kn polynomials $G_{ij}(x)$ ($i = 0, \ldots, k-1$; $j = 0, \ldots, n-1$) to describe the situation. We have

$$T_j(x) = \sum_{i=0}^{k-1} G_{ij}(x)I_i(x).$$

It is no longer possible to describe the encoding with one generator polynomial. We prefer the following way of describing rate k/n convolutional codes which makes them into block codes over a suitably chosen field.

Let $\mathscr{F}$ be the quotient field of $\mathbb{F}_2[x]$, i.e. the field of all Laurent series of the form

$$\sum_{i=r}^{\infty} a_i x^i, \qquad (r \in \mathbb{Z}, a_i \in \mathbb{F}_2).$$

We consider the k bits entering the different shift registers at time t as a vector in $\mathbb{F}_2^k$. This means that the input sequences are interpreted as a vector in $\mathscr{F}^k$ (like in Chapter 3 the vectors are row vectors). We now consider the kn polynomials $G_{ij}(x)$ as the elements of a generator matrix G. Of course the n output sequences can be seen as an element of $\mathscr{F}^n$. This leads to the following definition.

(11.1.2) Definition. A rate k/n binary *convolutional code* C is a k-dimensional subspace of $\mathscr{F}^n$ which has a basis of k vectors from $\mathbb{F}[x]^n$. These basis vectors are the rows of G.

Although this shows some analogy to block codes we are hiding the difficulty by using $\mathscr{F}$ and furthermore the restriction on the elements of G is quite severe. In practice all messages are finite and we can assume that there is silence for $t < 0$. This means that we do not really need $\mathscr{F}$ and can do everything with $\mathbb{F}[x]$. Since this is not a field, there will be other difficulties for that approach.

When discussing block codes, we pointed out that for a given code there are several choices of G, some of which may make it easier to analyze C. The same situation occurs for convolutional codes. For such a treatment of generator matrices we refer the reader to [23]. This is one of the few examples of a mathematical analysis of convolutional codes.

§11.2. Decoding of Convolutional Codes

There are several algorithms used in practice for decoding convolutional codes. They are more or less similar and all mathematically not very deep. In fact they resemble the decoding of block codes by simply comparing a received word with all codewords. Since the codewords of a convolutional code are infinitely long this comparison has to be truncated, i.e., one only considers the first l symbols of the received message. After the comparison one decides on say the first information symbol and then repeats the procedure for subsequent symbols. We sketch the so-called *Viterbi-algorithm* in more detail using the example of Figures 4 and 5.

Suppose the received message is 10 00 01 10 00.... The diagram of Figure 6 shows the possible states at time $t = 0, 1, 2, 3$, the arrows showing the path through Figure 5. Four of the lines in Figure 6 are dashed and these

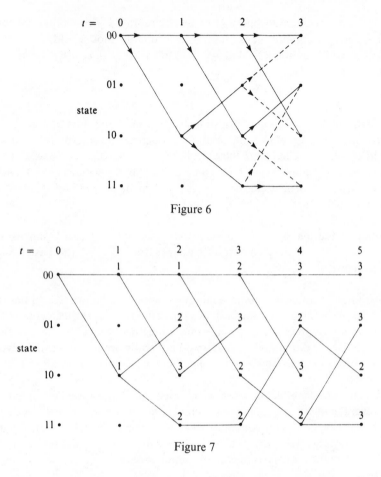

Figure 6

Figure 7

will be omitted in the next figure. To see why, let us assume that at $t = 3$ the register is in the state 00. One way to get in this state is the horizontal path which would correspond to output 00 00 00... and hence this assumption means that at $t = 3$ two errors have already been made. If, on the other hand the state 00 was reached via 10 and 01, there would have been output 11 01 11 and so there are already three errors. We do not know whether the register is in state 00 but if it is, then the horizontal path is the more likely way of having gotten there. Furthermore this path involves two errors. Let us extend Figure 6 to Figure 7 where $t = 4$ and $t = 5$ are included and we also show the number of errors involved in reaching the different stages.

Of course it can happen that there are two equally likely ways to reach a certain state in which case one chooses one of them and discards the other. Corresponding to each time and state, one can list the most likely outputs corresponding to that assumption. In this way Figure 7 would lead to the following list of outputs.

		$t = 1$	$t = 2$	$t = 3$	$t = 4$	$t = 5$
	00	00	00 00	00 00 00	00 00 00 00	00 00 00 00 00
state	01	—	11 01	00 11 01	11 10 01 10	00 00 11 10 10
	10	11	00 11	00 00 11	00 00 00 11	11 10 01 10 00
	11	—	11 10	11 10 01	00 00 11 10	00 00 11 10 01

Clearly at $t = 5$ a maximum likelihood decision would be that the register is in state 10, that two errors have been made and that the output was 11 10 01 10 00. The corresponding input can be found from Figure 7. The easiest way is to mark each edge with the input symbol corresponding to that edge. We leave it to the reader to invent several ways of continuing after truncation. It is clear that we have come upon problems of computing time and storage. A mathematically more interesting question is to calculate the effect of an incorrect decision on subsequent decoding decisions and also to find out what is the influence of the free distance of the code on the decoding accuracy. For a more detailed treatment of these questions we refer to [51].

§11.3. An Analog of the Gilbert Bound for Some Convolutional Codes

We consider a special class of rate k/n convolutional codes, namely those defined as follows. Take the k input sequences $I_0(x), \ldots, I_{k-1}(x)$ and form

$$I(x) := \sum_{i=0}^{k-1} x^i I_i(x^n).$$

This means that every n-tuple of information bits ends in $n - k$ zeros. Take a generator polynomial $G(x)$ and define output by $T(x) = G(x)I(x)$. This corresponds to a special choice of the polynomials $G_{ij}(x)$ in our earlier description of rate k/n codes. As before, we define the constraint length to be $l + 1 = 1 + $ degree $G(x)$ and we consider only codes for which $l + 1 \le mn$, where m is fixed. We are interested in the free distance d_f of such codes. Clearly $d_f \le l + 1$. By shifting the time scale, we see that in studying the encoding procedure we may make the restriction that $i_0 = t_0 = G(0) = 1$. For every initial mn-tuple $1 = t_0, t_1, \ldots, t_{mn-1}$ of an output sequence and every initial mk-tuple $1 = i_0, i_1, \ldots, i_{mk-1}$, there is exactly one polynomial $G(x)$ of degree $\le mn$ such that these initial sequences are in accordance with $T(x) = G(x)I(x)$. We wish to exclude all initial segments of $T(x)$ which have weight $< d$. This means that we exclude at most $2^{mk-1} \sum_{i=0}^{d-2} \binom{mm-1}{i}$ poly-nomials with $G(0) = 1$ as generators. Hence there is a choice of $G(x)$ yielding at least the required free distance if

$$2^{mk} \sum_{i=0}^{d} \binom{mn}{i} < 2^{mn}.$$

Taking $d = \lambda mn$ and writing $R := k/n$, we have from Theorem 1.4.5(i) by taking logarithms ·

$$\frac{1}{mn} \log \sum_{i=0}^{d} \binom{mn}{i} < H(\lambda) < 1 - R,$$

if

$$\lambda < H^-(1 - R).$$

Here λ is the quotient of the free distance and the constraint length. This bound should be compared with Theorem 5.1.9.

§11.4. Construction of Convolutional Codes from Cyclic Block Codes

Since quite a lot is known about block codes, it is not surprising that several authors have used good block codes to construct convolutional codes with desirable properties. In this section we describe one of the methods which were developed.

We use the notation of Section 4.5.

(11.4.1) Lemma. *Let* $q = 2^r$, $P(x) \in \mathbb{F}_q[x]$, $c \in \mathbb{F}_q \backslash \{0\}$, $n \geq 0$, $N \geq 0$. *Then*

$$w(P(x)(x^n - c)^N) \geq w((x - c)^N) \cdot w(P(x) \bmod (x^n - c)).$$

PROOF. Write $P(x)$ as $\sum_{i=0}^{n-1} x^i Q_i(x^n)$. Then by Theorem 4.5.2 we have

$$w(P(x)(x^n - c)^N) = \sum_{i=0}^{n-1} w(Q_i(x)(x - c)^N)$$

$$\geq \sum_{i=0}^{n-1} w(Q_i(c))w((x - c)^N)$$

$$= w((x - c)^N) \cdot w\left(\sum_{i=0}^{n-1} Q_i(c)x^i\right)$$

$$= w((x - c)^N) \cdot w(P(x) \bmod (x^n - c)). \qquad \square$$

REMARK. It is not difficult to prove Lemma 11.4.1 for an arbitrary field $\mathbb{F}_q$.

(11.4.2) Theorem. *Let* $g(x)$ *be the generator of a cyclic code of length* n *(odd) over* $\mathbb{F}_q$ *(*$q = 2^r$*) with minimum distance* d_g *and let* $h(x)$ *be the parity check polynomial and* d_h *the minimum distance of the code with generator* $h(x)$. *Then* *the convolutional code with rate $1/(2m)$ over the same field and with generator $G(x) = g(x)$ is noncatastrophic and satisfies $d_f \geq \min\{d_g, 2d_h\}$.*

PROOF.

(i) Write $G(x) = \sum_{j=0}^{2m-1} x^j (\hat{G}_j(x^m))^2$. If we consider the representation of the convolutional code with polynomials $G_0(x), \ldots, G_{2m-1}(x)$ as in Section 11.1, then for any irreducible common factor $A(x)$ of these polynomials $G(x)$ would be divisible by $A^2(x)$ which is impossible since n is odd and $g(x)$ divides $x^n - 1$. So the code is noncatastrophic.

(ii) Consider an information sequence $I_0(x)$. We have $T(x) = G(x)I_0(x^{2m}) = G(x)(\hat{I}_0(x^m))^2$, and therefore $T(x)$ has the form

$$T(x) = P(x)(g(x))^{2i+1}(h(x))^{2j}$$

with $i \geq 0$, $j \geq 0$, $P(x) \neq 0$, $P(x)$ not divisible by $g(x)$ or $h(x)$. We consider two cases:

(a) Let $i \geq j$. Then we find

$$T(x) = P(x)(g(x))^{2(i-j)+1}(x^n - 1)^{2j}$$

and then Lemma 11.4.1 yields

$$w(T(x)) \geq w((x - 1)^{2j}) \cdot w(P(x)(g(x))^{2(i-j)+1} \bmod(x^n - 1)) \geq d_g$$

since the second factor concerns a codeword in the cyclic code generated by $g(x)$.

(b) Let $i < j$. We then find

$$T(x) = P(x)(h(x))^{2(j-i)-1}(x^n - 1)^{2i+1}$$

and then Lemma 11.4.1 yields $w(T(x)) \geq 2d_h$ because

$$w((x - 1)^{2i+1}) \geq 2. \qquad \square$$

Before looking at more examples of this argument, we discuss a bound for the free distance. Consider a convolutional code with rate $1/n$ over $\mathbb{F}_q$ with generator polynomial $G(x) = \sum_{i=0}^{n-1} x^i G_i(x^n)$. Let

$$L := n(1 + \max\{\text{degree } G_i(x) | 0 \leq i \leq n - 1\}).$$

(Some authors call L the constraint length.) It is obvious that

$$d_f \leq L.$$

This trivial bound has a certain analogy with the Singleton bound $d \leq n - k + 1$ for block codes. We shall now describe a construction due to J. Justesen [38] of convolutional codes which meet this bound. First we show that this requirement yields a bound on L.

(11.4.3) Lemma. *If a rate $1/n$ convolutional code over $\mathbb{F}_q$ has $d_f = L$ then $L \leq nq$.*

PROOF. If $d_f = L$ then each of the polynomials $G_i(x)$ has weight L/n. We consider input sequences $I_0(x) = 1 + \alpha x$ where α runs through $\mathbb{F}_q \setminus \{0\}$ and determine the average weight $\bar{w}$ of the corresponding encoded sequences. We find

$$\bar{w} = (q-1)^{-1} \sum_{\alpha \in \mathbb{F}_q \setminus \{0\}} \sum_{i=0}^{n-1} w(G_i(x)(1 + \alpha x))$$

$$= (q-1)^{-1} n \left\{ 2(q-1) + \left(\frac{L}{n} - 1\right)(q-2) \right\}.$$

Since $\bar{w} \geq L$, we must have $L \leq nq$. □

By using a method similar to the one of Theorem 11.4.2, we can give an easy example of a convolutional code with $d_f = L$.

(11.4.4) EXAMPLE. Let α be a primitive element of $\mathbb{F}_4$. Let $g_1(x) := x^2 + \alpha x + 1$, $g_2(x) = x^2 + \alpha^2 x + 1$. Then $(x^5 - 1) = (x - 1)g_1(x)g_2(x)$ and $g_1(x)$ and $g_2(x)$ are relatively prime. We consider a rate $\frac{1}{2}$ convolutional code C over $\mathbb{F}_4$ with generator polynomial

$$G(x) := g_1(x^2) + xg_2(x^2).$$

The code is noncatastrophic. We write an information sequence as $I_0(x) = I_0'(x)(x^5 - 1)^N$ where N is maximal. By Lemma 11.4.1 we have

$$w(T(x)) = w(g_1(x)I_0(x)) + w(g_2(x)I_0(x))$$
$$\geq w((x-1)^N) \cdot \{w(g_1(x)I_0'(x) \bmod (x^5 - 1))$$
$$+ w(g_2(x)I_0'(x) \bmod (x^5 - 1))\}.$$

Now, if $I_0'(x)$ is not a multiple of $(x-1)g_1(x)$ or $(x-1)g_2(x)$, then the BCH bound shows that both terms in the second factor on the right are ≥ 3. If on the other hand $I_0'(x)$ is a multiple of $(x-1)g_1(x)$, then both terms on the right in the top line are even (because of the factor $x - 1$) and both are positive. If the second one is 2, then the first one is at least 4, again by the BCH bound. Therefore C has free distance at least 6. Since $L = 6$, we have $d_f = L$.

To generalize the idea behind Theorem 11.4.2 in order to construct rate $\frac{1}{2}$ codes over $\mathbb{F}_q$ we consider polynomials of the form

$$g_i(x) := (x - \alpha^m)(x - \alpha^{m+1})\ldots(x - \alpha^{m+d-2}),$$

where α is a primitive element of $\mathbb{F}_q$. We choose $g_1(x)$ and $g_2(x)$ in such a way that they both have degree $\lfloor \frac{1}{3}q \rfloor$ and that they have no zeros in common. Then $G(x) := g_1(x^2) + xg_2(x^2)$ generates a noncatastrophic convolutional code C over $\mathbb{F}_q$. The two cyclic codes with generators $g_1(x)$ and $g_2(x)$ both have minimum distance $\geq 1 + \lfloor \frac{1}{3}q \rfloor =: d$. Let these codes have check polynomials $h_1(x)$ and $h_2(x)$. An information sequence $I_0(x)$ for C is written as

$$I_0(x) = (x^{q-1} - 1)^r (h_1(x))^s (h_2(x))^t p(x),$$

where $p(x)$ is not a multiple of $h_1(x)$ or $h_2(x)$ and s or t is 0. First assume that $s = t = 0$. By Lemma 11.4.1 we have

$$w(T(x)) = w(g_1(x)I_0(x)) + w(g_2(x)I_0(x))$$

$$\geq \sum_{i=1}^{2} w((x - 1)^r) w(p(x)g_i(x) \bmod(x^{q-1} - 1))$$

$$\geq 2d.$$

If $s > 0$ we obtain in a similar way

$$w(T(x)) = w((x^{q-1} - 1)^r (h_1(x))^s g_1(x) p(x)) + w((x^{q-1} - 1)^r (h_1(x))^s g_2(x) p(x))$$

$$\geq w((x - 1)^{r+1}) w(p(x)(h_1(x))^{s-1} \bmod(x^{q-1} - 1))$$

$$\quad + w((x - 1)^r) \cdot w(p(x)(h_1(x))^s g_2(x) \bmod(x^{q-1} - 1))$$

$$\geq 2 + (q - \lfloor \tfrac{1}{3}q \rfloor) \geq 2 + 2\lfloor \tfrac{1}{3}q \rfloor = 2d.$$

From the construction we have $L = 2(1 + \lfloor \tfrac{1}{3}q \rfloor)$, so $d_f = L$. These examples illustrate that this is a good way to construct convolutional codes. The method generalizes to rate $1/n$. For details we refer to [38].

§11.5. Automorphisms of Convolutional Codes

We have seen, e.g., in the chapter on cyclic codes, that the requirement that a code is invariant under a certain group of permutations can lead to interesting developments. A lot of algebraic methods could be introduced and several good codes were found in this way. Therefore it is not surprising that attempts have been made to do something similar for convolutional codes. We shall sketch some of these ideas and define cyclic convolutional codes. We shall not give many details but hope that the treatment will be sufficient for the reader to decide whether he wishes to become interested in this area in which case he is referred to the work of Ph. Piret (cf. [59], [55]). This work was recast by C. Roos (cf. [59]). The ideas have led to some good codes and they are certainly worth further research.

We consider a convolutional code as defined in (11.1.2). If we call such a code cyclic if a simultaneous cyclic shift of the coefficients $\mathbf{a}_i$ of x^i ($\mathbf{a}_i \in \mathbb{F}_2^n$) leaves the code invariant, we do not get anything interesting. In fact the code is simply a block code. This shows that it is already difficult to define automorphisms in a sensible way. We do this as follows. Let K be the group of permutations acting on $\mathbb{F}_2^n$. Consider $K^{\mathbb{Z}}$, i.e. the set of all mappings $\varphi : \mathbb{Z} \to K$, which we make into a group by defining $\varphi_1 \varphi_2(n) := \varphi_1(n)\varphi_2(n)$. We shall write φ_n instead of $\varphi(n)$. Note that $\varphi_n \in K$. We then define an action of φ on elements of $\mathscr{F}^n$ by

(11.5.1) $$\varphi\left(\sum_{i=r}^{\infty} \mathbf{a}_i x^i\right) := \sum_{i=r}^{\infty} \varphi_i(\mathbf{a}_i) x^i.$$

(11.5.2) Definition. If C is a convolutional code, then the set of all elements $\varphi \in K^{\mathbb{Z}}$ such that $\varphi(C) = C$ is called the *automorphism group* of C.

From the definition of convolutional codes, it is obvious that multiplication by x leaves a code C invariant. So, if φ is an automorphism of C, then $\varphi^x := x^{-1}\varphi x$ is also an automorphism. Furthermore it is clear that if we consider only the action on a fixed position, say only φ_i, we obtain a permutation group on $\mathbb{F}_2^n$ which is the projection of the automorphism group on the ith coordinate. By our remark above and the fact that $\varphi_i^x(\mathbf{a}_i) = \varphi_{i+1}(\mathbf{a}_i)$, we see that all projections are the same group. So it seems natural to try to find codes for which this projection is the cyclic group. We shall do this using the same algebraic approach as we did for block codes. We introduce a variable z and identify $\mathbb{F}_2^n$ with $\mathbb{F}_2[z] \bmod(z^n - 1)$. Let π be an integer such that $(\pi, n) = 1$ and let σ be the automorphism of $\mathbb{F}_2^n$ defined by $\sigma: f(z) \to f(z^\pi)$. The elements of $\mathscr{F}^n$ can now be written as $\sum_{i=r}^{\infty} a_i x^i$ where $a_i = a_i(z)$ is a polynomial of degree $< n$ ($i \in \mathbb{Z}$). In $\mathscr{F}^n$ we define addition in the obvious way and a multiplication (denoted by $*$) by

(11.5.3) $$\sum_i a_i x^i * \sum_j b_j x^j := \sum_i \sum_j \sigma^j(a_i) b_j x^{i+j}.$$

Suppose we take the factor on the left to be z (i.e. $a_0 = z$, $a_i = 0$ for $i \neq 0$). Then from (11.5.3) we find

(11.5.4) $$z * \sum_j b_j x^j = \sum_j (z^{\pi^j} b_j) x^j.$$

This means that the coefficient $\mathbf{b}_j$ of x^j is shifted cyclically over $\pi^j \pmod{n}$ positions. The main point of the definition above is that $(\mathscr{F}^n, +, *)$ is an algebra which we denote by $\mathscr{A}(n, \pi)$.

(11.5.5) Definition. A *cyclic convolutional code* (notation CCC) is a left ideal in the algebra $\mathscr{A}(n, \pi)$ which has a basis consisting of polynomials.

Observe that by (11.5.4) we now indeed have a group of automorphisms of the code which has the cyclic group as its projection on any coordinate. The difference with the trivial situation is the fact that the cyclic shifts are not the same for every position. We give one example to show that we have a class of nontrivial objects worth studying. We define a rate $\frac{4}{7}$ binary convolutional code with memory one by the metrix G given by

(11.5.6) $$G = \begin{bmatrix} 1 & 1 & 1 & 1 & 1 & 1 & 1 \\ 1+x & 1 & 1 & x & 1 & x & x \\ 0 & 1 & 1+x & 1 & x & 1+x & x \\ 0 & x & 1 & 1+x & 1+x & x & 1 \end{bmatrix}.$$

We shall now identify elements of $\mathbb{F}_2^7$ with polynomials in $\mathbb{F}_2[z] \bmod(z^7 - 1)$. Writing $z^7 - 1 = (1 + z)(1 + z + z^3)(1 + z^2 + z^3) = m_0(z)m_1(z)m_3(z)$ we can then abbreviate G as follows:

(11.5.7)
$$G = \begin{bmatrix} m_1 m_3 \\ m_0 m_3 \\ z m_0 m_3 \\ z^2 m_0 m_3 \end{bmatrix} + \begin{bmatrix} 0 \\ m_0^3 m_1 \\ z^{-1} m_0^3 m_1 \\ z^{-2} m_0^3 m_1 \end{bmatrix} x.$$

We claim that G is the generator matrix for a CCC in $\mathscr{A}(7, -1)$. Since $\pi = -1$ we have from (11.5.4)

(11.5.8)
$$z * \sum_i c_i x^i = \sum_i (z^{(-1)^i} c_i) x^i.$$

To show that the code is a CCC it is sufficient to consider the words $(1000)G$, $(0100)G$, $(0010)G$, $(0001)G$ and multiply these on the left by z and then show that the product is in the code. For the first three this is obvious from the form of (11.5.7) and from (11.5.8). For example,

$$z * (0100)G = z * (m_0 m_3 + m_0^3 m_1 x)$$
$$= z m_0 m_3 + z^{-1} m_0^3 m_1 x = (0010)G.$$

Furthermore

$$z * (0001)G = z * (z^2 m_0 m_3 + z^{-2} m_0^3 m_1 x)$$
$$= z^3 m_0 m_3 + z^{-3} m_0^3 m_1 x$$
$$= (1 + z)m_0 m_3 + (1 + z^6) m_0^3 m_1 x$$
$$= (0110)G.$$

The main point of Piret's theory is to show that a CCC always has a generator matrix with a "simple" form similar to (11.5.7). This makes it possible to construct examples in a relatively easy way and then study their properties, such as their free distance.

§11.6. Comments

Convolutional codes were introduced by P. Elias in 1955 (cf. [20]). There has been quite a lot of controversy about the question whether convolutional codes are "better" than block codes or not. Despite the lack of a deep mathematical theory convolutional codes are used successfully in practice. Many of these codes were simply randomly chosen. For one of the deep space satellite missions ([1]) a scheme was proposed which combined block codes and convolutional codes. The idea was to take an information stream, divide it into blocks of twelve bits, and code these blocks with the [24, 12] extended

Golay code. The resulting stream would be input for a convolutional encoder. This is the same idea as in the concatenated codes of Section 9.2.

For a connection between quasi-cyclic block codes and convolutional codes we refer to a paper by G. Solomon and H. C. A. van Tilborg [66]. They show, e.g. that the Golay code can be encoded and decoded convolutionally.

In Section 3.2 we saw that in decoding block codes the procedure for estimating the error pattern does not depend on the transmitted word. The idea was to introduce the syndrome (cf. (3.2.6)). The same idea has been used very successfully for convolutional codes. For more about this idea we refer to a paper by J. P. M. Schalkwijk, A. J. Vinck, and K. A. Post [60]. Some results concerning the error probability after decoding convolutional codes can be found in [51, Section 9.3].

The most complete treatment of convolutional codes can be found in a recent book by Ph. Piret [79].

§11.7. Problems

11.7.1. Suppose that in Figure 4 we remove the connection of the third flip-flop with the adder for T_1. Show that the resulting code is catastrophic.

11.7.2. Let $g(x)$ be the generator polynomial of a cyclic code with minimum distance d. As in Section 11.1 we take two polynomials $G_0(x)$ and $G_1(x)$ to generate a rate 1/2 convolutional code. If we take these such that $g(x) = G_0(x^2) + xG_1(x^2)$ then by (11.1.1) all encoded sequences are multiples of $g(x)$. Give an example where nevertheless the free distance is less than d. Check the result by constructing the encoder as in Figure 4.

11.7.3. Determine the free distance of the CCC given by (11.5.7).

Hints and Solutions to Problems

Chapter 2

2.4.1.

$$\sum_{0 \le k < N/2} \binom{N}{k} q^k p^{N-k} < (pq)^{N/2} \sum_{0 \le k < N/2} \binom{N}{k}$$

$$= 2^{N-1}(pq)^{N/2} < (0.07)^N.$$

2.4.2. There are 64 possible error patterns. We know that 8 of these lead to 3 correct information symbols after decoding. To analyse the remainder one should realize that there are only 4 essentially different 3-tuples (s_1, s_2, s_3). Consider one possibility, e.g. $(s_1, s_2, s_3) = (1, 1, 0)$. This can be caused by the error patterns (101011), (011101), (110000), (010011), (100101), (000110), (111110) and of course by (001000) which is the most likely one. Our decision is to assume that $e_3 = 1$. So here we obtain two correct information symbols with probability $p^2 q^4 + 2p^4 q^2$ and we have one correct information symbol with probability $2p^3 q^3 + p^5 q$.

By analysing the other cases in a similar way one finds as symbol error probability

$$\tfrac{1}{3}(22p^2 q^4 + 36p^3 q^3 + 24p^4 q^2 + 12p^5 q + 2p^6)$$

$$= \tfrac{1}{3}(22p^2 - 52p^3 + 48p^4 - 16p^5).$$

In our example this is 0.000007 compared to 0.001 without coding.

2.4.3. Take as codewords all possible 8-tuples of the form

$$(a_1, a_2, a_3, \quad a_2 + a_3, \quad a_1 + a_3, \quad a_1 + a_2, \quad a_1 + a_2 + a_3).$$

This code is obtained by taking the eight words of the code of the previous problem and adding an extra symbol which is the sum of the first 6 symbols.

This has the effect that any two distinct codewords differ in an even number of places, i.e. $d(\mathbf{x}, \mathbf{y}) \geq 4$ for any two distinct codewords $\mathbf{x}, \mathbf{y}$.

The analysis of the error patterns is similar to the one which was treated in Section 2.2. For $(e_1, e_2, \ldots, e_7)$ we find

$$e_2 + e_3 + e_4 = s_1,$$
$$e_1 + e_3 + e_5 = s_2,$$
$$e_1 + e_2 + e_6 = s_3,$$
$$e_1 + e_2 + e_3 + e_7 = s_4.$$

There are 16 possible outcomes (s_1, s_2, s_3, s_4). Eight of these can be explained by an error pattern with no errors or one error. Of the remainder there are seven, each of which can be explained by three different error patterns with two errors, e.g. $(s_1, s_2, s_3, s_4) = (1, 1, 0, 0)$ corresponds to $(e_1, e_2, \ldots, e_7)$ being (0010001), (1100000) or (0001100). The most likely explanation of (1, 1, 1, 0) is the occurrence of three errors. Hence the probability of correct decoding is

$$q^7 + 7q^6 p + 7q^5 p^2 + q^4 p^3.$$

This is about $1 - 14p^2$, i.e. the code is not much better than the previous one even though it has smaller rate.

2.4.4.   For the code using repetition of symbols the probability of correct reception of a repeated symbol is $1 - p^2$. Therefore the code of length 6 with codewords $(a_1, a_2, a_3, a_1, a_2, a_3)$ has probability $(1 - p^2)^3 = 0.97$ of correct reception. The code of Problem 2.4.2 has the property that any two codewords differ in three places and therefore two erasures can do no harm. In fact an analysis of all possible erasure patterns with three erasures shows that 16 of these do no harm either. This leads to a probability $(1 - p)^3(1 + 3p + 6p^2 + 6p^3) = 0.996$ of correct reception. This is a remarkable improvement considering the fact that the two codes are very similar.

Chapter 3

3.7.1.   By (3.1.6) we have $\sum_{i=0}^{3}\binom{n}{i} = 2^l$ for some integer l. This equation reduces to $(n + 1)(n^2 - n + 6) = 3.2^{l+1}$, i.e. $(n + 1)\{(n + 1)^2 - 3(n + 1) + 8\} = 3.2^{l+1}$. If $n + 1$ is divisible by 16 then the second factor on the left is divisible by 8 but not by 16, i.e. it is 8 or 24 which yields a contradiction. Therefore $n + 1$ is a divisor of 24. Since $n \geq 7$ we see that $n = 7, 11$, or 23 but $n = 11$ does not satisfy the equation. For $n = 7$ the code $M = \{\mathbf{0}, \mathbf{1}\}$ is an example. For $n = 23$ see Section 4.2.

3.7.2.   Let $\mathbf{c} \in C$, $w(\mathbf{c}) \leq n - k$. There is a set of k positions where $\mathbf{c}$ has a coordinate equal to 0. Since C is systematic on these k positions we have

$\mathbf{c} = \mathbf{0}$. Hence $d > n - k$. Given k positions, there are codewords which have $d - 1$ zeros on these positions, i.e. $d \leq n - k + 1$. In accordance with the definition of separable given in Section 3.1 an $[n, k, n - k + 1]$ code is called a *maximum distance separable* code (MDS code).

3.7.3. Since $C \subset C^{\perp}$ every $\mathbf{c} \in C$ has the property $\langle \mathbf{c}, \mathbf{c} \rangle = 0$, i.e. $w(\mathbf{c})$ is even and hence $\langle \mathbf{c}, \mathbf{1} \rangle = 0$. However, $\langle \mathbf{1}, \mathbf{1} \rangle = 1$ since the word length is odd. Therefore $C^{\perp} \backslash C$ is obtained by adding $\mathbf{1}$ to all the words of C.

3.7.4. $|B_1(\mathbf{x})| = 1 + 6 = 7$. Since $7|C| = 63 < 2^6$ one might think that such a code C exists. However, if such a C exists then by the pigeon hole principle some 3-tuple of words of C would have the same symbols in the last two positions. Omitting these symbols yields a binary code C' with three words of length 4 and minimum distance 3. W.l.o.g. one of these words is $\mathbf{0}$ and then the other two would have weight ≥ 3 and hence distance ≤ 2, a contradiction.

3.7.5. By elementary linear algebra, for every i it is possible to find a basis for C such that $k - 1$ basis vectors have a 0 in position i and the remaining one has a 1. Hence exactly q^{k-1} code words have a 0 in position i.

3.7.6. The even weight subcode of C is determined by adding the row $\mathbf{1}$ to the parity check matrix of C. This decreases the dimension of the code by 1.

3.7.7. From the generator matrix we find for $\mathbf{c} \in C$

$$c_1 + c_2 + c_5 = c_3 + c_4 + c_6 = c_1 + c_2 + c_3 + c_4 + c_7 = 0.$$

Hence the syndromes

$$(s_1, s_2, s_3) = (e_1 + e_2 + e_5, e_3 + e_4 + e_6, e_1 + e_2 + e_3 + e_4 + e_7),$$

for the three received words are resp. $(0, 0, 0)$, $(0, 0, 1)$, $(1, 0, 1)$. Hence (a) is a code word; by maximum likelihood decoding (b) has an error in position 7; (c) has an error in position 1 or an error in position 2, so here we have a choice.

3.7.8. (i) If $p \equiv 1 \pmod 4$ then there is an $\alpha \in \mathbb{F}_p$ such that $\alpha^2 = -1$. Then $G = (I_4, \alpha I_4)$ is the generator matrix of the required code.

(ii) If $p \equiv 3 \pmod 4$ we use the fact that not all the elements of $\mathbb{F}_p$ are squares and hence there is an α which is a square, say $\alpha = \beta^2$, such that $\alpha + 1$ is not a square, i.e. $\alpha + 1 = -\gamma^2$. Hence $\beta^2 + \gamma^2 = -1$. Then

$$G = \begin{bmatrix} 1 & 0 & 0 & 0 & \beta & \gamma & 0 & 0 \\ 0 & 1 & 0 & 0 & -\gamma & \beta & 0 & 0 \\ 0 & 0 & 1 & 0 & 0 & 0 & \beta & \gamma \\ 0 & 0 & 0 & 1 & 0 & 0 & -\gamma & \beta \end{bmatrix}$$

does the job.

(iii) If $p = 2$, see (3.3.3).

3.7.9. $$R_k = \frac{n-k}{n} = \frac{2^k - 1 - k}{2^k - 1} \to 1, \qquad \text{as } k \to \infty.$$

3.7.10. (i) Let $(\bar{A}_0, \bar{A}_1, \ldots, \bar{A}_n, \bar{A}_{n+1})$ be the weight distribution of $\bar{C}$. Then $\bar{A}_{2k-1} = 0$ and $\bar{A}_{2k} = A_{2k-1} + A_{2k}$. Since $\sum A_{2k} z^{2k} = \frac{1}{2}\{A(z) + A(-z)\}$ and $\sum A_{2k-1} z^{2k-1} = \frac{1}{2}\{A(z) - A(-z)\}$, we find $\bar{A}(z) = \frac{1}{2}\{(1+z)A(z) + (1-z)A(-z)\}$.

(ii) From (i) and (3.5.2) we find the weight enumerator of the extended Hamming code of length $n + 1 = 2^k$ to be

$$\frac{1}{2}\left\{ \frac{(1+z)^{n+1} + (1-z)^{n+1}}{n+1} \right\} + \frac{n}{n+1}(1 - z^2)^{(n+1)/2}.$$

Now apply Theorem 3.5.3. The weight enumerator of the dual code is $1 + 2nz^{(n+1)/2} + z^{n+1}$, i.e. all the words of this code, except **0** and **1**, have weight 2^{k-1}.

3.7.11. The error pattern is a nonzero codeword **c**. If $w(\mathbf{c}) = i$ then the probability of this error pattern is $p^i(1-p)^{n-i}$. Therefore the probability of an undetected error is $(1-p)^n\{-1 + A(p/(1-p))\}$.

3.7.12. Let G_i $(i = 1, 2)$ be a generator matrix of C_i in standard form. Define $A_{ij} \in \mathcal{R}$ $(1 \le i \le k_1, 1 \le j \le k_2)$ as follows. The first k_1 rows of A_{ij} are **0** except for row i which is equal to the ith row of G_1 and similarly for the first k_2 columns except for column j which is the transpose of the jth row of G_2. It is easy to see that this uniquely determines an element A_{ij} in $\mathcal{R}$. The A_{ij} are $k_1 k_2$ linearly independent elements of $\mathcal{R}$ which generate the code C. If $A \in \mathcal{R}$ has a nonzero row then this row has weight $\ge d_1$, i.e. A has at least d_1 columns with weight $\ge d_2$. So C has minimum distance $\ge d_1 d_2$. In fact equality holds.

3.7.13. The subcode on positions 1, 9 and 10 is the repetition code which is perfect and single-error correcting. The subcode on the remaining seven positions is the [7, 4] Hamming code which is also perfect. So we have a unique way of correcting at most one error on each of these two subsets of positions. C has minimum distance 3 and covering radius 2.

3.7.14. (i) Consider the assertion $A_k :=$ "after 2^k choices we have a linear code and for $i < k$ the word length increases after 2^i steps". For $k = 1$ the assertion is true. Suppose A_k is true for some value of k. Consider the codeword $\mathbf{c}_{2^k}$. The list of chosen words looks like

$$
\begin{array}{c}
A\left\{
\begin{array}{l}
\mathbf{c}_0 \qquad\quad = 0 \ \ 0 \ \ \ldots \ \ 0 \ \ 0 \ \ \ldots \ \ 0 \\
\ \vdots \\
\mathbf{c}_{2^{k-1}-1} = * \ \ * \ \ \ldots \ \ 1 \ \ 0 \ \ \ldots \ \ 0
\end{array}
\right. \\[2em]
B\left\{
\begin{array}{l}
\mathbf{c}_{2^{k-1}} = * \ \ * \ \ \ldots \ \ * \ \ 11 \ \ \ldots \ \ 1 \\
\ \vdots \\
\mathbf{c}_{2^k - 1} = * \ \ * \ \ \ldots \ \ * \ \ 11 \ \ \ldots \ \ 1
\end{array}
\right.
\end{array}
$$

where the words in B are obtained by adding $\mathbf{c}_{2^{k-1}}$ to the words of A. If $\mathbf{c}_{2^k}$ has the same length as the words of B, since it is lexicographically larger, c_{2^k} must be of the form $c_{2^{k-1}} + x$ where x has 0s in the last positions. However $d \leq d(c_{2^{k-1}} + x, c_{2^{k-1}} + c_i) = d(x, c_i)$, where $0 \leq i < 2^{k-1}$, shows that we should have chosen x instead of $c_{2^{k-1}}$, a contradiction. So the length of the code increases when we choose c_{2^k}. Now suppose that we have shown that $c_{2^k+i} = c_{2^k} + c_i$ for $0 \leq i < j$ (it is true for $i = 0$). We have $d(c_{2^k} + c_j, c_{2^k} + c_i) = d(c_j, c_i) \geq d$, $d(c_{2^k} + c_j, c_i) = d(c_{2^k}, c_i + c_j) \geq d$ since by the assumption on linearity $c_i + c_j = c_v$ for some v. This proves that $c_{2^k} + c_j$ is a possible choice for the codeword c_{2^k+j}. The difficult part is to show that it is the least choice. On the contrary, suppose the choice should be $c_{2^k} + x$ where $c_{2^k} + x \prec c_{2^k} + c_j$ (we use $\prec$ for the lexicographic ordering). By the induction hypothesis $x \succ c_j$. These inequalities imply that c_j, x, and c_{2^k} look like

$$c_j \;=\; * \quad \ldots \quad * \quad 0 \quad a_1 a_2 \quad \ldots \quad a_t \quad 0 \; 0 \quad \ldots \quad 0 \; 0$$

$$x \;=\; * \quad \ldots \quad * \quad 1 \quad a_1 a_2 \quad \ldots \quad a_t \quad 0 \; 0 \quad \ldots \quad 0 \; 0$$

$$c_{2^k} \;=\; * \quad \ldots \quad * \quad 1 \quad ** \quad \ldots\ldots\ldots\ldots\ldots\ldots\ldots\ldots *1.$$

The assumption that $c_{2^k} + x$ is an admissible choice implies (again using linearity)

$$d(c_{2^k} + x, c_j + c_i) \geq d, \qquad \text{for } 0 \leq i < 2^k,$$

i.e.

$$d(c_{2^k} + x + c_j, c_i) \geq d, \qquad \text{for } 0 \leq i < 2^k.$$

But $c_{2^k} + x + c_j \prec c_{2^k}$, i.e. the choice for c_{2^k} was not the least, a contradiction. This completes the proof by induction of assertion A_k.

(ii) Now consider the case $d = 3$. Let n_k be the length of the code after 2^k vectors have been chosen. So $n_1 = 3$. Let C_k be the linear code after 2^k choices. If C_k is not perfect then there is a vector x of length n_k which has distance ≥ 2 to every word of C_k. So $(x, 1)$ is a possible choice for c_{2^k}. This gives us $n_{k+1} = n_k + 1$. If, on the other hand, C_k is perfect it is clear that $n_{k+1} = n_k + 2$ and $c_{2^k} = (1, 0, 0, \ldots, 0, 1, 1)$. The assertion $B_a :=$ "the length n_k equals $2^a + i$ for $k = 2^a - a - 1 + i$ and $1 \leq i < 2^a$" now follows by induction from the observations above. In each of the sequences mentioned in B_a the final code is a Hamming code.

Chapter 4

4.8.1. By (4.5.6) $\mathcal{R}(1, m)$ has dimension $m + 1$, i.e. it contains 2^{m+1} words of length $n = 2^m$. By Theorem 4.5.9 each of the $2(2^m - 1)$ hyperplanes of $AG(m, 2)$ yields a codeword of $\mathcal{R}(1, m)$, i.e. except for $\mathbf{0}$ and $\mathbf{1}$ every codeword is the characteristic function of a hyperplane. Take $\mathbf{0}$ and the codewords corresponding to hyperplanes through the origin. Replace 0 by -1 in each of these codewords. Since two hyperplanes intersect in 2^{m-1} points the n vectors are pairwise orthogonal.

4.8.2.   Since the code is perfect every word of weight 3 in $\mathbb{F}_3^{11}$ has distance 2 to a codeword of weight 5. Therefore $A_5 = 2^3\binom{11}{3}/\binom{5}{2} = 132$. Denote the 5-set corresponding to $\mathbf{x}$ by $B(\mathbf{x})$. Suppose $\mathbf{x}$ and $\mathbf{y} \notin \{\mathbf{x}, 2\mathbf{x}\}$ are codewords of weight 5 such that $|B(\mathbf{x}) \cap B(\mathbf{y})| > 3$. Then $w(\mathbf{x} + \mathbf{y}) + w(2\mathbf{x} + \mathbf{y}) \leq 8$ which is impossible because $\mathbf{x} + \mathbf{y}$ and $2\mathbf{x} + \mathbf{y}$ are codewords. Therefore the 66 sets $B(\mathbf{x})$ cover $66 \cdot \binom{5}{4} = \binom{11}{4}$ 4-subsets, i.e. all 4-subsets.

4.8.3.   By Theorem 1.3.8 any two rows of A have distance 6 and after a permutation of symbols they are (111, 111, 000, 00) and (111, 000, 111, 00). Any other row of A then must be of type (100, 110, 110, 10) or (110, 100, 100, 11). Consider the 66 words $\mathbf{x}_i$ resp. $\mathbf{x}_j + \mathbf{x}_k$. We have $d(\mathbf{x}_i, \mathbf{x}_i + \mathbf{x}_k) = w(\mathbf{x}_k) = 6$, $d(\mathbf{x}_i, \mathbf{x}_j + \mathbf{x}_k) = w(\mathbf{x}_i + \mathbf{x}_j + \mathbf{x}_k) = 4$ or 8 by the above standard representation. Finally, we have $d(\mathbf{x}_i + \mathbf{x}_j, \mathbf{x}_k + \mathbf{x}_l) \geq 4$ by two applications of the above standard form (for any triple $\mathbf{x}_i, \mathbf{x}_j, \mathbf{x}_k$). Since $d(\mathbf{x}, \mathbf{1} + \mathbf{y}) = 11 - d(\mathbf{x}, \mathbf{y})$, adding the complements of the 66 words to the set decreases the minimum distance to 3.

4.8.4.   Apply the construction of Section 4.1 to the Paley matrix of order 17.

4.8.5.   a) Show that the subcode corresponds to the subcode of the hexacode generated by $(1, \omega, 1, \omega, 1, \omega)$.
   b) As in the proof for $\mathscr{G}_{24}$, show that the subcode has dimension 4.
   c) Show that $d = 4$.

4.8.6.   Let C be an (n, M, d) code, d even. Puncture C. The new code C' is an $(n - 1, M, d - 1)$ code (if we puncture in a suitable way). The code $\overline{C}'$ is an (n, M, d) code because all words in $\overline{C}'$ have even weight.

4.8.7.   If R and S are 3 by 3 matrices then write

$$
\begin{bmatrix}
R & S & S & S \\
S & R & S & S \\
S & S & R & S \\
S & S & S & R
\end{bmatrix}
:= M(R, S).
$$

The rows of A, B, C, D have weight 5, 6, 8, 9, respectively. For two words $\mathbf{a}$, $\mathbf{b}$ we have $d(\mathbf{a}, \mathbf{b}) = w(\mathbf{a}) + w(\mathbf{b}) - 2\langle \mathbf{a}, \mathbf{b} \rangle$ where $\langle \mathbf{a}, \mathbf{b} \rangle$ is calculated in $\mathbb{Z}$. By block multiplication we find

$$AA^T = M(4I + J, 2J), \qquad BB^T = M(3I + 3J, 3J - I),$$

$$AB^T = M(5J, 3J) - 2B^T, \qquad \text{a matrix with entries 3 or 1.}$$

It follows that two rows of A resp. B have distance 6 or 8 and that a row of A and a row of B have distance 5 or 9. In the same way the fact that the remaining distances are at least 5 follows from

$$CA^T = (4J - 2I, 4J - 2I, 4J - 2I, 4J - 2I),$$

$$CB^T = (4J, 4J, 4J, 4J),$$

$$DA^T = 3J + D, \qquad DB^T = 3J + 2D,$$

$$CC^T = 4J + 4I, \qquad DD^T = 3I + 6J, DC^T = 6J.$$

(This construction is due to J. H. van Lint, cf. [43].)

4.8.8.   From Theorem 1.3.8 we have $A^T = -A$ and $AA^T = 11I$. It follows that over $\mathbb{F}_3$ any two rows of G have inner product 0, i.e. G generates a [24, 12] self-dual code C. Therefore $(A \quad I)$ is also a generator matrix for C. So, when looking for words of minimum weight we may assume that the first twelve positions contribute at most one half of the total weight. Since C is self-dual all weights are divisible by 3. Every row of G has weight $1 + 11 = 12$ and a linear combination of two rows has weight $2 + 7 = 9$ (this follows from $AA^T = 11I$). Therefore a linear combination of three rows has weight at least $3 + (11 - 7)$ and hence at least 9. This shows that C has minimum weight 9.

Remark. This code and the ternary Golay code are examples of *symmetry codes*. These codes were introduced by V. Pless (1972). The words of fixed weight in such codes often yield t-designs (even with $t = 5$) as in Problem 4.8.2. The interested reader is referred to [11].

4.8.9.   Let $\mathbf{1}, \mathbf{v}_0, \ldots, \mathbf{v}_{m-1}$ be the basis vectors of $\mathcal{R}(1, m)$. From (4.5.3)(i) and (ii) we then see that $\mathbf{1} = (\mathbf{1}, \mathbf{1})$, $\mathbf{w}_0 = (\mathbf{v}_0, \mathbf{v}_0)$, $\ldots$, $\mathbf{w}_{m-1} = (\mathbf{v}_{m-1}, \mathbf{v}_{m-1})$, $\mathbf{w}_m = (\mathbf{0}, \mathbf{1})$ are the basis vectors (of length 2^{m+1}) of $\mathcal{R}(1, m + 1)$. Therefore a basis vector of $\mathcal{R}(r + 1, m + 1)$ of the form $\mathbf{w}_{i_1} \ldots \mathbf{w}_{i_s}$ is of type $(\mathbf{u}, \mathbf{u})$ with $\mathbf{u}$ a basis vector of $\mathcal{R}(r + 1, m)$ if $\mathbf{w}_m$ does not occur in the product and it is of type $(\mathbf{0}, \mathbf{v})$, where $\mathbf{v}$ is a basis vector of $\mathcal{R}(r, m)$ if $\mathbf{w}_m$ does occur in the product. If $d(r, m)$ is the minimum distance of $\mathcal{R}(r, m)$ then from the $(\mathbf{u}, \mathbf{u} + \mathbf{v})$-construction we know that $d(r + 1, m + 1) = \min\{2d(r + 1, m), d(r, m)\}$ and then Theorem 4.5.7 follows by induction.

4.8.10.   (i) We consider the vectors $\mathbf{x}^*$ and $\mathbf{c}^* = \pm \mathbf{a}_i$ as vectors in $\mathbb{R}^n$. Clearly $\langle \mathbf{x}^*, \mathbf{c}^* \rangle = n - 2d(\mathbf{x}, \mathbf{c})$. We may assume that the $\mathbf{a}_i$ are chosen in such a way that $\langle \mathbf{x}^*, \mathbf{a}_i \rangle$ is positive $(1 \le i \le n)$. The vectors $\mathbf{x}^*$ and all $\mathbf{a}_i$ have length $\sqrt{n}$. Therefore $\sum_{i=1}^n \langle \mathbf{x}^*, \mathbf{a}_i \rangle^2 = n^2$, because the $\mathbf{a}_i$ are pairwise orthogonal. It follows that there is an i such that $\langle \mathbf{x}^*, \mathbf{a}_i \rangle$ is at least $\sqrt{n}$.

(ii) Now let $m = 2k$ and $\mathbf{c} \in \mathcal{R}(1, m)$. By definition $\mathbf{c}$ is the list of values of a linear function on $\mathbb{F}_2^m$ and $d(\mathbf{x}, \mathbf{c})$ is therefore the number of points in $\mathbb{F}_2^m$ where the sum of $x_1 x_2 + x_3 x_4 + \cdots + x_{2k-1} x_{2k}$ and this linear function takes the value 1. Observe that

$$x_1 x_2 + x_3 x_4 + \cdots + x_{2k-1} x_{2k} + x_1$$

$$= x_1 \bar{x}_2 + x_3 x_4 + \cdots + x_{2k-1} x_{2k}$$

where $\bar{x}_2 := x_2 + 1$. Therefore a sequence of coordinate transformations $\bar{x}_i := x_i + 1$ (for $\mathbb{F}_2^m$) changes the sum into an expression equivalent to $x_1 x_2 + \cdots + x_{2k-1} x_{2k}$ or to its complement (if the term $\mathbf{1}$ occurs in the linear function). We count the points $\mathbf{x}$, for which $x_1 x_2 + \cdots + x_{2k-1} x_{2k} = 1$. Call this number n_k. Clearly $n_k = 3n_{k-1} + (2^{2k-2} - n_k)$, from which we find $n_k = 2^{2k-1} - 2^{k-1}$. This can also be calculated by considering the vector $(x_1, x_3, \ldots, x_{2k-1})$. If this is not $\mathbf{0}$ then 2^{k-1} choices for $(x_2, x_4, \ldots, x_{2k})$ are possible. Hence $n_k = (2^k - 1)2^{k-1}$.

4.8.11. Since the ternary Hamming code is self-dual it follows that C is self-dual; $(J + I$ has rank 4 and hence C has dimension 6). Therefore the minimum distance of C is either 3 or 6. Clearly a linear combination of the first four rows of G has weight > 4. On the other hand a linear combination of the last two rows has weight 6. Again since $J + I$ has rank 4 a combination involving rows of both kinds cannot have weight 3.

Chapter 5

5.5.1. We construct a suitable parity check matrix for the desired code C by successively picking columns. Any nonzero column can be our first choice. If m columns have been chosen we try to find a next column which is not a linear combination of i previous columns for any $i \leq d - 2$. This ensures that no $(d - 1)$-tuple of columns of the parity check matrix is linearly dependent, i.e. the code has minimum distance at least d. The method works if the number of linear combinations of at most $d - 2$ columns out of m chosen columns is less than q^{n-k} (for every $m \leq n - 1$). So a sufficient condition is

$$\sum_{i=0}^{d-2} \binom{n-1}{i}(q-1)^i < q^{n-k}.$$

The left-hand side of the inequality in (5.1.8) is at least $n(q-1)/(d-1)$ times as large, the right-hand side only q times as large, i.e. Problem 5.5.1 is a stronger result in general.

5.5.2. By (5.1.3) we have $A(10, 5) = A(11, 6)$. The best bound is obtained by using (5.2.4) (also see the example following (5.3.5)). It is $A(11, 6) \leq 12$. From (1.3.9) (also see the solution of Problem 4.7.3) we find an $(11, 12, 6)$ code. Hence $A(10, 5) = 12$.

5.5.3. Equality in (5.2.4) can hold only if this is also the case for the inequalities used in the proof and that is possible only if $\frac{1}{2}M^2$ is an integer. So $M = l$ is impossible.

5.5.4. By Problem 4.7.4 we have $A(17, 8) \geq 36$. The best estimate from Section 5.2 is obtained by using the Plotkin bound. We find $A(17, 8) \leq 4A(15, 8) \leq 64$. A much better result is obtained by applying Theorem 5.3.4.

The reader can check that the result is $A(17, 8) \leq 50$. The best known bound, obtained by refining the method of (5.3.4), is $A(17, 8) \leq 37$ (cf. [6]).

5.5.5.   The columns of the generator matrix are the points $(x_1, x_2, x_3, x_4, x_5)$ of PG(4, 2). We know (cf. Problem 3.7.10) that all the nonzero codewords of the [31, 5] code have weight 16. By the same result the positions corresponding to $x_1 = x_2 = 0$ yield a subcode of length 7 with all nonzero weights equal to 4 and the positions with $x_3 = x_4 = x_5 = 0$ give a subcode of length 3 with all nonzero weights equal to 2. If we puncture by these ten positions the remaining [21, 5] code therefore has $d = 16 - 4 - 2 = 10$. From (5.2.6) we find $n \geq 10 + 5 + 3 + 2 + 1 = 21$, i.e. the punctured code meets the Griesmer bound.

5.5.6.   This is a direct consequence of the proof of Lemma 5.2.14 (the average number of occurrences of a pair of ones is $|C| \cdot \binom{w}{2} / \binom{n}{2} = A(n - 2, 2k, w - 2)$ and no pair can occur more than this many times).

5.5.7.   Let $n = 2^k - 2$. By Lemma 5.2.14 we have $A(n, 3, 3) \leq \frac{1}{6}n(n - 2)$. Hence Theorem 5.2.15 yields

$$A(n, 3) \leq 2^n / \left\{ 1 + n + \left(\binom{n}{2} - \frac{3n(n - 2)}{6} \right) / \binom{n}{2} \right\} = 2^{n-k}.$$

Hence the $[n, n - k, 3]$ shortened Hamming code is optimal.

5.5.8.   If two words $\mathbf{c}$ and $\mathbf{c}'$ of weight w have distance 2, say $c_j = c'_k = 1$, $c'_j = c_k = 0$, then $\sum_{i=0}^{n-1} ic_i - \sum_{i=0}^{n-1} ic'_i \equiv j - k \pmod{n}$. It follows that each of the codes C_l ($0 \leq l \leq n - 1$) has minimum distance 4. Therefore $A(n, 4, w) \geq 1/n \binom{n}{w}$, since $\sum_{l=0}^{n-1} |C_l| = \binom{n}{w}$. By Lemma 5.2.14 we have $A(n, 4, w) \leq \binom{n}{w} / (n - w + 1)$. Combining these inequalities the result follows. (For generalizations of this idea cf. [30].)

5.5.9.   Let C be a binary $(n, M, 2k)$ code. Define

$$S := \{(\mathbf{c}, \mathbf{x}) | \mathbf{c} \in C, \mathbf{x} \in \mathbb{F}_2^n, d(\mathbf{c}, \mathbf{x}) = w\}.$$

Clearly $|S| = \binom{n}{w} M$. For a fixed $\mathbf{x}$ there are at most $A(n, 2k, w)$ words $\mathbf{c}$ in C such that $d(\mathbf{c}, \mathbf{x}) = w$. Therefore $\binom{n}{w} M \leq 2^n A(n, 2k, w)$.

5.5.10.   (i) The proof of this inequality is essentially the same as the proof of Lemma 5.2.10. If a constant weight code has m_i words with a 1 in position i then, in our usual notation,

$$2k \binom{M}{2} \leq \sum_{i=1}^{n} m_i(M - m_i) \leq M^2 w - n \left(\frac{Mw}{n} \right)^2.$$

(ii) Let $2k/n \to \delta$ as $n \to \infty$. Let $w/n \to \omega$ as $n \to \infty$. Then $A(n, 2k, w)$
is bounded as $n \to \infty$ and Problem 5.5.9 yields $\alpha(\delta) \leq 1 - H_2(\omega)$.
We must still satisfy the requirement $1 - (w/k)(1 - (w/n)) > 0$.
So the best result is obtained if $1 - (2\omega/\delta)(1 - \omega) = 0$, i.e. $\omega = \frac{1}{2} - \frac{1}{2}\sqrt{1 - 2\delta}$, which is (5.2.12).

5.5.11.   We have $K_2(i) = 2i^2 - 2ni + \binom{n}{2}$ and this is less than $2d^2 - 2nd + \binom{n}{2}$ for $d \leq i \leq n - d$. Since $A_0 = A_n = 1$ (w.l.o.g.) and $A_i = 0$ for all other
values of i outside $[d, n - d]$, we find from (5.3.3)

$$2\binom{n}{2} + \left(2d^2 - 2nd + \binom{n}{2}\right) \sum_{i=d}^{n-d} A_i \geq 0.$$

This yields the required inequality.

5.5.12.   Consider the problem of determining $A(9, 4)$ with Theorem 5.3.4.
We find four inequalities for A_4, A_6, A_8. To this system we may add the
obvious inequality $A_8 \leq 1$. A rather tedious calculation yields the optimal
solution $A_4 + A_6 + A_8 \leq 20\frac{1}{3}$. So we have to consider the possibility of a
$(9, 21, 4)$ code. Taking $\omega = -1$ in the proof of Lemma 5.3.3 yields the
inequalities

$$21 \sum_{i=0}^{9} A_i K_k(i) \geq \binom{9}{k},$$

i.e. using

$$K_k(0) = \binom{9}{k},$$

$$\frac{20}{21} K_k(0) + \sum_{i=1}^{9} A_i K_k(i) \geq 0.$$

Since the code has 21 words, there are at most 10 pairs of codewords with
distance 8, i.e. $A_8 \leq \frac{20}{21}$. Therefore the numbers $\frac{21}{20} A_i$ must satisfy the same
inequalities which we solved to start with. This implies $A_4 + A_6 + A_8 \leq \frac{20}{21} \cdot \frac{61}{3} < 20$, a contradiction.

Chapter 6

6.12.1.   We generalize Sections 6.1 and 6.2. Over $\mathbb{F}_3$ we have $x^4 + 1 = (x^2 + x + 2)(x^2 + 2x + 2)$. Hence $x^2 + x + 2$ is the generator of a negacyclic $[4, 2]$ code which has generator matrix $\left(\begin{smallmatrix} 2 & 1 & 1 & 0 \\ 0 & 2 & 1 & 1 \end{smallmatrix}\right)$. By Definition
3.3.1 this is a $[4, 2]$ Hamming code.

6.12.2.   Since $x^4 + x + 1$ is primitive we can take it as generator for the
$[15, 11]$ Hamming code. Now follow the procedure of the proof of Theorem

6.4.1 to find $a(x)(x^4 + x + 1)$ which turns out to be $1 + (x + x^2 + x^4 + x^8)$ $+ (x^3 + x^6 + x^9 + x^{12})$, a sum of three idempotent corresponding to cyclotomic cosets. The method described after Theorem 6.4.4 and the example given there provide a second solution.

6.12.3. Consider the matrix E introduced in Section 4.5 and leave out the initial column. We now have a list of the points $\neq (0, 0, \dots, 0)$ in $AG(m, 2)$, written as column vectors. We can also consider this as a list of elements of $\mathbb{F}_{2^m}^*$. This is a cyclic group generated by a primitive element ξ of $\mathbb{F}_{2^m}$. The mapping $A: \mathbb{F}_{2^m} \to \mathbb{F}_{2^m}$ defined by $A(x) := \xi x$ is clearly a nonsingular linear transformation of $AG(m, 2)$ into itself and as a permutation of the points of $AG(m, 2)\backslash\{0\}$ it has order $2^m - 1$. The mapping A maps flats into flats. It now follows from Lemma 4.5.5(i), (4.5.6) and Theorem 4.5.9 that the permutation of coordinate places corresponding to A yields a cyclic representation of the shortened code.

6.12.4. Use $x^3 + 2x + 1$ to generate $\mathbb{F}_3^3$. If β is a primitive element $x^3 + 2x + 1$ is its minimal polynomial. Using a table of the field we find the minimal polynomial of β^2 to be $(x - \beta^2)(x - \beta^6)(x - \beta^{18}) = x^3 + x^2 + x + 2$ and the minimal polynomial of β^4 is $(x^3 + x^2 + 2)$. The product of these functions has β, β^2, β^3, β^4 among its zeros. So it generates the required code. The generator polynomial is $1 + x + 2x^2 + 2x^3 + 2x^4 + x^5 + x^6 + x^7 + 2x^8 + x^9$. The dimension of the code is 17.

6.12.5. First make a table of $\mathbb{F}_{2^5}$. By substitution we find $E(\alpha^i) = R(\alpha^i)$ for $i = 1, 2, 3, 4$. These are respectively $\alpha^{28}, \alpha^{25}, 1, \alpha^{19}$. We must determine $\sigma(z) = 1 + \sigma_1 z + \sigma_2 z^2$ from the equations $1 + \sigma_1 \alpha^{25} + \sigma_2 \alpha^{28} = 0, \alpha^{19} + \sigma_1 + \sigma_2 \alpha^{25} = 0$. We find $\sigma_1 = \alpha^{28}, \sigma_2 = \alpha^{10}$, i.e.

$$\sigma(z) = (1 - \alpha^{14} z)(1 - \alpha^{27} z).$$

So the codeword was

$$(1\ 0\ 0\ 1\ 0\ 1\ 1\ 0\ 1\ 1\ 1\ 1\ 0\ 0\ 1\ 0\ 1\ 1\ 0\ 1\ 0\ 1\ 0\ 1\ 0\ 1\ 1\ 0\ 1\ 1\ 1).$$

The generator of the code is $(1 + x^2 + x^5)(1 + x^2 + x^3 + x^4 + x^5)$, i.e. $g(x) = 1 + x^3 + x^5 + x^6 + x^8 + x^9 + x^{10}$. The codeword is

$$g(x)(1 + x^{11} + x^{20}).$$

6.12.6. Since the defining set of C contains $\{\beta^j | j = -2, -1, 1, 2\}$, it follows from Example 6.6.10 (with $d_A = 3$ and $|B| = 2$) that $d \geq 4$. Consider the even weight subcode C' of C. The words of this code have $\beta^{-2}, \beta^{-1}, \beta^0, \beta^1, \beta^2$ as zeros. Hence C' has minimum distance at least 6 by the BCH bound. It follows that $d \geq 5$.

6.12.7. Consider any $[q + 1, 2, q]$ code C'. This code is systematic on any two positions (cf. (3.7.2)). For the coefficients of the weight enumerator this implies

$$(q + 1)A_{q+1} + aAq = (q + 1)(q^2 - q).$$

Since $A_{q+1} + A_q = q^2 - 1$ we find that $A_{q+1} = 0$, i.e. every nonzero codeword has weight q. There is a unique codeword $\mathbf{c} = (c_0, c_1, \ldots, c_q)$ with $c_0 = c_{(q+1)/2} = 1$. Since exactly one coordinate of $\mathbf{c}$ is 0, a cyclic shift of $\mathbf{c}$ over $\frac{1}{2}(q + 1)$ positions does not yield the same word $\mathbf{c}$. Hence C' is not cyclic.

6.12.8.   Over $\mathbb{F}_3$ we have

$$x^{11} - 1 = (x - 1)(x^5 - x^3 + x^2 - x - 1)(x^5 + x^4 - x^3 + x^2 - 1),$$

where the factors are irreducible. So, as in (6.9.1), we can take $g_0(x) = (x^5 - x^3 + x^2 - x - 1)$ as generator of the ternary $[11, 6]$ QR code C. Both the BCH bound and Theorem 6.9.2 yield $d \geq 4$; in the latter case there is the restriction $c(1) \neq 0$. The code $C^\perp$ has generator $(x - 1)g_0(x)$ (cf. Section 6.2). Now consider the code $\overline{C}$ obtained by adding an overall parity check in the usual way. If G is a generator matrix for $C^\perp$, then a generator matrix for C is obtained by adding the row $\mathbf{1}$ and a generator matrix for $\overline{C}$ is given by

We see that $\overline{C}$ is self-dual. The inner product of a codeword with itself (over $\mathbb{R}$) is the number of nonzero coordinates. Hence every codeword in C has a weight divisible by 3. This proves $d \geq 5$. That C is perfect follows from the definition by using $1 + \binom{11}{1} \cdot 2 + \binom{11}{2} \cdot 2^2 = 3^5$.

6.12.9.   By (6.9.5) d is odd. By Theorem 6.9.2(ii) and (iii) we have $d^2 - d + 1 \geq 47$ (i.e. $d \geq 8$) and $d \equiv 3 \pmod 4$. Hence $d \geq 11$. By the Hamming bound (Theorem 5.2.7) we have, with $d = 2e + 1$,

$$\sum_{i=0}^{e} \binom{47}{i} \leq 2^{47}/|C|.$$

Since C has dimension 24, we find $e \leq 5$. It follows that $d = 11$.

6.12.10.   In the example of Section 6.9 and in Problem 6.12.8 we have already found the $[7, 4]$ Hamming code and the two Golay codes as examples of perfect QR codes. There is one other perfect QR code. That there are no others with $e > 1$ is a consequence of the results of Chapter 7. Suppose C is a QR code of length n over $\mathbb{F}_q$ and C is a perfect code with $d = 3$. Then by (3.1.6) we have

$$1 + n(q - 1) = q^{(n-1)/2}, \qquad (\text{or } q^{(n+1)/2}).$$

The two cases are similar. In the first we have

$$n = 1 + q + q^2 + \cdots + q^{(n-3)/2}.$$

If $n > 5$ then the right-hand side is at least

$$1 + 2 + \frac{n-5}{2} \cdot 4 = 2n - 7,$$

i.e. $n = 7$ and $q = 2$ and C is the $[7, 4]$ Hamming code. It remains to try $n = 3$ and $n = 5$. We find

$$1 + 3(q - 1) = q \qquad \text{resp.} \quad 1 + 5(q - 1) = q^2.$$

So the only solution is $n = 5$, $q = 4$.

6.12.11. Let β be a primitive element of $\mathbb{F}_n$. Define $R_v := \{\beta^i \in \mathbb{F}_n | i \equiv v \pmod{e}\}$, $0 \leq v < e$. Let α be a primitive nth root of unity in an extension field of $\mathbb{F}_q$. We define

$$g_v(x) := \prod_{r \in R_v} (x - \alpha^r), \qquad 0 \leq v < e.$$

Since $q \in R_0$ each of the g_v has coefficients in $\mathbb{F}_q$. Furthermore these polynomials all have degree $(n - 1)/e$ and

$$x^n - 1 = (x - 1)g_0(x)g_1(x)\ldots g_{e-1}(x).$$

The eth power residue code C has generator $g_0(x)$. The codes with generator $g_v(x)$ are all equivalent. The proof of Theorem 6.9.2(i) can be copied to yield $d^e > n$. If $n = 31$, $e = 3$, $q = 2$ this yields $d^3 > 31$ so $d \geq 4$. Since $5^3 = -1$ in $\mathbb{F}_{31}$ we see that $g_0(\alpha) = g_0(\alpha^{-1}) = 0$. Hence by Problem 6.12.6 we have $d \geq 5$. Furthermore, $d < 7$ by the Hamming bound. In fact the Hamming bound even shows that the code consisting of the 2^{20} words of C with odd weight cannot have $d = 7$. Hence $d = 5$.

6.12.12. (a) Since $\alpha, \alpha^2, \alpha^4, \alpha^5$ are zeros of codewords $d \geq 4$ is a direct consequence of Example (6.6.10).

(b) By the BCH bound we have $d \geq 3$. If $d = 3$ there would be a codeword with coordinates 1 in positions 0, i, j. Let $\xi = \alpha^i$, $\eta = \alpha^j$. Then $1 + \xi + \eta = 0$, $1 + \xi^5 + \eta^5 = 0$. We then find $1 = (\xi + \eta)^5 = (\xi^5 + \eta^5) + \xi\eta(\xi^3 + \eta^3)$, i.e. $\xi^3 + \eta^3 = 0$. This is a contradiction because $2^m - 1 \not\equiv 0 \pmod 3$, so $x^3 = 1$ has the unique solution $x = 1$, whereas $\xi \neq \eta$.

6.12.13. Consider the representation of (6.12.8). Let α be a primitive element of $\mathbb{F}_{3^5}$. Then α^{22} is a primitive 11th root of unity, i.e. a zero of $g_0(x)$ or $g_1(x)$. So the representations of 1, α^{22}, α^{44}, ..., α^{220} as elements of $(\mathbb{F}_3)^5$ are the columns of a parity check matrix of C. Multiply the columns corresponding to α^{22i} with $i > 5$ by $-1 = \alpha^{121}$ and reorder to obtain 1, α^{11}, α^{22}, ..., α^{110} corresponding to a zero of $x^{11} + 1$. This code is equivalent to C which is known to be unique and this representation is negacyclic.

6.12.14. The defining set of this code is

$$R = \{\alpha^i | i = 1, 2, 4, 5, 7, 8, 9, 10, 14, 16, 18, 19, 20, 25, 28\}.$$

Show that the set R contains AB, where $A = \{\alpha^i | i = 8, 9, 10\}$ and $B =$

$\{\beta^j \mid j = 0, 1, 3\}, \beta = \alpha^{10}$. This implies $d \geq 6$. For the even weight subcode take $A = \{\alpha^i \mid i = 4, 7, 8, 9\}, B = \{\beta^j \mid j = 0, 3, 4\}, \beta = \alpha^8$. Apply Theorem 6.6.9 with $|I| = 6$.

Chapter 7

7.7.1. Let C be the code. Since the Hamming code of length $n + 1 = 2^m - 1$ is perfect with $e = 1$, C has covering radius 2. Substitute $n = 2^m - 2$, $|C| = 2^{n-m}$, $e = 1$ in (5.2.16). We find equality. It follows that C is nearly perfect.

7.7.2. Suppose $\rho(\mathbf{u}, C) = 2$, i.e. $\mathbf{u} = \mathbf{c} + \mathbf{e}$, where $\mathbf{c} \in C$ and $\mathbf{e}$ has weight 2. So $c(\alpha) = c(\alpha^3) = 0$ and $e(x) = x^i + x^j$ for some i and j. We calculate in how many ways we can change three positions, labelled x_1, x_2, x_3, and thus find a codeword. So we are calculating the number of solutions of

$$x_1 + x_2 + x_3 + \alpha^i + \alpha^j = 0,$$

$$x_1^3 + x_2^3 + x_3^3 + \alpha^{3i} + \alpha^{3j} = 0.$$

Substitute $y_i := x_i + e(\alpha)$. We find

$$y_1 + y_2 + y_3 = 0$$

$$y_1^3 + y_2^3 + y_3^3 = s := \alpha^{i+j}(\alpha^i + \alpha^j),$$

where $s \neq 0$ and $y_k \notin \{\alpha^i, \alpha^j\}$.

From the first equation we have $y_3 = y_1 + y_2$ which we substitute in the second equation. The result is

$$y_1 y_2 (y_1 + y_2) = s.$$

Since $s \neq 0$ we have $y_2 \neq 0$. Define $y := y_1/y_2$. The equation is reduced to

$$y(1 + y) = s/y_2^3.$$

Since $(3, n) = (3, 2^{2m+1} - 1) = 1$ it follows that for every value of y, except $y = 0$, $y = 1$, this equation has a unique solution y_2 (in $\mathbb{F}_{2^{2m+1}}$). Hence we find $n - 1$ solutions $\{y_1, y_2\}$ and then y_3 follows. Clearly, each triple is found six times. Furthermore, we must reject the solution with $y_1 = \alpha^i$, $y_2 = \alpha^j$ because these correspond to $x_1 = \alpha^j, x_2 = \alpha^i, x_3 = 0$ (or any permutation). So $\rho(\mathbf{u}, C) = 2$ implies that there are $\frac{1}{6}(n - 1) - 1$ codewords with distance 3 to $\mathbf{u}$. In a similar way one can treat the case $\rho(\mathbf{u}, C) > 2$.

7.7.3. The code C is the Preparata code of length 15. However, we do not need to use this fact. Start with the $(16, 256, 6)$ Nordstrom-Robinson code $\overline{C}$ and puncture to obtain a $(15, 256, 5)$ code C. These parameters satisfy (5.2.16) with equality.

7.7.4. That C is not equivalent to a linear code is easily seen. If it were, then C would in fact be a linear code since $\mathbf{0} \in C$. Then the sum of two words of C

would again be in C. This is obviously not true. To show that C is perfect we must consider two codewords $\mathbf{a} = (\mathbf{x}, \ \mathbf{x} + \mathbf{c}, \ \sum x_i + f(\mathbf{c}))$ and $\mathbf{b} = (\mathbf{y}, \ \mathbf{y} + \mathbf{c}', \ \sum y_i + f(\mathbf{c}'))$. If $\mathbf{c} = \mathbf{c}'$ and $\mathbf{x} \neq \mathbf{y}$ it is obvious that $d(\mathbf{a}, \mathbf{b}) \geq 3$. If $\mathbf{c} \neq \mathbf{c}'$ then $d(\mathbf{a}, \mathbf{b}) \geq w(\mathbf{x} - \mathbf{y}) + w(\mathbf{x} + \mathbf{c} - \mathbf{y} - \mathbf{c}') \geq w(\mathbf{c} - \mathbf{c}') \geq 3$. Since $|C| = 2^{11}$ and $d = 3$ we have equality in (3.1.6), i.e. C is perfect.

7.7.5. For the two zeros of Ψ_2 we find from (7.5.2) and (7.5.6)

$$x_1 + x_2 = n + 1 \quad \text{and} \quad x_1 x_2 = 2^{l-1}.$$

Hence $x_1 = 2^a$, $x_2 = 2^b$ ($a < b$). From (3.1.6) we find $n^2 + n + 2 = 2^c$ (where $c \geq 3$ since $n \geq 2$).

So

$$(2^a + 2^b)(2^a + 2^b - 1) + 2 = 2^c.$$

Since on the left-hand side we have a term 2, the other term is not divisible by 4. Therefore $a = 0$ or $a = 1$. If $a = 0$ we find $2^b(2^b + 1) + 2 = 2^c$, i.e. $b = 1$ and $n = 2$ corresponding to the code $C = \{(00)\}$. If $a = 1$ we find $2^{2b} + 3 \cdot 2^b + 4 = 2^c$, i.e. $b = 2$ and then $n = 5$ corresponding to the repetition code $C = \{(00000), (11111)\}$.

7.7.6. First use Theorem 7.3.5 and (1.2.7). We find the equation

$$4x^2 - 4(n + 1)x + (n^2 + n + 12) = 0,$$

with zeros $x_{1,2} = \frac{1}{2}(n + 1 \pm \sqrt{n - 11})$.

It follows that $n - 11 = m^2$ for some integer m. From (7.3.6) we find

$$12 \cdot 2^n = |C| \cdot (n^2 + n + 12) = |C|(n + 1 + m)(n + 1 - m).$$

So $n + 1 + m = a \cdot 2^{\alpha+1}$, $n + 1 - m = b \cdot 2^{\beta+1}$ with $ab = 1$ or 3. First try $a = b = 1$. We find $n + 1 = 2^\alpha + 2^\beta$, $m = 2^\alpha - 2^\beta$ ($\alpha > \beta$) and hence

$$2^\alpha + 2^\beta - 12 = 2^{2\alpha} - 2^{\alpha+\beta+1} + 2^{2\beta},$$

i.e.

$$-12 = 2^\alpha(2^\alpha - 2^{\beta+1} - 1) + 2^\beta(2^\beta - 1),$$

an obvious contradiction.

Next, try $b = 3$. This leads to $n + 1 = a \cdot 2^\alpha + 3 \cdot 2^\beta$, $m = a \cdot 2^\alpha - 3 \cdot 2^\beta$ and hence

$$3 \cdot 2^\beta(3 \cdot 2^\beta - 2^{\alpha+1} - 1) + 2^\alpha(2^\alpha - 1) + 12 = 0.$$

If $\alpha > 2$ then we must have $\beta = 2$ and it follows that $\alpha = 4$. Since $\alpha \leq 2$ does not give a solution and the final case $a = 3$ also does not yield anything we have proved that $n + 1 = 2^4 + 3 \cdot 2^2$, i.e. $n = 27$.

The construction of such a code is similar to (7.4.2). Replace the form used in (7.4.2) by $x_1 x_2 + x_3 x_4 + x_5 x_6 + x_5 + x_6 = 0$. The rest of the argument is the same. We find a two-weight code of length 27 with weights 12 and 16 and then apply Theorem 7.3.7.

Chapter 8

8.8.1.   In Theorem 8.3.1 it was shown that if we replace $g(z)$ by $\hat{g}(z) := z + 1$ we get the same code. So $\Gamma(L, g)$ has dimension at least 4 and minimum distance $d \geq 3$. As was shown in the first part of Section 8.3, d might be larger. We construct the parity check matrix $H = (h_0 h_1 \ldots h_7)$ where h_i runs through the values $(\alpha^j + 1)^{-1}$ with $(j, 15) = 1$. We find that H consists of all column vectors with a 1 in the last position, i.e. $\Gamma(L, g)$ is the $[8, 4, 4]$ extended Hamming code.

8.8.2.   Let **a** be a word of even weight in C. By (6.5.2) the corresponding Mattson-Solomon polynomial $A(X)$ is divisible by X. By Theorem 8.6.1 the polynomial $X^{n-1} \circ A(X)$, i.e. $X^{-1}A(X)$, is divisible by $g(X)$. Since C is cyclic we find from (6.5.2) that $X^{-1}A(X)$ is also divisible by $g(\alpha^i X)$ for $0 < i \leq n - 1$. If $g(X)$ had a zero different from 0 in any extension field of $\mathbb{F}_2$ we would have $n - 1$ distinct zeros of $X^{-1}A(X)$, a contradiction since $X^{-1}A(X)$ has degree $< n - 1$. So $g(z) = z^t$ for some t and C is a BCH code (cf. (8.2.6)).

8.8.3.   This is exactly what was shown in the first part of Section 8.3. For any codeword $(b_0, b_1, \ldots, b_{n-1})$ we have $\sum_{i=0}^{n-1} b_i \gamma_i^r = 0$ for $0 \leq r \leq d_1 - 2$, where $\gamma_i = \alpha^i$ (α primitive element). So the minimum distance is $\geq (d_2 - 1) + (d_1 - 2) + 2 = d_1 + d_2 - 1$.

8.8.4.   Let $G^{-1}(X)$ denote the inverse of $G(X)$ in the ring $(T, +, \circ)$. The definition of GBCH code can be read as

$$P(X) \cdot (\Phi a)(X) = Q(X)G(X) + R(X)(X^n - 1),$$

where $Q(X)$ has degree $< n - t$. This is equivalent to

$$(G^{-1}(X) \circ P(X))(\Phi a)(X) = Q(X) + R^*(X)(X^n - 1),$$

for a suitable $R^*(X)$. The same condition, including the requirement that degree $Q(X) < n - t$, is obtained if we take the pair $(\hat{P}(X), X^t)$, where

$$\hat{P}(X) = X^t \circ G^{-1}(X) \circ P(X).$$

8.8.5.   In (6.6.1) take $l = 5$ and $\delta = 2$. We find that C is a BCH code with minimum distance $d \geq 2$. Since $(x + 1)(x^2 + x + 1) = x^3 + 1 \in C$ we have $d = 2$. If in (8.2.4) we take $g(x)$ of degree > 1 then by Theorem 8.2.7 the Goppa code $\Gamma(L, g)$ has distance at least 3. If $g(z)$ has degree 1 then Theorem 8.3.1 yields the same result. So C is not a Goppa code.

Chapter 9

9.4.1.   The words of C_α have the form $(a(x), \alpha(x)a(x))$ where $a(x)$ and $\alpha(x)$ are polynomials mod $x^6 + x^3 + 1$. To get $d > 3$ we must exclude those $\alpha(x)$ for which a combination $a(x) = x^i$, $\alpha(x)a(x) = x^j + x^k$ is possible and also the inverses of these $\alpha(x)$. Since $(1 + x)^8 = 1 + x^8 = x^{-1}(x + x^9) = x^{-1}(x + 1)$ it is easily seen that each nonzero element of $\mathbb{F}_{2^6}$ has a unique representation $x^i(1 + x)^j$ where

$$i \in \{0, \pm1, \pm2, \pm3, \pm4\}, \qquad j \in \{0, \pm1, \pm2, \pm4\}.$$

So the requirement $d > 2$ excludes nine values of $\alpha(x)$ and $d > 3$ excludes the remaining 54 values of $\alpha(x)$. This shows that for small n the construction is not so good! By (3.7.14) there is a [12, 7] extended lexicographically least code with $d = 4$. In (4.7.3) we saw that a nonlinear code with $n = 12$, $d = 4$ exists with even more words.

9.4.2.   Let $\alpha(x)$ be a polynomial of weight 3. Then in $(a(x), \alpha(x)a(x))$ the weights of the two halves have the same parity. So $d < 4$ is only possible if there is a choice $a(x) = x^i + x^j$ such that $\alpha(x)a(x) \equiv 0 \bmod(x^6 - 1)$. This is so if $\alpha(x)$ is periodic, i.e. $1 + x^2 + x^4$ or $x + x^3 + x^5$. For all other choices we have $d = 4$.

9.4.3.   Let the rate R satisfy $1/(l + 1) < R \le 1/l$ ($l \in \mathbb{N}$). Let s be the least integer such that $m/[(l + 1)m - s] \ge R$. We construct a code C by picking an l-tuple $(\alpha_1, \alpha_2, \ldots, \alpha_l) \in (\mathbb{F}_{2^m})^l$ and then forming $(\mathbf{a}, \alpha_1\mathbf{a}, \ldots, \alpha_l\mathbf{a})$ for all $\mathbf{a} \in \mathbb{F}_2^m$ and finally deleting the last s symbols. The word length is $n = (l + 1)m - s$.

A nonzero word $\mathbf{c} \in C$ corresponds to 2^s possible values of the l-tuple $(\alpha_1, \ldots, \alpha_l)$. To ensure a minimum distance $\ge \lambda n$ we must exclude

$$\le 2^s \sum\nolimits_{i < \lambda n} \binom{n}{i}$$ values of $(\alpha_1, \ldots, \alpha_l)$. We are satisfied if this leaves us a choice

for $(\alpha_1, \ldots, \alpha_l)$, i.e. if

$$2^s \sum_{i < \lambda n} \binom{n}{i} < 2^{ml}.$$

From Theorem 1.4.5 we find

$$s + nH(\lambda) < ml,$$

i.e.

$$H(\lambda) < \frac{ml - s}{n} = 1 - \frac{m}{n} = 1 - R + o(1), \qquad (m \to \infty).$$

Chapter 10

10.5.1.   Consider the sequence $r, r^2, r^3, \ldots$. There must be two elements in the sequence which are congruent mod A, say $r^n - r^m \equiv 0 \pmod{A}$ $(n > m)$.

10.5.2.   Let $m = r^n - 1 = AB$, where A is a prime $> r^2$. Suppose that r generates a subgroup H of $\mathbb{F}_A^*$ with $|H| = n$ which has $\{\pm c | c = 1, 2, \ldots, r - 1\}$ as a complete set of coset representatives. Consider the cyclic AN code C of length n and base r. Clearly every integer in the interval $[1, m]$ has modular distance 0 or 1 to exactly one codeword. So C is a perfect code. (Since

$w_m(A) \geq 3$ we must have $A > r^2$.) A trivial example for $r = 3$ is the cyclic code {13, 26}. Here we have taken $m = 3^3 - 1$ and $A = 13$.

The subgroup generated by 3 in $\mathbb{F}_{13}^*$ has index 4 and the coset representatives are ± 1 and ± 2.

10.5.3. We have $455 = \sum_{i=0}^{5} b_i 3^i$ where $(b_0, b_1, \ldots, b_5) = (2, 1, 2, 1, 2, 1)$. The algorithm described in (10.2.3) replaces the initial 2, 1 by -1, 2. In this way we find the following sequence of representations:

$$(2, 1, 2, 1, 2, 1) \to (-1, 2, 2, 1, 2, 1) \to (-1, -1, 0, 2, 2, 1)$$

$$\to (-1, -1, 0, -1, 0, 2) \to (0, -1, 0, -1, 0, -1).$$

So the representation in CNAF is

$$455 \equiv -273 = -3 - 3^3 - 3^5.$$

10.5.4. We check the conditions of Theorem 10.3.2. In $\mathbb{F}_{11}^*$ the element 3 generates the subgroup {1, 3, 9, 5, 4}; multiplication by -1 yields the other five elements. $r^n = 3^5 = 243 = 1 + 11.22$. So we have $A = 22$, in ternary representation $A = 1 + 1.3 + 2.3^2$. The CNAF of 22 is $1 - 2.3 + 0.3^2 + 1.3^3 + 0.3^4$ (mod 242). The code consists of ten words namely the cyclic shifts of $(1, -2, 0, 1, 0)$ resp. $(-1, 2, 0, -1, 0)$. All weights are 3.

Chapter 11

11.7.1. Using the notation of Section 11.1 we have

$$G(x) = (1 + (x^2)^2) + x(1 + x^2) = 1 + x + x^3 + x^4.$$

The information stream 1 1 1 1 1 ... would give $I_0(x) = (1 + x)^{-1}$, and hence

$$T(x) = (1 + x^2)^{-1} G(x) = 1 + x + x^2,$$

i.e. the receiver would get 1 1 1 0 0 0 0 ....

Three errors in the initial positions would produce the zero signal and lead to infinitely many decoding errors.

11.7.2   In Theorem 11.4.2 it is shown how this situation can arise. Let $h(x) = x^4 + x + 1$ and $g(x)h(x) = x^{15} - 1$. We know that $g(x)$ generates an irreducible cyclic code with minimum distance 8. Consider the information sequence 1 1 0 0 1 0 0 0 0 ..., i.e. $I_0(x) = h(x)$. Then we find

$$T(x) = h(x^2)g(x) = (x^{15} - 1)h(x),$$

which has weight 6. By Theorem 11.4.2 this is the free distance. In this example we have $g(x) = x^{11} + x^8 + x^7 + x^5 + x^3 + x^2 + x + 1$. Therefore $G_0(x) = 1 + x + x^4$, $G_1(x) = 1 + x + x^2 + x^3 + x^5$. The encoder is

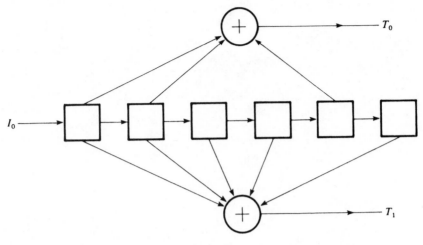

Figure 8

and

$$I_0 = 1\ 1\ 0\ 0\ 1\ 0\ 0\ 0\ldots \qquad \text{yields as output}$$

$$T = 11\ 00\ 10\ 00\ 00\ 00\ 00\ 01\ 10\ 01\ 00\ 00\ldots$$

11.7.3.   Consider a finite nonzero output sequence. This will have the form $(\mathbf{a}_0 + \mathbf{a}_1 x + \cdots + \mathbf{a}_l x^l)G$, where the $\mathbf{a}_i$ are row vectors in $\mathbb{F}_2^4$. We write G as $G_1 + xG_2$ as in (11.5.7). Clearly the initial nonzero seventuple in the output is a nonzero codeword in the code generated by m_3; so it has weight ≥ 3. If this is also the final nonzero seventuple, then it is $(11\ldots 1)$ and the weight is 7. If the final nonzero seventuple is $\mathbf{a}_l G$, then it is a nonzero codeword in the code generated by $m_0 m_1$ and hence has weight at least 4. However, if $\mathbf{a}_l = (1000)$, then $\mathbf{a}_l G = \mathbf{0}$ and the final nonzero seventuple is a nonzero codeword in the code generated by m_1 and it has weight ≥ 3. So the free distance is 6. This is realized by the input $(1100) * (1000)x$.

References*

1. Baumert, L. D. and McEliece, R. J.: *A Golay-Viterbi Concatenated Coding Scheme for MJS '77*. JPL Technical Report 32-1526, pp. 76–83. Pasadena, Calif.: Jet Propulsion Laboratory, 1973.
2. Berlekamp, E. R.: *Algebraic Coding Theory*. New York: McGraw-Hill, 1968.
3. Berlekamp, E. R.: *Decoding the Golay Code*. JPL Technical Report 32-1256, Vol. IX, pp. 81–85. Pasadena, Calif.: Jet Propulsion Laboratory, 1972.
4. Berlekamp, E. R.: Goppa codes. *IEEE Trans. Info. Theory*, **19**, pp. 590–592 (1973).
5. Berlekamp, E. R. and Moreno, O.: Extended double-error-correcting binary Goppa codes are cyclic. *IEEE Trans. Info. Theory*, **19**, pp. 817–818 (1973).
6. Best, M. R., Brouwer, A. E., MacWilliams, F. J., Odlyzko, A. M. and Sloane, N. J. A.: Bounds for binary codes of length less than 25. *IEEE Trans. Info. Theory*, **23**, pp. 81–93 (1977).
7. Best, M. R.: *On the Existence of Perfect Codes*. Report ZN 82/78. Amsterdam: Mathematical Centre, 1978.
8. Best, M. R.: Binary codes with a minimum distance of four. *IEEE Trans. Info. Theory*, **26**, pp. 738–742 (1980).
9. Bussey, W. H.: Galois field tables for $p^n \le 169$. *Bull. Amer. Math. Soc.*, **12**, pp. 22–38 (1905).
10. Bussey, W. H.: Tables of Galois fields of order less than 1,000. *Bull. Amer. Math. Soc.*, **16**, pp. 188–206 (1910).
11. Cameron, P. J. and van Lint, J. H.: *Designs, Graphs, Codes and their Links*. London Math. Soc. Student Texts, Vol. 22. Cambridge: Cambridge Univ. Press, (1991).
12. Chen, C. L., Chien, R. T. and Liu, C. K.: On the binary representation form of certain integers. *SIAM J. Appl. Math.*, **26**, pp. 285–293 (1974).
13. Chien, R. T. and Choy, D. M.: Algebraic generalization of BCH-Goppa-Helgert codes. *IEEE Trans. Info. Theory*, **21**, pp. 70–79 (1975).
14. Clark, W. E. and Liang, J. J.: On arithmetic weight for a general radix representation of integers. *IEEE Trans. Info. Theory*, **19**, pp. 823–826 (1973).

---

* References added in the Second Edition are numbered 72 to 81.

15. Clark, W. E. and Liang, J. J.: On modular weight and cyclic nonadjacent forms for arithmetic codes. *IEEE Trans. Info. Theory*, **20**, pp. 767–770 (1974).

16. Curtis, C. W. and Reiner, I.: *Representation Theory of Finite Groups and Associative Algebras*. New York–London: Interscience, 1962.

17. Cvetković, D. M. and van Lint, J. H.: An elementary proof of Lloyd's theorem. *Proc. Kon. Ned. Akad. v. Wetensch.* (A), **80**, pp. 6–10 (1977).

18. Delsarte, P.: An algebraic approach to coding theory. *Philips Research Reports Supplements*, **10** (1973).

19. Delsarte, P. and Goethals, J.-M.: Unrestricted codes with the Golay parameters are unique. *Discrete Math.*, **12**, pp. 211–224 (1975).

20. Elias, P.: *Coding for Noisy Channels*. IRE Conv. Record, part 4, pp. 37–46.

21. Feller, W.: *An Introduction to Probability Theory and Its Applications*, Vol. I. New York–London: Wiley, 1950.

22. Forney, G. D.: *Concatenated Codes*. Cambridge, Mass.: MIT Press, 1966.

23. Forney, G. D.: Convolutional codes I: algebraic structure. *IEEE Trans. Info. Theory*, **16**, pp. 720–738 (1970); *Ibid.*, **17**, 360 (1971).

24. Gallagher, R. G.: *Information Theory and Reliable Communication*. New York: Wiley, 1968.

25. Goethals, J.-M. and van Tilborg, H. C. A.: Uniformly packed codes. *Philips Research Reports*, **30**, pp. 9–36 (1975).

26. Goethals, J.-M.: The extended Nadler code is unique. *IEEE Trans. Info. Theory*, **23**, pp. 132–135 (1977).

27. Goppa, V. D.: A new class of linear error-correcting codes. *Problems of Info. Transmission*, **6**, pp. 207–212 (1970).

28. Goto, M.: A note on perfect decimal AN codes. *Info. and Control*, **29**, pp. 385-387 (1975).

29. Goto, M. and Fukumara, T.: Perfect nonbinary AN codes with distance three *Info. and Control*, **27**, pp. 336–348 (1975).

30. Graham, R. L. and Sloane, N. J. A.: Lower bounds for constant weight codes. *IEEE Trans. Info. Theory*, **26**, pp. 37–40 (1980).

31. Gritsenko, V. M.: Nonbinary arithmetic correcting codes, *Problems of Info. Transmission*, **5**, pp 15–22 (1969).

32. Hall, M.: *Combinatorial Theory*. New York–London–Sydney–Toronto: Wiley (second printing), 1980.

33. Hartmann, C. R. P. and Tzeng, K. K.: Generalizations of the BCH bound. *Info. and Control*, **20**, pp. 489–498 (1972).

34. Helgert, H. J. and Stinaff, R. D.: Minimum distance bounds for binary linear codes. *IEEE Trans. Info. Theory*, **19**, pp. 344–356 (1973).

35. Helgert, H. J.: Alternant codes. *Info. and Control*, **26**, pp. 369–380 (1974).

36. Jackson, D.: *Fourier Series and Orthogonal Polynomials*. Carus Math. Monographs, Vol. 6. Math. Assoc. of America, 1941.

37. Justesen, J.: A class of constructive asymptotically good algebraic codes. *IEEE Trans. Info. Theory*, **18**, pp. 652–656 (1972).

38. Justesen, J.: An algebraic construction of rate $1/v$ convolutional codes. *IEEE Trans. Info. Theory*, **21**, 577–580 (1975).

39. Kasami, T.: An upper bound on k/n for affine invariant codes with fixed d/n. *IEEE Trans. Info. Theory*, **15**, pp. 171–176 (1969).

40. Levenshtein, V. I.: Minimum redundancy of binary error-correcting codes. *Info. and Control*, **28**, pp. 268–291 (1975).

41. van Lint, J. H.: Nonexistence theorems for perfect error-correcting-codes. In: *Computers in Algebra and Theory*, Vol. IV (SIAM–AMS Proceedings) 1971.

42. van Lint, J. H.: *Coding Theory*. Springer Lecture Notes, Vol. 201, Berlin–Heidelberg–New York: Springer, 1971.

43. van Lint, J. H.: A new description of the Nadler code. *IEEE Trans. Info Theory*, **18**, pp. 825–826 (1972).
44. van Lint, J. H.: A survey of perfect codes. *Rocky Mountain J. Math.*, **5**, pp. 199–224 (1975).
45. van Lint, J. H. and MacWilliams, F. J.: Generalized quadratic residue codes. *IEEE Trans. Info. Theory*, **24**, pp. 730–737 (1978).
46. MacWilliams, F. J. and Sloane, N. J. A.: *The Theory of Error-correcting Codes*. Amsterdam–New York–Oxford: North Holland, 1977.
47. Massey, J. L.: *Threshold Decoding*. Cambridge, Mass.: MIT Press, 1963.
48. Massey, J. L. and Garcia, O. N.: Error-correcting codes in computer arithmetic. In: *Advances in Information Systems Science*, Vol. 4, Ch. 5. (Edited by J. T. Ton). New York: Plenum Press, 1972.
49. Massey, J. L., Costello, D. J. and Justesen, J.: Polynomial weights and code construction. *IEEE Trans. Info. Theory*, **19**, pp. 101–110 (1973).
50. McEliece, R. J., Rodemich, E. R., Rumsey, H. C. and Welch, L. R.: New upper bounds on the rate of a code via the Delsarte–MacWilliams inequalities. *IEEE Trans. Info. Theory*, **23**, pp. 157–166 (1977).
51. McEliece, R. J.: *The Theory of Information and Coding*. Encyclopedia of Math. and its Applications, Vol. 3. Reading, Mass.: Addison-Wesley, 1977.
52. McEliece, R. J.: The bounds of Delsarte and Lovasz and their applications to coding theory. In: *Algebraic Coding Theory and Applications*. (Edited by G. Longo, CISM Courses and Lectures, Vol. 258. Wien–New York: Springer, 1979.
53. Peterson, W. W. and Weldon, E. J.: *Error-correcting Codes*. (2nd ed.). Cambridge, Mass.: MIT Press, 1972.
54. Piret, Ph.: Structure and constructions of cyclic convolutional codes. *IEEE Trans. Info. Theory*, **22**, pp. 147–155 (1976).
55. Piret, Ph.: Algebraic properties of convolutional codes with automorphisms. Ph.D. Dissertation. Univ. Catholique de Louvain, 1977.
56. Posner, E. C.: Combinatorial structures in planetary reconnaissance. In: *Error Correcting Codes*. (Edited by H. B. Mann). pp. 15–46. New York–London–Sydney–Toronto: Wiley, 1968.
57. Preparata, F. P.: A class of optimum nonlinear double-error-correcting codes. *Info. and Control*, **13**, pp. 378–400 (1968).
58. Rao, T. R. N.: *Error Coding for Arithmetic Processors*. New York–London: Academic Press, 1974.
59. Roos, C.: On the structure of convolutional and cyclic convolutional codes. *IEEE Trans. Info. Theory*, **25**, pp. 676–683 (1979).
60. Schalkwijk, J. P. M., Vinck, A. J. and Post, K. A.: Syndrome decoding of binary rate k/n convolutional codes. *IEEE Trans. Info. Theory*, **24**, pp. 553–562 (1978).
61. Selmer, E. S.: Linear recurrence relations over finite fields. Univ. of Bergen, Norway: Dept. of Math., 1966.
62. Shannon, C. E.: A mathematical theory of communication. *Bell Syst. Tech. J.*, **27**, pp. 379–423, 623–656 (1948).
63. Sidelnikov, V. M.: Upper bounds for the number of points of a binary code with a specified code distance. *Info. and Control*, **28**, pp. 292–303 (1975).
64. Sloane, N. J. A. and Whitehead, D. S.: A new family of single-error-correcting codes. *IEEE Trans. Info. Theory*, **16**, pp. 717–719 (1970).
65. Sloane, N. J. A., Reddy, S. M. and Chen, C. L.: New binary codes. *IEEE Trans. Info. Theory*, **18**, pp. 503–510 (1972).
66. Solomon, G. and van Tilborg, H. C. A.: A connection between block and convolutional codes. *SIAM J. Appl. Math.*, **37**, pp. 358 – 369 (1979).
67. Szegö, G.: *Orthogonal Polynomials*. Colloquium Publications, Vol. 23. New York: Amer. Math. Soc. (revised edition), 1959.

68. Tietäväinen, A.: On the nonexistence of perfect codes over finite fields. *SIAM J. Appl. Math.*, **24**, pp. 88–96 (1973).
69. van Tilborg, H. C. A.: Uniformly packed codes. Thesis, Eindhoven Univ. of Technology, 1976.
70. Tricomi, F. G.: *Vorlesungen uber Orthogonalreihen.* Grundlehren d. math. Wiss. Band 76. Berlin–Heidelberg–New York: Springer, 1970.
71. Tzeng, K. K. and Zimmerman, K. P.: On extending Goppa codes to cyclic codes. *IEEE Trans. Info. Theory*, **21**, pp. 712–716 (1975).
72. Baker, R. D., van Lint, J. H. and Wilson, R. M.: On the Preparata and Goethals codes. *IEEE Trans. Info. Theory*, **29**, pp. 342–345 (1983).
73. van der Geer, G. and van Lint, J. H.: *Introduction to Coding Theory and Algebraic Geometry.* Basel: Birkhäuser, 1988.
74. Hong, Y.: On the nonexistence of unknown perfect 6- and 8-codes in Hamming schemes $H(n, q)$ with q arbitrary. *Osaka J. Math.*, **21**, pp. 687–700 (1984).
75. Kerdock, A. M.: A class of low-rate nonlinear codes. *Info and Control*, **20**, pp. 182–187 (1972).
76. van Lint, J. H. and Wilson, R. M.: On the Minimum Distance of Cyclic Codes. *IEEE Trans. Info. Theory*, **32**, pp. 23–40 (1986).
77. van Oorschot, P. C. and Vanstone, S. A.: *An Introduction to Error Correcting Codes with Applications.* Dordrecht: Kluwer, 1989.
78. Peek, J. B. H.: Communications Aspects of the Compact Disc Digital Audio System. *IEEE Communications Magazine*, Vol. 23, No. 2 pp. 7–15 (1985).
79. Piret, Ph.: *Convolutional Codes, An Algebraic Approach.* Cambridge, Mass.: The MIT Press, 1988.
80. Roos, C.: A new lower bound for the minimum distance of a cyclic code. *IEEE Trans. Info. Theory*, **29**, pp. 330–332 (1983).
81. Tsfasman, M. A., Vlădut, S. G. and Zink, Th.: On Goppa codes which are better than the Varshamov-Gilbert bound. *Math. Nachr.*, **109**, pp. 21–28 (1982).

Index

Graduate Texts in Mathematics

continued from page ii